POLITICS AS A MORAL PROBLEM

D1722363

POLITICS
AS A MORAL PROBLEM

by

János Kis

C E U PRESS

Central European University Press
Budapest • New York

© 2008 by János Kis
English translation © 2008 by Zoltán Miklósi

Published in 2008 by

Central European University Press
An imprint of the
Central European University Share Company
Nádor utca 11, H-1051 Budapest, Hungary
Tel: +36-1-327-3138 or 327-3000
Fax: +36-1-327-3183
E-mail: ceupress@ceu.hu
Website: www.ceupress.com

400 West 59th Street, New York NY 10019, USA
Tel: +1-212-547-6932
Fax: +1-646-557-2416
E-mail: mgreenwald@sorosny.org

All rights reserved. No part of this publication may be reproduced,
stored in a retrieval system, or transmitted,
in any form or by any means, without the permission
of the Publisher.

Translated by Zoltán Miklósi

ISBN 978-963-9776-34-0 paperback

The Library of Congress has cataloged
the hardcover edition as follows:
[CIP data for the hardcover edition]

Kis, János, 1943-
 [Politika mint erkölcsi probléma. English]
 Politics as a moral problem / by János Kis.
   p. cm.
 Includes bibliographical references and index.
 ISBN 978-9639776227 (cloth : alk. paper) 1. Political science--Philosophy. I.
Title.
 JA71.K56713 2008
 172--dc22
                                        2008030062

Printed in Hungary by
Akaprint Nyomda

CONTENTS

CHAPTER ONE

INTRODUCTION

1.1 The problem at first sight

In 1989, the community of democratic nations was euphoric. The Soviet empire was crumbling. Its successor states were undergoing a sweeping regime change, most of them adopting constitutional democracy. History seemed to be moving towards a happy ending, with the liberal-democratic project appearing as the only game in town.[1]

Less than twenty years later the community of democratic countries finds itself in a state of deep malaise. That the post-communist societies feel frustrated and disappointed should be no surprise. Their makeshift institutions are not solid enough to bear the burden of the high expectations placed on them. Their political establishments emerged, in a hasty selection process, from groups of former dissidents, communist party cadres, officers of the secret services, intellectuals, church-affiliated people, and new arrivists. Their societies suffered unusually deep economic recession and social dislocation. All these ills may be interpreted as pangs of the transition from communism to democracy and a capitalist market economy. As long as the old democracies stand fast and remain self-assured, there is hope that, sooner or later, the pessimism of the citizens of the new democracies will be dissipated.

But the old democracies seem to be experiencing a similar frustration and disappointment. The bad feelings that are taking hold of them have multiple and heterogeneous sources: immigration, the demise of the welfare state and steep rise in social inequality, the ambiguous impact of the mass media on the quality of public political debate, the challenge of international terrorism, the growth of multinational corporations evading the control of national governments, the risk of democratically unaccountable supra-national institutions limiting the sovereignty of the nation state, the costs of apparently unavoidable economic reforms, and so on.

There is a further reason, more specifically related to the quality of the democratic process itself, why democracy is in trouble. Citizens of democratic states tend to feel that politicians as a class are betraying their moral expectations. The loss of trust in politicians is fairly evenly spread over the democratic world. It is almost as noticeable in Western Europe and the United States as in post-communist East Central Europe.[2] There is a widespread sense that democratic politics is in a state of moral decay.

Is that feeling justified? Are today's democratic politicians on average more selfish and dishonest than their predecessors fifty or a hundred years ago? Not necessarily. Politics is clearly more transparent now than it used to be. The vices of politicians are more visible, too. The public receives more frequent, more detailed, and more explicit reports of their misdeeds. This may give rise to the illusion that they have become more immoral.

Since the mid-twentieth century, three important changes have caused what might be called a transparency explosion in democratic politics. Television has brought the political leaders into the citizens' living rooms; the internet has dramatically reduced the costs of information for ordinary people and decentralized the flow of information; and freedom of information acts have made it an obligation for state institutions to make documents of a general interest publicly accessible. What we are experiencing as moral decay may simply consist in a time lag between the explosion in transparency and the rise in accountability.

An illustration: before the adoption of freedom of information acts, the press and civil groups depended on the good will of government officials to meet their requests for data of public interest. Under the freedom of information acts currently in force in many democratic states, they may go to the courts and demand that the right of the public to know be enforced. Very probably, more information is disclosed now than was in the past, but the adversarial process of litigation makes governments appear more reluctant to provide the information requested.

So the feeling of a moral *decay* may not be justified. This does not mean that dissatisfaction with the *lack of improvement* in the ethics of public action is unjustified. There is a wide gap between the standards that apply to persons who act in the name of the citizenry and their actual conduct. This fact is a moral problem in itself. It is a problem, furthermore, because it damages the apparent integrity of democratic politics. It weakens the citizens' willingness to support policies whose costs are felt immediately but whose benefits come to fruition only in the long run. It makes the citizenry suspicious of the rule of law and the competitive process that is the living nerve of modern multi-party democracy. In sum, it makes the public increasingly accessible to populist rhetoric.

The moral standards of political leadership are believed by many to be soft constraints that politicians may disregard at their convenience. But the violations backfire. They erode other constraints that seem to be hard. To put it bluntly, the moral deficit gives rise to budgetary and other deficits.[3]

So the moral problem of politics must be taken seriously. But it is very hard to deal with or even to grasp. Citizens seem to be confused about the ethical standards of political leadership. Their instincts pull in opposite directions.

On the one hand, politicians occupy public offices and since the expectations against holders of public office are more demanding than those against ordinary people, their faults are judged more strictly. We regard it as natural for a private person to make greater efforts for the well-being of his own family than for the well-being of strangers, but we find it outrageous for a person to favor his own family in his capacity as public official. We praise an uncle who pays for the education of his poor nephew, but we condemn him if he wangles a lucrative government job for the young man. In sum, we would like to see our interests represented by honorable people of higher-than-average integrity.

On the other hand, in order to gain public office, politicians must engage in electoral competition, and we would not like to see our candidate lose because of his praiseworthy moral character. We are reluctant to vote for a champion of virtue whom we do not expect to find his way in the morass of political struggle. We condemn a politician who accepts campaign funding from private sources on the understanding that the donors will be compensated from the taxpayers' money. But we are not pleased if our candidates are always defeated because they, unlike their rivals, are unwilling to accept contributions from private sources. To put it briefly, we tend to think that the norms of political morality should not be always seen to be more demanding than the norms of private ethics. Sometimes, they actually seem to be more lenient. But the occasions when they are stricter and those when they are more relaxed are difficult to identify.

There is something to this ambiguity of the ordinary attitudes to the moral problem of politics. We have good reason to look with suspicion at politicians who promise to transform politics into a domain of incorruptible virtue. Over the history, such people proved to be hypocrites or fanatics. A sincere moralizer easily turns into a champion of terror. It seems to be better to have Fouché and Talleyrand rather than Saint-Just and Robespierre.

Any plausible theory of political morality must be able to show how our moral judgments on politics may form a consistent whole. Its basic tenets must be compatible with the widely shared sense that the good workings of the democratic institutions must not depend on the politicians' being paragons of virtue. It must cohere with a convincing explanation of why our ordinary judgments on the morality of political action are as cloudy as they are. And it must shed some light on how the moral standards of political action could be better identified and enforced than they currently are. The ambition of this book is to show that the ambiguity of the democratic public's attitude towards the ethics of public conduct can indeed be accounted for in a consistent manner. I want to offer an account that does not pull either in the direction of a moralizing utopia or of complacency towards the mores of the democratic political leadership as they now typically are.

I do not agree with those who, like Karl Popper, reject utopian thinking as necessarily harmful or useless. Utopias invite us to engage in thought experiments about what the world would be like should one or other of the general constraints on our lives (such as the scarcity of resources, fallibility, or the impossibility of having complex organizations without a hierarchy) be removed. Such thought experiments may help society better to understand how the world really is. From time to time, they lead us to realize that what we believed to be unavoidable consequences of a hard constraint may be changed without running up against the constraint. At other times they teach us to look critically at things that we cannot radically alter. Or they may reveal to us that an ideal we believed to be worth pursuing, although incapable of being fully realized, is not really appealing. Losing the capacity for utopia makes one uncritically accept reality as it is. By contrast, the utopian spirit that is also critically self-reflective may be a source of productive dissatisfaction both with the world and with the ideals that are accepted as valid.

But utopia is no replacement for thinking within the constraints of human nature and the world. This book is intended to be an exercise in the latter. It takes the basic principles and institutional schemes of liberal democracy for granted. The known alternatives to liberal democracy are morally unacceptable, and given what we know about the general circumstances of politics, I think there is reason to be skeptical about the possibility of an alternative that, rather than dealing better with the moral tensions of political action, would eliminate them altogether.

We have to understand the complexities of the relationship between politics and morality precisely in order to see how partial but progressive reforms may be implemented.

Politics involves a variety of characters: the voter, the journalist, the career civil servant, the legislator, the member of government, even the constitutional judge who pronounces a controversial ruling, and so on. In what follows, the journalist, the civil servant, or the constitutional judge will be mentioned only occasionally. The moral problem of (democratic) politics will be understood as specifically referring to those individuals who compete to gain and to retain elected office. For the purposes of this book, the Politician is a representative of the citizenry, who runs for or holds an office that a representative may occupy. Therefore, depending on the context, I will speak about politicians, or representatives, or holders of an elected office.

It is relevant that politicians run for elected office: this is what distinguishes them from any other participant of the political process who is not a politician. And it is relevant that they want to keep their office for more than one electoral cycle: this is what distinguishes a career politician from someone whose participation in politics is temporary and occasional. Even within the category of career politicians, I want to narrow the focus of attention further. What interests me in this book is not all elected officials but only those occupying leading positions: frontbenchers and holders of such governmental jobs as a member of parliament may assume without resigning from his or her mandate. When I speak about the Politician, I will have the prime minister, the members of the cabinet, the party bosses, and the influential legislators in mind. In other words, this book is about the ethics of political *leadership*.

However, I will not discuss the subject from the point of view of the way the *political leaders* themselves should reflect on and react to the moral problems involved in their actions. Rather, I will address the issue from the point of view of how *ordinary citizens* should judge the way the leaders respond to the challenge of morality.

In a legitimate polity, the citizenry is sovereign: it is the source of all authority. What the leaders may do depends, ultimately, on the judgments the citizenry makes about their doings. This is a robust normative claim about politics in general, and it entails a modest empirical claim about democratic politics. When the leaders as a class are seen for long periods as not living up to the moral standards of their office, then there is something wrong not only with them but with the way the citizenry is able and willing to hold them to account.

Niccolò Machiavelli, the father of modern political thought, wrote his work with the ambition to give the prince advice. In contrast, this book is *about* the prince but not written *for* him. For whom, then, is it written? For the people, I would hasten to respond if I were not so keenly aware of the irony of this statement.

1.2 A political debate

The idea of my book was conceived in the heat of political debate. In the summer of 2002, a few weeks after a socialist-liberal government took office in Hungary, the right-wing press leaked that Prime Minister Péter Medgyessy had been a covert counter-intelligence officer during the communist dictatorship.

At that time I was a member of the junior coalition party and a critical supporter of the government. In an editorial on the scandal I wrote that Medgyessy must go. My argument went as follows.

The communist counter-intelligence was certainly not a politically neutral tool of national security. Its mission was defined as struggle against "external and internal enemies." It was supposed to investigate and report about the political and ideological views and personal relations of Hungarian citizens. It enjoyed cozy relationships with the KGB, the Stasi, and the other communist secret services, and it sponsored terrorist groups. If a man with a history of collaborating with the communist counter-intelligence decides to pursue a political career after the transition to democracy, he is expected not to treat this aspect of his past as a private matter. The voters have a right to make an informed decision as to whether they want to have a former secret agent to be their prime minister. They have a right to hold the information about his past against him. This may be a serious campaign disadvantage for the former agent, but he voluntarily accepts it when he decides to stand for elected office. From the moment Medgyessy announced his intention to run for prime minister, he was under an obligation to give an account of his past. Medgyessy had violated this unwritten obligation. I argued that by refusing to make him resign, the coalition would undermine its own moral integrity, preparing the ground for its demise.[4]

After some hesitation, Medgyessy decided to stay. The socialists stood firmly behind him. The liberals first demanded that he leave but they soon changed their minds. It took two years for the socialist-liberal coalition to come to the view that Medgyessy was a liability and to force him to leave. His eventual fall was not directly linked to the secret agent affair. He was dropped because the parties of government, the socialists in particular, were afraid that his timid attempts to cut government spending would undermine their chances of re-election. By that time, measures of austerity were long overdue, but the socialists adamantly resisted to a change of course in economic policy. And Medgyessy who remained prime minister by their grace was not in a position to tell them: This is what we must do—you either follow me or look for someone irresponsible enough to continue the untenable course of deficit financing. In this indirect way his demise in 2004 was indeed related to the secret agent scandal of 2002. But his belated dismissal did not help the general public to learn the right lesson from his inglorious premiership.

The June 2002 crisis, however, gave rise to an illuminating public debate. The center-left coalition won by a narrow margin, and its position was perceived as highly uncertain. There were great fears that the departure of the prime minister would bring about the collapse of the majority. Most arguments were related to these fears. But some went beyond the moment into a highly abstract consideration of the standards by which the Medgyessy scandal was to be assessed.

The most interesting claim made in the prime minister's defense was this: When a politician violates a moral obligation, his conduct may be condemned, and such a condemnation may be a sufficient

reason for his friends and acquaintances to change their *private* relationship with him. It is not a reason for citizens to *publicly* demand his
resignation, however. It is only by violating a *legal* obligation that a
politician will make himself liable to suffer public sanctions. The law
in force did not require candidates for elected office to disclose their
past collaboration with the communist counter-intelligence. Therefore,
Medgyessy had no reason to resign. As writer Péter Nádas put it in an
interview,

> Democratic politics [...] is not about making moral judgments. If I
> need moral advice, I turn to my friend, or a priest, or a psychiatrist.
> Democratic parliaments are not suited to discuss moral issues.
> Such issues do not belong there. Stalinism and Hitlerism come to
> my mind when I see Parliament discussing moral issues. Dictato-
> rial regimes. Parliaments are meant to discuss pieces of legislation,
> and representatives see to it that others, the parties and the minis-
> ters also comply with these laws.[5]

The laws themselves must not express moral judgment, Nádas continues: "There is no such thing as a moral law, moral conceptions
cannot be the object of political legislation."
    In sum, Nádas made two claims. First, between two elections, no
breach of the norms of the ethics of public conduct should have practical consequences unless those norms are spelled out as law. Second,
however, moral norms are never spelled out as law in a democracy for
democratic legislation is not about moral matters. Thus, democratic
politicians must not be held accountable at all, between two elections,
for violating moral norms.
    This was perhaps more than Nádas really intended to say. In a re-
ply to the author of this book, he replaced his second claim that
"moral conceptions cannot be the object of political legislation" by a
statement to the effect that, on the contrary, "[i]t is hard to imagine a
democracy where the laws would not be based on moral principles ...
In a democracy, the only link connecting morality with politics is the
law." But he reiterated his main point:

> If you did not break the law, then you did not break the law. Po-
> litical rationality has to take this into account even though one
> may have justified reservations against another. It may sound dis-

heartening, but in democracies there is no instance higher than the law.[6]

In the course of the debate on the Medgyessy affair, I named this position *the separation thesis*[7] in witness of the fact that it called for separating democratic political (as distinct from legal) accountability from moral judgment.[8]

In the Medgyessy controversy, two arguments were raised in support of the separation thesis: an argument from democracy and another one from the rule of law. The first runs as follows: democracy is based on the agreement that political offices are filled through elections. The only source of the authority of office-holders is the consent expressed by the vote they receive from the citizens. The participants agree that those, and only those, who win the election will hold political office. By implication, they also agree that a political office may not be lost except by suffering defeat in an election. Politicians may err or sin, but as long as they do not break the law, their only punishment is being voted out of their job.[9]

The argument from the rule of law states that everybody must be subject to the law, and only to the law. Citizens are protected against the arbitrary or biased use of power by the requirement that no power be used without legal authorization and legal constraints. But the rule of law does not protect ordinary citizens only. The same protection is extended to the holders of power. Politicians, too, are protected against sanctions other than those provided by the law.[10]

Although persuasive, these arguments do not lend the separation thesis the required support.

Consider the argument from democracy. First, not all political leaders receive their authority directly from the voters. In a parliamentary regime, voters elect legislators and the head of government is elected by the legislature. The principle of democratic authorization is not violated if between two elections the legislature withdraws its confidence from the prime minister and empowers another person to form a government.

Second, even directly elected presidents may be removed from office in exceptionally grave cases. Constitutional democracies with the presidential form of government typically adopt some version of the impeachment procedure. Clear criminal law violations represent impeachable offenses, but for the impeachment procedure to be started, criminal law violation is not necessary. Any misconduct that is judged to undermine the integrity of the office may be raised to the level of impeachable offense.[11]

Third, even where there are no procedures to remove an elected official, his parliamentary group or the opposition or the press may demand his resignation, thus starting a political process that may eventually lead to his departure. It is not clear why such a practice would violate the principle of democratic authorization. That principle does not imply that the mandate received from the people would be non-returnable; and whether the call for resignation is justified depends entirely on the reasons to which it appeals.

Let us now look briefly at the argument from the rule of law. In a polity ordered by law, the *state* holds every citizen accountable for complying with the law, and only with the law. This also applies to political leaders. But from this it does not follow that *the public* should not hold the political leaders accountable for anything other than complying with the law. The state backs its instructions with coercive force, and claims a monopoly, within its jurisdiction, of deciding who can use coercive force, when, and against whom. Such a monopoly cannot be justified unless its exercise is subjected to the rule of law. The political sanctions that a democratic public may legitimately impose do not include the use of the coercive power of the state. It is not clear why, in holding a leader politically accountable for his actions and omissions, the public should be restricted in the same stringent manner as the state in administering coercive force.

Thus the separation thesis is not sustained either by the argument from democracy or by the argument from the rule of law. Nor are its practical consequences particularly attractive. In the 2002 debate I attributed its popularity to its capacity of accommodating the view that Medgyessy's conduct was morally dubious with the claim that its dubiousness should not matter politically. But even if I thought that the thesis is wrong in itself and that it played a disgraceful role in the unfolding of the secret agent scandal, I found it interesting in many ways.

First, it gave expression to the insight that there may be a tension between the moral judgment about particular political acts and the public reaction that is appropriate to those acts. The conduct of the politician may be morally reprehensible and justifiable at the same time. That tension is genuine, and it is at the core of the moral problem of politics, even though the thesis is mistaken about its nature and sources.

There is a further feature to the separation thesis that I found appealing: it aspired to give a principled answer to the question of how the moral problem of politics should be dealt with. Any acceptable answer must, in my view, begin with the ideals of democracy and the rule of law, and the underlying moral principles such as equality, self-government, and the like. But the relationship between these ideals and principles, on the one hand, and the way the tension between moral judgment and public practical reactions in politics is to be treated is more complex and indirect than the separation thesis suggests.

The thesis makes a general statement about moral misconduct in politics, without distinguishing between violations of norms committed in pursuit of selfish advantage and violations of norms committed in pursuit of the common good. If a moral prohibition does not coincide with a legal prohibition, the act that disregards it should involve no political sanction, so the thesis goes. This is utterly implausible. The moral problem of politics has nothing to do with the alleged principle that politicians shall be immune to punishment for the legally unsanctioned wrongs they commit while seeking private gain. It is related to what is called *the problem of dirty hands*. Under certain conditions, political leaders aiming to promote the public interest, find themselves unable to do this unless they commit morally reprehensible acts. The question is: what are the relevant conditions, why does politics regularly reproduce them, and are there any ways to limit their reproduction? Rather than offering an answer, the separation thesis begs the question.

Since it has no room for the question, the separation thesis cannot offer any means to discuss the role the citizenry plays or should play in developing practices to limit the conditions under which dirtying one's hands may be justified. It is insensitive to the problem of how the public controversy over dirty-handed political acts may contribute to setting and enforcing rules that will limit their permissibility.

Thus, although the questions in this book were raised by a debate about what I have called the separation thesis, it will be best to set that thesis aside once our argument starts.

1.3 A brief outline of the argument

This book will set out from what I would call the classical doctrine. The core of the classical doctrine can be understood as two related theses: the *thesis of realism* and the *thesis of indirect motivation*.

The realist thesis originates with Machiavelli. Pre-modern political authors tried to identify the virtues that make a prince a praiseworthy and exemplary person. In Machiavelli's view, this attempt is misguided. The good prince cannot assume that if he displays virtue in his dealings with his rivals, allies, and followers, they will likewise behave in a virtuous way towards him. Politics is not the domain of moral exemplariness. Realizing one's political goals requires gaining power, and the participants in the struggle for power are inclined to violate the requirements of general morality. Therefore, if the good prince always acted within the bounds of prepolitical moral principles, he would certainly be defeated by his rivals who deliberately employ evil means. If he failed in the struggle for power, he would not be able to carry out his mission. Thus, strict compliance with moral principles is neither rational under the circumstances of the struggle for power, nor is it required by the politician's responsibilities.

Machiavelli's advice to the good prince is to act against his immoral adversaries in the same manner as they act against him. The classical thesis of realism translates this advice into a moral judgment. In the version that I believe can be rightly attributed to Machiavelli, it holds that a prince who aims to promote the common good may be permitted to commit morally reprehensible acts.

Machiavelli had a particular view about the struggle for power. For him, the struggle of the good prince to gain and retain power was, at the same time, a struggle to consolidate the institutions of a failed state, a struggle conducted in conditions of political instability and extreme insecurity. On such assumptions, it was natural for him to believe that non-compliance with morality was total, and that, therefore, the good prince was permitted to do literally anything that was necessary for him to gain and retain power. I will call this view the *unconstrained thesis of realism*.

This version of the thesis has its drawbacks. It endorses a political strategy that is extremely risky for the participants in the power struggle, and brings a great deal of suffering and destruction to the people. The costs would be lower if the competitors could be confident that the others will comply with the demands of morality. But is it at all possible to raise the level of compliance with the moral norms? This question was first posed explicitly by Thomas Hobbes and, then, by David Hume and Immanuel Kant.

Unlike Machiavelli, Hobbes did not assume that most men are evil by nature. An evil person wants other people's lives to go badly. Hobbes's man is not evil—rather, he is a psychological egoist completely uninterested in the value (whether positive or negative) of other lives. Egoists, unlike truly evil men, are capable of co-operating for mutual advantage. If we want them to co-operate in accordance with the basic requirements of morality—"the laws of nature"—they must be given incentives in terms of their selfish interests, Hobbes suggested. In Hume's view, men are driven by benevolence towards others as well as by self-interest. Kant, too, thought that men are not driven by their inclinations alone: as rational beings, they are capable of being motivated to comply with the moral law for its own sake. But both Kant and Hume took it for granted that humans are finite beings; benevolence and respect for the moral law are less reliable regulators of their conduct than self-interest. Therefore, the question of how social institutions may secure the cooperation of individuals biased in favor of themselves and ready to act against the moral law was central for them, too. Their answer was that this was possible, but not through institutions that demanded more of people than they were capable of delivering by their nature. Institutional rules should be designed in such a way that they made self-interested choices coincide with the choices dictated by morality. This is a version of what I call the indirect motivation thesis—a version that leaves no room for moral motivation and virtue in the domain of social institutions but recommends that they be replaced completely by incentives appealing to self-interest. I call it, therefore, the *narrow thesis of indirect motivation*.

The two theses supply the *classical theory* of the morality of political action. As I will try to show, the classical doctrine, although it fits well the official conception of the classics of modern political theory, is neither tenable nor fully faithful to the complexities of their thought. But I do not believe that liberal democracy could be perfected to such a degree as to leave the theses of realism and indirect motivation fully behind. Rather, I will argue for amending the two theses, and call their amended versions, respectively, the *constrained thesis of realism* and the *wide thesis of indirect motivation*. Together, they will underpin a theory of political morality that we may call *neoclassical* as it seriously amends the classical theory without completely abandoning it.

The amendments to be proposed will help to identify the place of moral motivation and common deliberation as well as of holding political agents morally accountable in (democratic) politics. Or so I hope.

I will proceed as follows. First, I will briefly summarize the central ideas of modern political theory on the nature and the constraining circumstances of politics (Chapter Two). This summary will focus on two faces of politics: politics as the identification and realization of collective aims that require control over the state to come true, and politics as an ongoing struggle for the control over the state. Next, I will try to reconstruct the classical doctrine: the unconstrained thesis of realism (Chapter Three) and the narrow thesis of indirect motivation (Chapter Four). Chapter Five will show that the classical doctrine needs to be revised. Once a state with a monopoly of force is firmly established (and as long as it is capable of effectively maintaining this monopoly) the realist thesis becomes subject to constraints; it is no longer permissible to violate certain moral minima (5.1). From here, we will turn to indirect motivation. I will show that, on the one hand, self-interest cannot fully replace moral reasons in moving people to co-operate for promoting the common good within the bounds of justice. Workable institutions economize on moral virtue rather than fully dispensing with it. On the other hand, the mechanisms of indirect motivation do not make void the right of those subject to political authority to hold the bearers of authority accountable, to ask them to justify their acts, and to punish them if those acts are unacceptable. This analysis will lead to what I will call the wide thesis of indirect motivation (5.2 and 5.3).

The classical doctrine suggests that a political agent should approach the others *strategically*. In other words, he should take their desires and beliefs as predictors of their conduct, adjust his own actions to what he expects of them, and try to influence their motivation through a variety of incentives. The revision leads to the view that politics is not exhausted by the strategic approach: *common deliberation* on the principles that guide or ought to guide politics is an irreducible component of politics. Thus, the neoclassical theory has its complexities: it gives room for a constraint on the realist principle and for forms of indirect motivation that rather than replacing moral motivation by self-interest, they mix and allow for a combination of strategic interaction with common deliberation. This raises the question of how the content of the constraint is determined and how its workings are integrated into the realist thesis (Chapter Six) and further, how the wide thesis of indirect motivation unites deliberation and strategy (Chapter Seven).

Chapter Three introduces the realist thesis as a thesis about the conditions under which a political leader is morally permitted to dirty his hands. This understanding involves two problems that will be addressed by Chapters Eight and Nine, respectively. First, according to the constrained thesis of realism, the permission to dirty one's hands is subject to respecting certain moral minima. Chapters Six and Seven try to show that those moral minima are identified and enforced in a process in which agents are being held *politically accountable* for their deeds. But it is not clear how this process would work in the cases of justified dirty hands. Max Weber, while acknowledging the existence of moral minima (by claiming that, in extreme cases, the ethics of conscience defeats the ethics of responsibility), insists that they make the leader accountable to his own conscience and to it alone. His own argument in favor of this position is defective, but Chapter Eight proposes and discusses a quasi-Weberian argument that seems to be more promising than Weber's own. The core of that argument is the observation that the first-person and third-person reactions to justified dirty-handed acts part company: the agent has good reasons for feeling badly about the act but third parties have no reason to react with indignation, scorn, or any other negative attitude to it. The discrepancy seems to make the justifiable dirty-handed act immune to any claim of accountability *to others*. In order to meet this objection, I would point out that the participants in the political process tend to be divided by honest disagreements as to whether or not a particular dirty-handed act is indeed justified. I will show that under such conditions of disagreement politicians should not be exempted from being held accountable for their dirty-handed acts.[12]

Chapter Nine addresses the paradox of dirty hands. The paradox was stated by Machiavelli as follows: In order to promote the good, the good prince must learn how not to be good. Since doing what is not good is necessary for averting some great harm, it must be morally acceptable. But since it is not good, it is morally unacceptable.

How can an act be morally acceptable and morally unacceptable at the same time? The answer in Chapter Nine will outline a theory of dirty hands. According to that theory, acts are morally evaluated from two different perspectives: from the perspective of their outcomes and from that of the way they treat their object. An act whose outcomes are better than those of any of the alternatives open to the agent may be impermissible nevertheless if it treats its object in contravention of its value. Sometimes, however, the loss from not taking the better course of action is so great that it makes treating the object in contravention of its value permissible. Taking the better course of action is morally acceptable in such cases. However, the same act may still count as violating the norms that apply to the treatment of its object. Violating those norms is morally unacceptable. Although the agent is not required to refrain from carrying out this act, he is required to face up to the fact that what he does contravenes the norms of treating the object of his action with due concern and respect for its value. Chapter Nine will argue that the analysis of (justified) dirty hands along these lines may also help to account for the problem of moral dilemmas.

The Appendix is dedicated to Václav Havel's seminal essay "The Power of the Powerless." This was the most influential attempt to make sense of the kind of politics pursued by the democratic oppositions of communist East Central Europe in the decade and a half before the collapse of the Soviet empire. Havel's reflections on dissident politics were informed by a deep moral dissatisfaction with modern liberal democracy and by a hope that the experience of the anti-totalitarian movements might offer an alternative to the democratic process as we know it. As I was involved in the same broad movement, "The Power of the Powerless" played an important role in providing concepts, images and metaphors for my own political self-understanding. The brief Appendix is meant as a partial discharge of my debt of gratitude to Havel. At the same time, it may shed some light on the diversity of the approaches to politics taken by dissident intellectuals in those years.

*

In Section 1.2 and in the footnotes to it, I mentioned several authors who gave inspiration to my work by expressing disagreement with what I said in the Medgyessy-debate. Let me mention some others who helped me by making arguments parallel to mine. I am indebted, among others, to Loránd Ambrus-Lakatos, Tamás Bauer, Péter Hack, Ferenc Huoranszki and Zoltán Miklósi. I owe special thanks to the late István Eörsi (1932–2006), writer and columnist, an old friend from the dissident movement of the 1970s and '80s, for his critical support.

Notes

1 For a symptom of this self-congratulatory mood, see F. Fukuyama: "The End of History?" In *The National Interest,* Summer 1989.

2 According to the GfK Trust Index for 2005, the politicians' index was at 11 in East Central Europe, 14 in Western Europe, and 15 in the US. At the same time, the index for business leaders was 32, 33, and 32, respectively; the index for priests was 61, 54, and 70; that for the armed forces 67, 73, and 72. See *GfK Custom Research Worldwide, Trust Index, 2005.*

3 See V. Braithwaite, V.–M. Levi, eds.: *Trust and Governance.* New York: Russell Sage Foundation 1998; D. Győrffy: "Governance in a Low-Trust Environment: The Difficulties of Fiscal Adjustment in Hungary." In *Europe-Asia Studies.* 58 (2006) 239–259.; C. Offe–U. K. Preuss: "Democratic Institutions and Moral Resources." In D. Held, ed.: *Political Theory.* Cambridge: Polity Press, 1991.

4 J. Kis: "Medgyessynek mennie kell." (Medgyessy must go) *Magyar Hírlap* June 19, 2002. The article made it clear that the fact of past collaboration with the communist counter-intelligence was not, in itself, a reason for excluding the former agent from elected office. I mentioned the case of Gyula Horn, prime minister between 1994 and 1998, who was member of the communist party's paramilitary organization in the months after the crushing of the 1956 revolution. As I said, Horn was very probably responsible for much more serious wrongdoings than Medgyessy. But his past was known to the public, and he fought his campaign by confronting the charges about his membership in the communist militia. The reason why Medgyessy ought to have gone was, I maintained, that he kept his past as an officer of the counter-intelligence secret.

5 "A fruitless and futile controversy: An interview with Péter Nádas by Zsófia Mihancsik." In *Magyar Narancs,* June 27, 2002.

6 P. Nádas: "The Risk of Reason" in *Élet és Irodalom,* January 4, 2003. This brief piece was written in response to my article "The Moral Minimum," protesting that I attributed to him the separation thesis. I returned to this controversy in my article "Politics as a Moral Problem," *Élet és Irodalom,* May 23, 2003.

7 J. Kis, "The Moral Minimum," in *Élet és Irodalom,* December 20, 2002. Political theory knows several different separation theses. One, put forward by legal positivism, holds that a proposition is a proposition of law independently of its moral content: it can be immoral and still part of the law, or it can express a true

moral principle without having legal status. Another, rooted in political liberalism, maintains that well-ordered political regimes separate the private and the
public domains from each other. The pre-theoretical claim that I call here the
separation thesis has nothing to do with the thesis of legal positivism. It shares
some features with the liberal thesis of the separation of the private from the
public but it is essentially different by virtue of its claim that the moral judgment
on the public activities of politicians must be treated as if it were a private affair.

8 A very similar claim has been put forward in 2006 in Great Britain, in a controversy over the suspension from office of Ken Livingstone, the mayor of London. See J. Ashley: "Livingstone's Suspension Is an Affront to Democracy."
Guardian, February 27, 2006, and K. Livingstone: "An Attack on Voters' Rights."
Guardian, March 1, 2006.

9 See the editorial of *Magyar Narancs,* June 27, 2002, and an article by András
Lányi: "Korunk hőse" (A Hero of Our Times), in *Heti Válasz,* June 28, 2002.

10 See Z. Fleck, "A moralisták ellen" (Against Moralists), *Élet és Irodalom,*
April 11, 2003.

11 See M. J. Gerhardt: *The Federal Impeachment Process.* Princeton, N. J.: The
University Press, 1996, 103. Nixon's legal counsel represented the view before the
Senate Judiciary Committee that the process could be started only for criminal
acts. By contrast, the committee held that it was sufficient if the president was
proved to have committed an act that "threatens the integrity of his office." See
"Impeachment" in the *Encyclopedia Americana.* The more than 430 constitutional
lawyers who argued against impeaching Clinton were not arguing that Clinton
had done nothing illegal but that impeachment must be based on "grossly derelict
exercise of official power," while the acts with which Clinton had been charged
were unrelated to the exercise of presidential powers. See Bernard J. Hibbits,
"More Than 430 Law Professors Send Letter to Congress Opposing Impeachment," *The Jurist,* November 7, 1998.

12 As it may become apparent from this brief summary, the reflections of this
book aim to elucidate the problem of dirty hands as it is raised by democratic
politics. The expression "dirty hands" itself does not, however, originate in democratic thought. It dates back to Jean-Paul Sartre's drama, *Dirty Hands,* a *mor-
alité* on revolutionary politics. The communist leader Hoederer tells Hugo, his
young comrade-in-arms: "How you cling to your purity, young man! How afraid
you are to soil your hands! All right, stay pure! What good will it do? Why did
you join us? Purity is an idea for a yogi or a monk. You intellectuals and bourgeois anarchists use it as a pretext for doing nothing. To do nothing, to remain
motionless, arms at your sides, wearing kid gloves. Well, I have dirty hands. Right
up to the elbows. I have plunged them in filth and blood. But what do you hope?
Do you think you can govern innocently?" Hoederer's tirade is directed against
what he sees as petty-bourgeois sentimentalism. But he has another adversary,
who remains hidden in the play. The leaders of the Bolshevik revolution viewed

the sentimental rejection of dirty means with the same contempt as did Sartre, the fellow-traveller of a later generation. But their view was based on a very different conception. Morality, they insisted, is always class morality, its standards are relative to the class that holds it. The prohibition against unlawful violence is a norm of bourgeois morality. The morality of the proletariat rejects this prohibition as nothing but a means to sustain the rule of the bourgeoisie. What ultimately decides the contest of conflicting class moralities is the historic role of the classes whose interests they serve. The progressive class's morality is progressive, the reactionary class's morality is reactionary. In an earlier historical period, the bourgeoisie used to play the role of the progressive class, and so its morality also played a progressive role. By now, however, history has left the bourgeoisie behind, and elevated the proletariat to the status of the progressive class. To the extent that it is an effective means of the proletarian revolution, unlawful violence is morally acceptable. This standpoint may be characterized as a mixture of moral nihilism, relativism, and consequentialism; it is best summarized in Trotsky's writings. See his polemics against Kautsky in *Terrorism and Communism* (originally published in 1920; English translation Ann Arbor: University of Michigan Press, 1961), and his essay "Their Morals and Ours" that responded to the criticism of John Dewey (see L. Trotsky, *The Basic Writings*. New York: Basic Books, 1968). On Lenin's and Trotsky's views see S. Lukes: *Marxism and Morality* (Oxford: The University Press, 1987). Hoederer is neither a nihilist nor a consequentialist or a relativist. Rather, he is motivated by despair, and his despair is driven by deep moral concerns: he knows that the necessity of acting with dirty hands does not make the agent's hands any less dirty. (Sartre's conception is further complicated by the fact that he viewed revolutionary violence not only as a means to an end but also as an act of self-liberation: see J.-P. Sartre, *Cahiers pour une morale*. Paris: Gallimard 1983, 412–421, and his foreword to Frantz Fanon's *Les damnés de la terre* (Paris: Maspéro, 1963). – I will not address the moral problem of revolutionary politics in this book. I have discussed it in great detail in an essay about the young György Lukács's commitment to the communist movement, and his reflections on revolutionary violence; see J. Kis: "Lukács György dilemmája" (The Dilemma of György Lukács), in *Holmi*, 5/2003.

CHAPTER TWO

THE CIRCUMSTANCES OF POLITICS

2.1 Two faces of politics

Politics is an ongoing activity through which political communities shape their identity, set goals for themselves, identify principles for regulating their internal conflicts, and resolve those conflicts in accordance with accepted principles.

A community is a relatively stable social group, whose members are related to each other through shared institutions, such as marriage and the family, ownership and inheritance, contract, association, and dispute management. A community is political if its constitutive institutions include a state. States are organizations that have successfully claimed a monopoly of control over the use of coercive force in a given territory. According to an apt formulation by Robert Nozick,

> A state claims a monopoly on deciding who may use force when; it says that only it may decide who may use force and under what conditions; it reserves for itself the sole right to pass on the legitimacy and permissibility of any use of force within its boundaries; furthermore it claims the right to punish all those who violate its claim of monopoly.[1]

If the use of coercive power is to be legitimate, it must be authorized by an appropriate organ of the state. When force is used in a territory where there is no state to authorize it, the coercive act may be just or unjust but it cannot be legitimate or illegitimate: it is simply *non-legitimate*. When force is used within the jurisdiction of an existing state without that state's authorization, the coercive act is *illegitimate*.

But a state's claim of exclusive control over the use of coercive force must also pass the test of legitimacy. For this to be the case, its claim must be beyond effective challenge.[2]

To have unchallenged control over the use of force in a territory is not, however, a sufficient condition for a state to be legitimate. The monopoly of control over the use of coercive force creates unequal relationships between those occupying official positions in the government and those subjected to their rule. Officials may issue directives backed by coercion to their subjects who, on their part, are supposed to obey and to avoid using coercive force without official authorization. But the moral relationship between human beings is egalitarian. None is inherently superior to the other. As the classics of modern political philosophy have put it, "men are born free and equal."[3] Human beings are capable of acting for reasons, of setting short-term and long-term goals for their activity, and of subjecting their acts to the hierarchy of those goals. They have the capacity to make something of their lives, and this capacity is possessed by virtually all to a sufficiently high degree. No normal adult human being needs systematic guidance from others in order to lead his own life.[4] Although the rational capacities of different individuals vary, the differences of degree that exist between normal adults do not justify the claim that some are born to live under the rule of others. And if nobody is born to be ruled, then nobody can be born to rule, either.[5]

No state has *legitimate* monopoly of coercive force unless its claim of monopoly can be shown to be compatible with the fundamental moral relationship between human beings, which involves freedom and equality.

Anarchists insist that states are essentially incompatible with this requirement.[6] The only—or at least the predominant—function of their monopoly of control over coercive force is to make the majority unfree and to allow a minority to take unfair advantage of the unfreedom of the many. There can be no human emancipation, they argue, without the abolition of any organization that monopolizes the control over the means of coercion.

Conservatives deny that humans merely as humans can possess that fundamental moral standing which is supposed to make them each other's equals. Liberals affirm the principle of fundamental moral equality. The liberal project can be understood as one of meeting anarchism on its own territory.

The liberal argument consists of two parts. First, it shows that a society without a supreme organization monopolizing the control over the use of force would not be a peaceful association of free and

equal individuals but a theater of unregulated struggle of private coercive organizations competing with each other for power and economic
resources. It is not necessary to assume that those who band together
into coercive organizations do this with the unjust aim of subjugating
and exploiting the rest. One may concede to the anarchists that the
withering away of the state would make all humans infinitely benevolent and strictly abiding by their duties, and still find that a stateless
society would be a society torn by permanent internal wars. For such
a finding to hold, it is sufficient to assume that the withering away of
the state does not remove the possibility of good-faith disagreements.
Suppose that all individuals seek justice but that they do not agree on
what is it that justice requires. Suppose members of a group of individuals honestly believe that the current distribution of burdens and
benefits in their society is deeply unjust, and suppose they are unable
to convince the members of another group that the existing distribution of resources is unjust, nor can the others convince them that justice requires that the existing distribution be preserved. Then, for the
latter, changing by force the existing distribution would be a matter of
unjust interference with just economic relationships while, for the
former, protecting it by force would count as unjust interference with
a process of change required by justice. Naked force would be opposed to naked force, not because one of the sides seeks unjust advantages but because the two sides, both seeking justice, disagree on
whether the existing distribution of advantages and disadvantages or a
proposed alternative to it is just.[7]

Thus, early liberals agree with Hobbes that

> In such condition, there is no place for Industry; because the fruit
> thereof is uncertain: and consequently no Culture of the Earth; no
> navigation, nor use of the commodities that may be imported by
> Sea; no commodious Building; no Instruments of moving, and
> removing such things as require much force; no Knowledge of the
> face of the Earth; no account of Time; no Arts; no Letters; no So-
> ciety; and which is worst of all, continuall feare, and danger of vio-
> lent death; And the life of man, solitary, poore, nasty, brutish, and
> short.[8]

Contemporary liberals share this view. The first political question
is that of "securing of order, protection, safety, trust, and the condi-

tions of cooperation," Bernard Williams insists, for example. Solving this question is "the condition of solving, indeed posing, any others."[9] If political communities capable of enforcing moral standards in the relationships of their members are to exist, states must exist, too. This is the first condition of political legitimacy, that I mentioned above.

Once states exist, the moral standing of human individuals as free and equal persons confronts them with the second requirement of political legitimacy. There must be a set of basic rights that all human beings possess, and that they all possess equally: a state that treats its subjects as equals is one that respects and ensures respect for those rights within its jurisdiction with regard to all and without discrimination. Furthermore, human individuals must not be subjected to coercive power arbitrarily but under the constraints of specific rules: the use of coercive power must be regulated by laws; the laws must be relatively stable and accessible to all; they must be general in form and apply impartially; they must be prospective rather than retroactive; and the rules under which they are made, repealed, amended and applied must in their turn be relatively stable and widely known. In other words, human beings of an equal moral standing have a right to be governed within the bounds of the rule of law. Moral equality also demands that none should have privileged access to the official roles of coercive institutions. Official roles must be open to all those, and only to those, who are subjected to the state's power and authority; the offices must be filled, directly or indirectly, by the collective choice of all the subjects, and all the participants in the choice procedure must have an equal vote. Finally, the elected officials must pursue, in their official capacity, the good of the community of the subjects; in so doing, they must treat the status and interests of all members of the community with equal concern and respect, and they must be accountable to the community for their official actions and omissions. In a legitimate state the political community is self-governing. Wherever constitutional democracy is a realistic option, no state can be legitimate without being a constitutional democracy.

However, legitimacy is not to be understood as an all-or-nothing property; it admits of dimensions and degrees. Rather than being either fully legitimate or completely illegitimate, a state may be more or less legitimate. Even contemporary constitutional democracies are far from completely matching the criteria of legitimacy listed above.[10] And even non-democratic states may command some legitimacy.

For an organization to be something else than a warlord with his private army, it must genuinely aspire to satisfy the criteria of legitimacy. Furthermore, it must leave room for criticism of its actual practices and procedures. And if the aspiration to live up to the promises of a legitimate state is genuine, the state must be responsive to criticism: it must include procedures of self-correction that bring it closer to the ideal of the self-government of equals even if no state is likely ever to meet that ideal completely.

To the extent that an organization with a monopoly of control over the use of coercive force meets these requirements of claim, aspiration, critical public space and responsiveness, it is a legitimate state rather than a warlord's private army.

Once the concept of a—legitimate—state is given, we can identify a political community as a group bounded by the boundaries of their state. A human population caught up in the power struggle of mutually excluding coercive organizations can form no political community. In this sense, states are constitutive of political communities by virtue of their first condition of legitimacy—the monopoly of control over the coercive force in a given territory. At the same time, the second set of legitimacy conditions—which requires them to treat their subjects in accordance with their moral status as free and equal persons—involves that legitimate states are owned by their community and serve it as a means to define and pursue its collective aims.

This finding allows us to make explicit a hidden aspect of the definition of politics with which the present chapter started. For the aims of this book, politics is an ongoing activity through which political communities shape their identity, set common goals for themselves, identify principles for regulating their internal conflicts, and resolve those conflicts *by way of deciding what their state shall do and what principles it shall observe in doing what they want it to do.*

Of course, there is also a great deal of struggle between private coercive organizations in stateless conditions. Such struggles may count as politics, provided that they aim at consolidating a state over a particular territory and transforming the population of that territory into a political community. The mere confrontation of private coercive organizations, however, has nothing to do with politics as a communal activity.

As a state-bound activity, politics has a second aspect, not included in the definition at the beginning of this section. Politics is inherently related to the struggle for the control over the state's apparatuses.

Under very special conditions, the control over the state apparatus may be conceived as directly held by the community at large, as in a Rousseauian direct democracy. But in contemporary societies those special conditions are absent, and the control over the state is delegated to a group of office-holders, that is a small fraction of the community, who act as its *representatives*.

To the extent that politics includes action through representatives, it also includes procedures to select the representatives from the larger community. In all political regimes, those procedures have an enormous impact on what collective aims the state will pursue. The processes through which political issues are defined and political decisions are reached are inextricably linked with the processes which decide who shall occupy the positions of control over the state's apparatus.

Thus, as a state-bound activity, politics is not reducible to common deliberation and decision-making. It is at the same time *struggle for power*. Which of the competing policy platforms will obtain the go-ahead does not depend exclusively on the force of arguments but, most importantly, on who will be the winner in that struggle.

As holders of office, representatives are supposed to proceed in the name and for the benefit of the represented, to pursue the public interest rather than their own private interest or that of their extended family and friends, and to give, in the process of deliberating on the common good, an impartial consideration to the interests of all. "Statesmen may have their own interests when they hold office, but they must be selfless in their judgments and assessments of their society's fundamental interests, and must not be swayed ... by passions of vindictiveness," John Rawls claims.[11] And Ronald Dworkin insists that while in our private lives "we have particular responsibilities toward those with whom we have special relationships," in the political life of the community, we have to work "for policies that ... treat every citizen as equal."[12] Selflessness and impartiality inform the ideal of the statesman.

Yet even in a democracy, before a politician can live up to this ideal he must first occupy political office, and the selection process is a zero-sum competitive game. As competitors for office, politicians cannot be required to be guided by the impartially determined common good alone. If that were the case, they would have to subordinate the fight for their own victory to the fight for the victory *of the best candidate*, whoever that person might be. We would find such a fight unintelligible.

Participants in power struggles are permitted to be biased in favor of *their own* victory. This doesn't mean that they are permitted to do whatever may improve their chances of gaining and retaining power. Not all means are morally acceptable. The competitive character of the selection of office-holders does not make diverting public resources to private aims, nepotism, or selling official influence permissible, for example. Furthermore, running for political office cannot be justified unless it is part of a larger project to serve the community, and to serve it with an impartial concern for all its members. But those who run for political office are permitted to seek power *for themselves*, rather than for another, whose advancement would be most desirable from an impersonal point of view.

This finding would be of limited significance if the struggle *for* power were neatly separable from the struggles politicians fight while *in* power; in other words, if the competition for office were neatly separable from the competition between policies. But there is no sharp line to separate the two sets of activities. As is often repeated in the press, the next electoral campaign begins on the day the results of the present election are announced. Whatever an incumbent does or omits to do is rightly perceived as having some impact on his chances to stay in power. And the permission to be partial must apply to at least some of the choices which are likely to affect these chances. Therefore it is not the case that while as a participant in the struggle for power a representative is allowed to give special consideration to his own career interests, as a power-holder, he must give strict priority to the impartially determined common interest. At all stages of his career, he is permitted to strike some balance between his other-regarding and impartial concerns as a representative of the community and his self-regarding reasons as a participant in an ongoing competition for the position of representative.

In sum, politics in a modern state is a Janus-faced activity. Its two faces are intimately related to the two aspects of the state's legitimacy: the moral aspect and the monopoly of power aspect. On the one hand, representatives are subjected to heightened moral expectations.

As agents of the community, they are supposed to seek selflessly to advance the common good and to treat the interests of all with an impartial concern. They are supposed to be faithful and trustworthy servants of the community. As participants in the competition for office, however, they are allowed, within limits, to pursue their own advancement.

In order to fully grasp the significance of this dualism, we have to consider another complexity characteristic of politics. There is no community without a shared aim to settle on common principles to regulate the interaction of its members, on common objectives to pursue together, and on common policies to realize those objectives. Individuals in search of shared principles, objectives, and policies are parties to *common deliberation* on what is best for them collectively to do. Representatives are supposed to facilitate and promote collective deliberation by way of giving impartial consideration to the interests of all, and straightforwardly expressing their views on the common good as determined subject to the constraint of impartiality. But common deliberation and straightforward argument are not the only dimension of legitimate politics. Even assuming full agreement on principles, objectives, and policies, there is room for what is generally called *strategic action*. In its most abstract understanding, strategic action means action that is responsive to the way other agents may choose and act. Without being responsive in this way, agents cannot co-ordinate their action to reach their coinciding objectives. So strategic interaction aiming to reach coinciding objectives is morally unproblematic.[13]

Politicians as competitors for power do not, however, pursue shared aims. They compete for the limited good of elected office. Their strategic responses to each other's expected acts are conflictual rather than cooperative, adversarial rather than friendly. Since they are morally permitted to fight for their own victory, they are also permitted to think and to express their thoughts in terms of adversarial strategy. Permissible political action is not reducible to common deliberation-cum-decision and what I would call co-ordination strategy. It is also essentially linked to strategies of conflict, strategies of an adversarial nature. A politician of good intentions but of little talent for the strategy of conflict is not a good politician; a good politician has considerable capacities to win allies for his cause and to neutralize his enemies, to make good bargains, to use the means of threat effectively, and to reveal or to conceal his aims depending on the necessities of the political game.

The struggle for power is a systematic source of the presence of adversarial strategies in the political process. There are further sources as well. Politicians represent interests that often compete with each other for scarce resources and opportunities, and they represent ideals, principles, or aspirations that tend to be objects of deep disagreement. Adversarial strategy is, thus, a pervasive phenomenon of politics.

I do not mean to suggest that all strategic moves that may promote a morally defensible cause are permissible. The question of the moral limits of permissible strategy is one of the key questions this book will try to address. What we can establish at this point is that no moral limits of political action may be as strict as to exclude from politics all kinds of adversarial strategy.

2.2 Insufficient compliance

Strategic choices react to the expected choices and acts of others. The relevant expectations depend to a large extent on whether those others can be relied on to comply faithfully with moral norms and institutional rules. The problem of the degree of compliance to be expected in a society is at the core of a distinction made by John Rawls, in *A Theory of Justice*, between ideal and non-ideal theory.

Ideal theory, Rawls says, "works out the principles that characterize a well-ordered society under favorable circumstances," while non-ideal theory applies "under less happy conditions."[14] What is a well-ordered society?

It is, first, a society whose members accept the principles of justice; they all accept the same principles, and everybody knows that everybody else accepts the same principles. Secondly, it is a society whose basic institutions work in conformity with the generally accepted principles of justice, and this, too, is known by everybody. These two conditions are summarized by Rawls in the statement that well-ordered societies are governed by a "public conception of justice."[15] Finally, the members of a well-ordered society "have a strong and normally effective desire to act as the principles of justice require,"[16] and this is also common knowledge among them.[17]

Together, these assumptions imply that all members of a well-ordered society normally abide by all the directives of the institutions of their society on all occasions. Rawls calls this "strict compliance."[18]

An individual may be motivated to act in contravention to moral principles or institutional rules either directly or indirectly. He may be directly motivated to act in this manner by his desire to take unfair advantage of the sacrifices of others. Or he may be motivated to do so indirectly by the fear that others will take advantage of his sacrifices. The first motive is neutralized by the assumption that in well-ordered societies everybody is guided by an effective sense of justice. Since in well-ordered societies the institutional rules are consistent with the generally accepted principles of justice, and since everyone knows this, the desire not to take advantage of the sacrifices of others moves everyone to abide by the rules. Similarly, it is easy to see why the second motive remains inert in a society where everybody is governed by an effective sense of justice, and where everybody knows this about everybody else. Under such conditions, nobody has any reason to fear that others will unfairly exploit his cooperative efforts. Where people are not only individually motivated to comply with the institutional rules but know that everybody else is motivated in the same way, all can be assured that they will not suffer any unfair disadvantage as a result of their compliance (with institutions that are presumed to be just).[19]

Note that a well-ordered society would not demand too much from its members. The assumption that everybody is effectively motivated by a sense of justice does not imply that individuals are required to make greater sacrifices than an ordinary human being can be expected to make. Well-ordered societies are just societies, rather than societies beyond justice, and Rawls explicitly refers to limited altruism as one of the circumstances, alongside moderate scarcity of resources, that make justice both necessary and possible. At the same time, just institutions leave great freedom for everyone to pursue his personal aims. To borrow an expression from Thomas Nagel, a well-ordered society arranges a kind of moral division of labor between institutions and individuals.[20] It is up to the institutions to determine the requirements of justice the individuals must abide by, and to make sure that those requirements are met. If the combination of individual choices and efforts results in an unjust distribution of burdens and benefits, it is

the working of the basic structure of society that is supposed to restore justice. The individuals can rest contented with obeying the institutions; within the limits of obedience, they are free to pursue their
own personal ends, and those limits are permissive enough. The institutions are indifferent to any pursuit that does not impose any unjust
burdens on others: the principles of justice, Rawls maintains, "do not
rank the system of ends."[21]

Thus, strict compliance with just institutions is not excessively demanding. It leaves room for a morally permissible pursuit of personal
interests. And yet, strict compliance at best marks out a vanishing
point that actual human interaction in existing societies may approximate to various degrees without ever reaching it. Although limited altruism is taken care of by the idea of a well-ordered society,
other imperfections of human nature are not.

The sense of justice in human individuals is generally of a limited
efficacy, and the intentions, dispositions or attitudes of one are not
fully transparent to another. As a rule, individuals cannot be sure how
effectively their fellow-individuals are motivated by a sense of justice.
But if we drop the assumptions of a normally effective desire to act in
conformity with the principles of justice, and of a general knowledge
that this desire is normally effective in all members of the community,
the implication of strict compliance falls away. Presumably, many
individuals will be directly motivated to choose non-compliance on
many occasions, and many others will fear that even more people are
motivated to choose non-compliance on even more occasions. As a
result, the latter will be indirectly motivated to choose non-compliance
themselves. A theory of justice that accounts for the anthropological
circumstances of justice in a realistic manner must be a "partial
(rather than strict) compliance theory."[22]

If this is true in general, it must be true in particular about the circumstances of politics that include the struggle for power, a zero-sum
game. Constitutional democracies are special, but not in the way of
eliminating the competition for office from politics. They pacify it,
subject it to the principle of equality, impose regular procedures on it,
and turn it into the service of public deliberation and decision-
making. But they don't make it obsolete.

Section 2.1 concluded with the finding that politics by representation may never be fully reduced to common deliberation, decision,
and co-ordination: it is at the same time a process of strategic interac-

tion (of an adversarial character). We can now add that political strategy is necessarily based on the assumption that the competitors, adversaries, and possible allies do not fully comply with the principles and rules of politics.

When distinguishing non-ideal or partial compliance theory from ideal or strict compliance theory, Rawls identifies the object of the first as a family of problems such as punishment, compensation for unjustly caused harm, or just war. These issues are all related to the question of what the society is required or permitted to do in order to minimize or rectify the wrongs from partial compliance.[23] The focus on rectification and damage minimalization involves a simple binary disjunction between strict and partial compliance. Thus, for Rawls, compliance is either strict ("yes") or it is partial ("no"). The fact that partial compliance may depart from strict compliance to various degrees does not matter for him. But of course compliance varies in degrees. And when we apply Rawls's distinction to the domain of political struggles, the fact that compliance may be partial to different degrees becomes relevant. Here, the question is not reducible to the one asking, what to do in order to rectify or minimize the wrongs due to non-compliance. The struggle for power is strategic interaction and partial compliance is a factor in such interaction. When one moves downward on the compliance slope, one may reach a critical boundary. Above that boundary, even if the condition of full compliance is not met, its failure to obtain does not morally justify defection on the part of a particular person. Once the level of compliance drops to the critical boundary, its fall makes defection permissible. Above the boundary, enough others comply with the rules on enough occasions. Below that boundary, too many others defect on too many occasions. I will call the levels of compliance that stop short of affecting the reasons for complying "sufficient compliance," while all the levels below this will be called "insufficient compliance."

To sum up, politics is a domain where insufficient compliance is the rule rather than the exception. Political action is a type of strategic action under the conditions of insufficient overall compliance.

Proposing a distinction between strict compliance and partial compliance, Rawls makes it clear that, in order to identify the principles of justice, political theory must set out from an assumption of strict compliance. It would be perverse to allow the standards of fairness and justice to be manipulated by the failure to comply with the requirements of morality and the rules of social institutions. More generally, a theory of justice that allows the standards of just distribution to depend on strategic behavior cannot be a true theory of justice.

This may explain why Rawls's *Theory* is silent about strategy. It may also explain why it is silent about politics as we know it. The upshot is that the assumptions of a plausible theory of political action cannot be restricted to the assumptions of the theory of justice. Following Hume, Rawls calls these the circumstances of justice and characterizes them as a combination of identity of interests with conflicts of interest; as many individuals living together in a definite geographical territory; as people being roughly similar in physical and mental powers and in their vulnerability to attacks; as a moderate scarcity of goods; as shortcomings of knowledge, thought, judgment, and the like.[24] It is reasonable to assume that the circumstances of politics include all these conditions and more. Jeremy Waldron suggests that we add the combination of a need to cooperate and an absence of any general agreement on the principles of just cooperation. This, he says, is what gives rise to the need for the law and the state.[25] I would like to add four further conditions: the existence of an organization monopolizing the legitimate control over coercive force, competition for the positions of control over this organization, strategic interaction, and insufficient compliance.

This chapter has argued for the plausibility of the assumptions of strategic interaction and of insufficient compliance, based on the other two assumptions we added to the circumstances of politics: that politics as we know it is a state-bound activity and that, as a consequence, power struggles are constitutive of it. That argument did not imply that state power and power struggles would be *necessary* conditions for the presence of strategy and insufficient compliance. It was only meant to show that they are *sufficient* conditions. I am not suggesting that they are the only conditions. But they are the most important conditions that, in the domain of politics, *systematically* generate strategic action and insufficient compliance.

2.3 Preliminary remarks on politics as a moral problem

Politics is a set of practices through which a community shapes its own identity, adopts the aims and means of collective action, and distributes its burdens and benefits. As such, it is inseparable from common deliberation on shared aims and principles.

At the same time, politics is constituted by strategic interaction, often of an adversarial character. The core of political strategy is competition for control over the state, but strategy has its place in all walks of life where political decisions are taken.

Political strategies are usually devised on the assumption of an insufficient degree of general compliance. Given insufficient compliance, agents cannot be expected to comply with the principles and rules disregarded by others. "Cannot be expected to comply" does not simply mean that it may not be rational for them to comply. It also means that they may be morally permitted not to comply. To comply with a rule disregarded by others may amount to allowing oneself to be made the victim of unfair treatment, and nobody can be morally required to do that. The principle that one cannot be required to allow oneself to be treated unfairly applies to all conceivable strategic situations, including those arising in a community of equals that is not ordered by state institutions. A more specific principle applies to representatives or office-holders in a state, who are expected to act in the name and for the benefit of those who jointly—as a political community—own the state in question. Representatives bear special responsibility for the outcome of their actions since the purpose of representation is to serve the represented. Their conduct is judged to a larger than usual extent by the consequences of what they choose to do, and this circumstance, too, contributes to making it morally permissible for them to proceed, sometimes in a non-compliant manner.

When insufficient overall compliance makes it permissible for an agent to act in contravention of the generally disregarded rule, there may be nothing wrong with his non-compliant action. But that is not always the case. Acting in contravention of a generally disregarded rule may be permissible and yet censured in moral terms. It may be permissible, in certain circumstances, to mislead the public, to betray an ally, or to cooperate with corrupt people. But misleading the public, betraying an ally, cooperating with corrupt people remains morally reprehensible even if that is what the agent may be permitted to act in these ways. It is in such cases that one tends to say that the agent got his hands dirty.

The problem of dirty hands makes the phenomenon of strategic action under insufficient compliance particularly difficult for the theory of morality to deal with. Both main currents of contemporary moral philosophy—consequentialism and deontology—are perplexed by this problem.

Consequentialism in its simpler, act-consequentialist, version holds that an act is right if, all things considered, it brings about at least as good a state of affairs as any of the alternatives open to the agent. The moral considerations that count against carrying out a right act must be given their due weight in the overall balance of reasons for and against it. But the question whether the act is morally acceptable is decided by the overall balance alone. Once a particular reason has made its contribution to that balance, it has no further role to play. It follows that no act can be right and reprehensible at the same time— we have simply no conceptual resources to make such a judgment.

Rule-consequentialism is capable of accounting for the *appearance* of acting justifiably with dirty hands, but not for the claim that a particular act is *really* right and dirty-handed at the same time. According to rule-consequentialism, an act is right if it is permitted or required by a system of moral rules the general acceptance of which results in at least as good a result as the general acceptance of any of its alternatives. In other words, an act that is allowed by the best system of moral rules is right, while an act that is prohibited by that system is wrong. The best moral system would qualify its rules with appropriate exception clauses so as to minimize the possibility of conflict among them, and it would entail second-order priority rules to decide which rule is to be acted upon if two rules that do not lend themselves to further amendment should come into conflict with each other. Such a moral system would identify any acts as either non-ambiguously right or non-ambiguously wrong. It would not allow for conflicts between right acts and dirty hands. And since the claim that an act is really right means that it is endorsed by the best system of moral rules, and the claim that an act is really wrong means that it is disapproved of by the best system, the best system rules out the possibility of an act being *really* both right and dirty-handed at the same time.

Deontological theories claim that the criteria of the moral assessment of actions proposed by consequentialism are either wrong or at
least incomplete. When acts are assessed for their moral worth, it is
not the comparative value of their outcomes alone that matters. It
matters, too, whether they treat their object—above all, human beings—properly. An act may bring about the best outcome and yet be
morally impermissible because it counts as violation of a moral right,
or as offending human dignity, or treating a person as a mere means.
Thus, deontology is capable of making judgments that distinguish
between an act being best in terms of its outcomes and wrong in terms
of the way it deals with its object. As a consequence, deontology also
has the tools for judging an act with the best possible outcomes as
dirty-handed: one acts with dirty hands if one treats the object of the
action in a way that counts as violating a deontological constraint. But
deontology seems to imply that dirty-handed acts are simply to be
avoided as violations of some moral prohibition or other.

This is so because of the insistence of deontology that the constraints of morality do not compete with outcome-related reasons. A
constraint is not a very weighty reason, capable of overriding all the
outcome-related reasons, whether separately or in combination.
Rather, it is a higher-order principle that prohibits us to act for certain types of reason on certain occasions, no matter how great a
good would be produced by the act in question. Accordingly, to
claim that a constraint is overridden by the consequentialist value of
an act seems to misstate the relationship between constraints and
consequences. Nor must a constraint be ignored on the ground that
it conflicts with some other constraint. Deontologists tend to share
with rule-consequentialists the assumption that true moral standards
are endowed with the requisite exception clauses. They tend to hold
that, sometimes, deontological standards appear to conflict with
each other but, properly amended, can always be satisfied together.
Apparently, they also tend to deny the possibility of an act being
right and dirty-handed at the same time.

For consequentialists, no act can be morally objectionable if it
maximizes the good or if it is allowed by a system of moral rules that
maximizes the good. For deontologists, no act can be permissibly
performed if it is morally objectionable.

I believe that the moral problem of politics cannot be made sense
of unless one succeeds in showing that good-maximizing acts may be

morally objectionable, and that morally objectionable acts may be permissible under certain circumstances. One of the central aims of this book is to elucidate this general idea and to give some support to it. But before I address the question of how to interpret the possibility of permissible dirty hands in terms of moral theory, I will complete the political argument.

In this book, the claim that, under certain circumstances, dirty-handed acts are morally permissible, will be called the *thesis of realism*. It is part of the heritage of classical political theory. Another classical thesis holds that the scope of permissibly dirty hands may be narrowed by devising institutions that encourage overall compliance with moral norms at a higher level, but that such institutions should predominantly appeal to non-moral interests. I will call this the *thesis of indirect motivation*. We have inherited both theses from classical doctrine in a specific form: the thesis of realism unconstrained, the thesis of indirect motivation narrowly understood. In Chapters Three and Four I will reconstruct the two theses in their classical form. This may help us better to understand why political theory, as inherited from the past, is unable to cope with the central moral problems of political action. Chapters Five to Seven will be devoted to the revision of the classical theses.

Notes

1 R. Nozick: *Anarchy, State, and Utopia*. Oxford: Blackwell, 1973, 23. The standard, Weberian definition of the state speaks about the (legitimate) monopoly of possessing and using the means of violence. Nozick's definition focuses on the monopoly of control over the use of the means of violence. It is neutral between controlling coercive force by monopolizing its legitimate *use* and controlling it by monopolizing the ultimate *decision* on who may use it. This definition allows an organization to be a state even if it gives licence to private firms to police the streets, to manage prisons, and so on. Whether we approve it or not, outsourcing coercion is a phenomenon of increasing dimensions in contemporary states, and Nozick's definition, unlike Weber's, is capable of accommodating this phenomenon. I, for one, find the rise of outsourcing of the coercive functions of the state a troublesome tendency, but I agree that even if it affects the moral quality of the modern state, it does not necessarily undermine its statehood.

2 The claim that states have exclusive control over the use of force in a territory does not imply that in order for an organization to qualify as state it must

command absolute sovereignty. Our definition is compatible with the existence of supra-state bodies that limit the sovereign power of states so long as the rights of these bodies to interfere with a state's internal affairs is delegated by the state in question and so long as the delegation is revocable. Thus, our identification of a state is not conceptually tied to the Westphalia order of international relations.

3 "[A]ll men equally are by nature free." T. Hobbes: *Leviathan.* Cambridge: The University Press, 1991, 150. "Thus, we are born free as we are born rational..." J. Locke: *Two Treatises of Government.* Cambridge: The University Press, 1960, 308.

4 "The freedom ... of man and liberty of acting according to his own will is grounded on his having reason which is able to instruct him in that law he is to govern himself by and make him know how far he is left to the freedom of his own will." Locke: *Two Treatises,* 309.

5 "Age or virtue give men a just precedency; excellence of parts and merit may place others above the common level; birth may subject some and alliance or benefits others to pay an observance to those to whom nature, gratitude or other respects may have made it due; and yet all this consists with the equality which all men are in respect of jurisdiction or dominion one over the other..." Ibid., 304.

6 Classical Marxism shares this view.

7 See I. Kant: *The Metaphysics of Morals.* In Kant: *Practical Philosophy.* M. J. Gregor, ed. Cambridge: The University Press, 1996, 455 f.

8 T. Hobbes: *Leviathan.* Cambridge: The University Press, 1991, 89.

9 B. Williams: "Realism and Moralism in Political Theory." In Williams: *In the Beginning Was the Deed.* Princeton–Oxford: Princeton University Press, 2005, 3.

10 Think of the poor quality of political deliberation, of the low level of accountability of public officials, and of the enormous role private money plays in the political process.

11 J. Rawls: *The Law of Peoples.* Cambridge–London: Harvard University Press, 1999, 97 f.

12 R. Dworkin: "Liberal Community". In Dworkin: *Sovereign Virtue.* Cambridge–London: Harvard University Press, 2000, 235.

13 Here is a famous example: *A* and *B* agree to meet at 7 in the evening, but they forget to arrange for the place. There is no way for them to get in touch before 7 pm. But they both want to see the other. What shall they do? Clearly, they have to coordinate their action without talking to each other. They have to identify the place where the other is most likely to go, and go there. But if *A* finds out that *B* is most likely to go to *b*, and *B* finds out that *A* is most likely to go to *a*, and if *A* goes to *b* while *B* going to *a*, then they won't meet. Once *A* understands this, he has to ask himself if it is not better for him to go to *a* rather than to *b*. But if *B* reasons in the same manner, then she will go to *b* and they will not meet, and so on. Unless one of them has a cue about the likely choice of the other, they cannot coordinate.

14 J. Rawls: *A Theory of Justice*. Cambridge, Mass.: Harvard University Press, 1971, 245 f.

15 *Theory*, 4 f.

16 Ibid., 5.

17 *Theory*, 5, 454.

18 See *Theory*, 8 f, 245 f, 351.

19 Ibid., 497. More precisely, Rawls makes the following assumption with respect to the second motivation: even though the members of well-ordered societies know that other members are motivated to comply with the rules of institutions, they cannot be absolutely sure that this motivation will be sufficient under all circumstances. Their knowledge is not enough to make mutual trust perfect. The suspicion that some may violate the rules will loom large, and this intuition will force everyone to violate the rules, at least every once in a while. Therefore, even well-ordered societies need to support institutions with the threat of force. Only this can provide guarantees to members of the society that others will comply with the rules the same way as they do. Rawls calls this the Hobbes thesis, acknowledging the fact that here he is making a conscious concession to the stringent stipulations of ideal theory. However, the correspondence with Hobbes's arguments is only partial; in Hobbes's state of nature both motivations for violating the rules are present—the desire to gain unjustified benefits and the fear of unjustified benefits gained by others. By contrast, Rawls's well-ordered society leaves room only for the second. Therefore, Rawls believes, in well-ordered societies a mere threat of coercion may suffice to secure strict compliance; actual use of punitive measures may never have to occur. See *Theory*, 240.

20 I. T. Nagel: *Equality and Partiality*. Oxford: The University Press, 1991, 86.

21 *Theory*, 19.

22 *Theory*, 8 f.

23 Ibid. Another example given by Rawls is "weighing one form of institutional injustice against another". This issue, too, boils down to minimizing the injustices due to partial compliance.

24 Ibid., 126 ff.

25 See J. Waldron: *The Dignity of Legislation*. Cambridge: The University Press, 1999.

CHAPTER THREE

REALISM: THE UNCONSTRAINED THESIS

3.1 Machiavelli's paradox

The rise of modern political thinking was intimately linked to two key ideas. The first holds that politics is a secular enterprise. The second insists that politics is essentially an ongoing struggle for power. Niccolò Machiavelli was the most influential advocate of these related ideas.

The struggle for power, Machiavelli insisted, requires the prince to adjust his moves to what his potential allies and followers, and his potential rivals and their allies and followers are expected to do, rather than to what they are required to do by morality and religion: "[I]t must be understood," he says, "that a ruler, and especially a new ruler, cannot always act in ways that are considered good because, in order to maintain his power, he is often forced to act treacherously, ruthlessly or inhumanely, and disregard the precepts of religion."[1]

Should the ultimate aim of the prince consist in attaining personal salvation, the moral standards applying to his action would not depend on what other people do. Whether one is worthy of salvation depends exclusively on the life one leads. If the prince's deeds reveal a pious character he will be redeemed, whether or not he succeeds in the struggle for power. If he leads a vicious life he will forfeit his chances of salvation, no matter how successful he may prove to be in defeating his adversaries.

However, the prince's calling is not defined in terms of personal salvation. His accomplishments are related to his capacity for gaining and retaining power. Machiavelli understood this task differently from the way it appears to us citizens of stable constitutional democracies. We take the rules of the system—including the rules for the orderly change of these rules—for granted. For us, the struggle for power presupposes the existence of official positions and of rules in accordance with which one can obtain and retain office. It determines who shall occupy the positions of control over the state's apparatus, but not whether there should be any such positions or whether those who occupy them can expect obedience on the part of their subordinates and other subjects of the state. To Machiavelli, the two considerations did not appear separable. He lived in an Italy divided into many highly unstable principalities. The prince he meant to address was a man driven by the aspiration to unite Italy under one strong and solid government, rather than just to obtain and retain power for himself.

Machiavelli's teachings are about the art of gaining and retaining power, but he is not giving advice to just anyone who wants to become or to remain a ruler. His intended listener is the prince, for whom *salus populi suprema lex esto*, the "prudent orderer of a republic who has the intent to wish to help not himself but the common good, not for his own succession but for the common fatherland."[2]

He addresses the good prince, whom he likes to see as an "armed prophet."[3] On the one hand, he wants his listener to be a prophet who rallies the people around a new message. On the other hand, he wants him to bear arms, for it is his firm conviction that solid power is never built on the attraction of the ruler's message but rather on the coercive force that he commands.

As he cannot count on the disciplining effect of any stable rules of political competition, such a prince is well-advised, Machiavelli insists, not to assume that his potential allies, rivals, and their potential allies act upon selfless moral considerations. There would be nothing wrong with such an assumption if "people were good... but they are of evil nature."[4] This psychological axiom provides the grounds for the precepts Machiavelli puts forward as guides of action for a good prince:

[H]ow men live is so different from how they should live that a ruler who does not do what is generally done, but persists in doing what ought to be done, will undermine his power rather than maintain it. If a ruler who wants always to act honourably is surrounded by many unscrupulous men his downfall is inevitable. Therefore, a ruler who wishes to maintain his power must be prepared to act immorally when this becomes necessary.[5]

Machiavelli's heroes are the great founders, "Moses, Cyrus, Romulus, Theseus, and the like," the most excellent of "those who became princes by their own virtue."[6] Yet the key to his conception is the figure of the vicious politician: Agathokhles who had the whole senate of Syracuse slaughtered, Cesare Borgia who was notorious for his cruelty, Pope Alexander VI who never failed to break his word, and their likes. Virtuous princes must compete with vicious rivals, under terms set by the latter, by means chosen by the latter, *The Prince* insists.

A good man is disinclined to do what evil people do without qualms. But the "armed prophet" must do what evil people are prepared to do. I call this Machiavelli's paradox. It takes two forms. As a *paradox of action* it states that the good prince must do what a good man is disinclined to do. As a *paradox of character* it states that the good prince's conduct must not be dominated by the inclinations characteristic of good men.

Paradoxes are troubling because they put logic and rationality to a test. They are doubly troubling when, as in the case of Machiavelli, they challenge our deeply ingrained moral convictions.

The paradoxes that have occupied philosophers for millennia are of a conceptual nature. They are related to some inherent properties of our concepts such as the vagueness of the boundaries of their scope. Machiavelli's paradox is not like that. It relies on empirical circumstances that changed dramatically over the centuries, but not to the degree of disappearing completely, and that are likely to stay with us in the future, as long as politics will continue. Thus, before addressing the question of how, if at all, it can be resolved, we have to make an attempt to explain it.

The next section will try to sketch an explanation that, I hope, is faithful to Machiavelli's thinking. I will begin with what I called the paradox of action.

3.2 Explaining the paradox

The question is why the good prince should adjust his conduct to that of his vicious rivals rather than the other way round. Consider a stylized story. Machiavelli was concerned primarily with internal power struggles, but the structure of the argument remains the same if we examine it in the context of interstate conflict:

Two Princes–1. Two Italian princes, called Balducci and d'Agostino, rule in adjacent realms. Their military and economic might is roughly equal. Because of the weather, the opportunity for them to wage war against each other is limited to the summer months. They must either invade the neighboring country in June or give up hope of occupying it in that year. Of course, both d'Agostino and Balducci may decide not to attack their neighbor. If so, neither will be in a position to annex the neighboring realm to his own, but nor will either lose his principality. The status quo will be preserved, and it will be preserved at no cost. A second possibility is for d'Agostino to mobilize his troops and attack, while Balducci fails to mobilize; d'Agostino wins, forces his rival into exile, and annexes his country. Third, the same thing can happen with the roles reversed: Balducci mobilizes and, striking while d'Agostino fails to mobilize, wins and conquers. Fourth, when June arrives both princes attack; the war is fought at the border, and each side causes serious losses to the other, without conquering any territory.

Since they are rational, both princes can be expected to choose the alternative that ranks highest on their list of priorities. Therefore, in order to answer the question of what they should do, we must know their preference ordering. Suppose that they have a twofold interest: power and glory. And suppose provisionally that they are of "evil nature." In other words, they are ready to subject others to extreme suffering if that can marginally increase their power and/or glory. Should this be the case, they will rank the alternatives in the following order.

For d'Agostino, the best scenario is the one in which he strikes and Balducci does not, because then his realm or power is doubled. If both mobilize and strike virtually at the same time, d'Agostino's realm may remain intact at the cost of lives, money and other resources, but he may increase his military glory. Perhaps the increase in glory will fully compensate him for the material costs of the war while the costs of war offset the advantages of greater glory. Then d'Agostino will be at the point of indifference between the scenario of mutual attack and the scenario in which neither of the two princes attacks the other. If the costs of war outweigh the benefit it should bring in terms of glory, d'Agostino's second preference will be the peaceful option and mutual attack will be relegated to third place on his list of priorities. If the benefit in terms of glory outweighs the costs of war, the order of the two alternatives will be reversed. And the worst scenario from d'Agostino's point of view will be that in which Balducci mobilizes and strikes while he fails to mobilize, because in this case he will lose everything.

Suppose, for the sake of simplicity, that the costs of war, for d'Agostino, outweigh the benefits in terms of glory. Then, his ranking will be: 1. I strike, while he doesn't; 2. I don't strike, and neither does he; 3. I strike, and so does he; 4. I don't strike, but he does. Balducci will make the same ordering from his own point of view, so that d'Agostino's option 1 will become his option 4, and d'Agostino's option 4 his option 1, with options 2 and 3 remaining the same for both princes.

Given these rankings, it will always be rational for d'Agostino to attack, no matter what Balducci should do. And the same will hold for Balducci. They will both strike, thus causing serious losses to each other while remaining unable to change the status quo. Given their ordering of the options, they would prefer that neither of them is attacked, but the structure of their interests will involve them in a war of simultaneous aggression.

Let us now modify the assumption that *both* princes are of an "evil nature." This is the configuration that Machiavelli had in mind.

Two Princes–2. Everything is as in the original version, except for the motivation of the two princes. Balducci continues to lack any moral qualms. D'Agostino, however, is now a good man who believes that his highest responsibility is to secure peace and happiness for his people.

D'Agostino's moral commitment to peace alters his ranking of the possible scenarios. It will no longer be true that, for him, the best option is to attack while Balducci refrains from attacking. The preferred combination would now be for neither of the princes to mount an attack on the other. Would the option where d'Agostino does not strike but Balducci does rise to second place in the order of alternatives? It would not, because d'Agostino is supposed to take his responsibility for his people seriously. Should he put non-resistance to violence in second place, he would forfeit his throne and abandon his subjects to the mercy of the enemy. Does it follow, then, that attacking an unprepared Balducci remains at least the second best option on d'Agostino's list? It does not, because as a good man, d'Agostino must attribute great importance to not taking advantage of any sufferings inflicted on other people. His ordering will, then, look like this: 1. I don't attack, and neither does Balducci; 2. I attack, and so does he; 3. I attack, but he does not; and 4. I don't attack, but he does.

Given this change in his structure of preferences, it will no longer be rational for d'Agostino to attack, no matter what Balducci should do. He will have reason to mount an attack on Balducci if, and only if, he has reason to expect Balducci to attack him.

But Balducci is the same evil man that he was in Two Princes–1. Thus, he must be expected to attack, regardless of what d'Agostino might do. It would then be a mistake, on the part of d'Agostino, not to attack as well. He may be a peace-lover, but even so, it will be rational for him to act as if he were a born warlord. It is d'Agostino who must adjust his action to what Balducci is likely to do, rather than the other way around.

This is not yet the full story. For d'Agostino's problem is not simply deciding what he should do but also making himself capable of doing it. What he has most reason to do in his rivalry with Balducci is similar in nature to what Balducci is likely to do against him. But a good man is disinclined to do such things. If he were not, he would not be such a good man. But goodness also means dedication to the *salus populi*, and so it demands that he should not allow his reluctance to perform evil deeds to prevent him from acting in the same manner as his evil enemy. In other words, it demands that he make himself a less good man.

The reluctance of a virtuous man to do things that the virtues of his role may require him to do is itself a mark of virtue. Even if we admire the good prince for overcoming his reluctance and doing what his responsibility orders him to do, we would admire him less if he did it easily, without having to overcome any aversions.

A good person may realize that the welfare of his community is more important than his own admirable moral record, but he will continue to be repelled by what he has to do, and will do it against strong inner resistance. That he is repelled by the act *ex ante* and has pangs of conscience about it *ex post* proves that he is a good person. Even if we value him for his readiness to do what the common good demands of him, we would find him less good if he acted without scruples. But if the good person is a prince engaged in the struggle for power, his moral scruples put him at a serious disadvantage in relation to his unscrupulous rivals. He is tormented by doubts where those people act without hesitation. His indecision condemns him to drop out of the political game.

Dedication to the common cause demands that the good prince resolve the conflict by making himself less good overall, or so Machiavelli argues. In order to be able to act resolutely, he must make himself less morally sensitive than he initially is; he must unlearn the sensibilities and dispositions characteristic of a good man. Unless the good prince successfully accomplishes this process of unlearning, he will not be able to live up to his responsibilities as a good ruler. "[O]ne should not be troubled about becoming notorious for those vices without which it is difficult to preserve one's power," Machiavelli urges.[7]

3.3 From explanation towards solution

The explanation of the paradox, if correct, restricts the scope of possible solutions: no solution can be valid unless it is compatible with the correct explanation. But the correct explanation does not necessarily exclude all solutions except one. In order to identify a uniquely valid solution, further argument is needed.

Machiavelli himself was gesturing towards three different solutions. There are passages in his works that suggest that, in power politics, all norms are those of mere prudence or practical rationality: power politics is a domain to which no moral norms apply. In other words, power politics is *morally neutral*. On this reading Machiavelli is a moral skeptic. Other passages, however, seem to imply that power politics is subject to moral assessment, but that in this domain any act that an agent who wants to promote the common good finds unavoidable is *morally permissible*. On this second reading Machiavelli is an early act-consequentialist.

To understand the third conception hinted at in Machiavelli's remarks, we must recall the brief characterization of act-consequentialism given in the previous chapter. Act-consequentialism holds that an act is right if it yields results that, all things considered, are at least as good as any of the alternatives open to the agent. If that is the case the act in question is permissible. Act-consequentialism is capable of accounting for the intrinsic value or disvalue of acts. It may, for example, count the fact of carrying out the act as one of its outcomes: in so doing, the act-consequentialist simply adds the intrinsic goodness or badness of the action to the goodness or badness of what it brings about. But the (dis)value of the act does not count, for such a theory, independently of the aggregate value of the outcomes. Once a particular reason has made its contribution to the overall balance, it has no further, independent role to play. As I noted in Chapter Two (2.2), it follows from this that no act can be both right and vicious. Now the third conception amounts to a denial of this conclusion. It does not deny the significance of consequences. On the contrary, it explicitly acknowledges that the prince's decisions and acts involve consequences on an unusually large scale and that, as the head of his community, he bears special responsibility for those consequences. It also pays attention to the fact that the prince is engaged in a continuous struggle for power, which is characterized by a low overall level of compliance with moral principles and institutional rules. And it holds that under such circumstances the responsibility for consequences may require the prince to carry out acts that are morally reprehensible even if they are justified. As today's moral theory would put it, the prince may be permitted or—sometimes—even required to act with dirty hands.

There is a fourth conception that Machiavelli did not contemplate at all. It agrees with the conception of dirty hands both in its claim that the circumstances of power struggles involve heightened consequentialist standards for the assessment of political action and in its claim that some acts that are justified by their consequences may be intrinsically reprehensible nevertheless. It adds that political action is subject to constraints: certain moral minima remain in force in politics. I will return to the discussion of the fourth conception in Chapter Five (5.1). Here, I will offer a brief sketch of the first three.

Let us begin by considering a Machiavelli-based argument in favor of the conception of moral skepticism about politics. I concluded the previous section by a quotation to the effect that "one should not be troubled about becoming notorious for those vices without which it is difficult to preserve one's power." This statement seems to argue for the skeptical position. But on a closer reading it does not. It does not say that the good prince should not be troubled about *actually* assuming vicious character traits. Rather, it says that he should not be troubled about *becoming notorious* for vicious character traits. Notoriety for vice matters to the prince for reasons that are very different from those for which vice itself may matter to him. Acting viciously matters for its own sake, because vice is intrinsically morally reprehensible. Having the reputation of someone who tends to act viciously is something about which we may care for its own sake, too: a person who wants to be moral necessarily also wants to have the reputation of being moral. Machiavelli insists, however, that the good prince should not care about his reputation of being virtuous or vicious for its own sake but instrumentally, with a view to its impact on the conduct of his subjects, rivals and external enemies. In other words, according to Machiavelli, he must care about his moral reputation as a means of, or an obstacle to, gaining and retaining power. He is well advised to polish his reputation of being a good man as long as this helps him to establish and consolidate his rule. But whenever his rule is likely to be better served by the reputation of being vicious, he must do, without any scruples whatever will earn him such a reputation: "I say that each prince must desire to be considered merciful and not cruel," Machiavelli stresses. "Nonetheless, he must be wary not to use this mercy badly. ... [A] prince must not care about the infamy of cruelty in order to keep his subjects united and faithful."[8]

If Machiavelli thought that the role of moral virtues in politics extended only as far as the reputation of virtuousness—which was good for the prince when it helped him in his struggle for power, and bad for him when it frustrated his ambition to rule—then he was a mere technician of power whose recommendations are but precepts of practical rationality. In this reading, politics appears as a morally neutral domain. Benedetto Croce suggested that we read Machiavelli in this way.[9]

The skeptical reading can easily be made internally consistent. It presupposes that whenever we apply moral judgments to the domain of politics, we mistakenly extend the claims of morality beyond its proper jurisdiction. Once we come to redraw the limits of morality in conformity to the nature of political struggles, the paradox dissolves.

This reading, however, presents great difficulties when it comes to accommodating other Machiavellian statements, such as the celebrated passage from the *Discourses* where Machiavelli insists that

It is very suitable that when the deed accuses him, the effect excuses him, and when the effect is good, as was that of Romulus, it
will always excuse the deed; for he who is violent to spoil, not he
who is violent to mend, should be reproved.[10]

That a deed producing good effects is always excused by those effects is a controversial claim, but it amounts to a straightforward
moral judgment. It holds that political agents should not be blamed
for any acts that accuse them if the consequences excuse them; or, to
put it differently, an act that accuses the agent is permissible if it is
necessary for reaching the desired good outcomes. What is judged as
morally permitted is not judged as morally indifferent. This is the act-
consequentialist reading of Machiavelli.

Johann Gottlieb Fichte proposes a similar interpretation of the
moral permissibility view. He does not attribute to Machiavelli the view
that moral concepts do not apply to the political domain. His interpretation goes like this: The moral concepts that apply to politics are different from those that apply to ordinary life. Our understanding of Machiavelli, Fichte argues, is confounded by his terminology. Machiavelli
used the terms of "popular language" to denote the virtues and, thus,
"he called the real virtues, such as wise parsimony or the strength of
character that transcends the law ... by the names of vices, speaking of
greed and cruelty."[11] In Fichte's view, therefore, when the prince acts in
a manner contrary to ordinary morality, his acts do not count as immoral in politics. There are routine cases in which political action disregards the moral requirements of private life but it does this rightly, since
in its own place there is nothing immoral to it. What counts as morally
impermissible in the domain of ordinary life, may be permitted by political morality.

There is some support for this reading in Machiavelli. He maintains, for example, that the interests of the state sometimes require the
ruler to do things that "*seem* vicious," while doing things that "*seem*
virtuous" may cause the fall of the state.[12]

If this were Machivelli's last word on the matter, we would have a
second solution to the paradox. According to this solution, the paradox
is only apparent, and its appearance is due to our tendency to misapply
the concepts of ordinary morality to the political domain, where different moral concepts are in force. Once we realize that under the conditions of insufficient overall compliance, which are characteristic of

political struggles, morality permits certain actions that would be impermissible under sufficient compliance, there is no longer an inconsistency.

But this is not Machiavelli's last word. Elsewhere he reveals his awareness that non-consequentialist considerations may matter for the evaluation of an act that is made permissible by its good consequences: He insists, for example, that

> it cannot be called virtue to kill one's fellow-citizens, to betray one's friends, to be treacherous, merciless and irreligious; power may be gained by acting in such ways, but not glory.[13]

This statement lends new meaning to his claim that "a ruler who wishes to maintain his power must be prepared to act immorally when this becomes necessary."[14] Even if it is necessary for such a ruler to act immorally, his action still remains immoral. The prohibition is suspended without invalidating the judgment that what the agent did was morally objectionable.

Machiavelli clearly thought that acts that bear witness to cruelty, mendaciousness, fraudulence, and the like are permissible under certain conditions. But he also thought that, even if permissible, such acts made the hands of the agent dirty.

This reading allows for an act to be right and reprehensible at the same time: a property for which there is no room in an act-consequentialist account. The virtue of the prince consists, according to this reading, in being prepared to get his hands dirty by taking an inherently deplorable option if doing so is necessary for reaching a sufficiently important public aim.

Machiavelli does not seem to have been conscious of the differences between the three conceptions. Nor, insofar as the third is concerned, did he have the conceptual tools necessary for raising, let alone for solving, the question of how an act can be right and morally objectionable at the same time. The paradox of dirty hands seems too complex to be analyzed within the conceptual framework of Machiavelli's views. I will return to it in Chapter Nine, which is meant to conclude my argument.

The remaining sections of the present chapter will continue the progression towards what I called the classical thesis of realism. In order to elucidate some of its features, I will now turn to Thomas

Hobbes. First, as we will see, the realist thesis has the form of a dis-
junctive moral proposition. Sufficient compliance either obtains or it
does not. If it does, each particular person is morally required to
comply. If it does not, a particular person may be morally permitted
to avoid complying (subject to certain conditions). Hobbes' discussion of the laws of nature is of precisely such structure.

Second, Machiavelli's account of insufficient compliance is somewhat restricted. As Two Princes–2 illustrates, Machiavelli tended to
assume that the good prince is permitted to act with dirty hands on
condition that his internal supporters and rivals, external enemies,
and/or their supporters are of vicious character. Reading Hobbes will
help us, or so I hope, to see that the assumption of viciousness is no
necessary condition for the permission to hold.

Finally, reading Hobbes will help to prepare the transition from the
thesis of realism to that of indirect motivation.

3.4 Hobbes' treatment of the laws
of nature

The "fundamental laws of nature" are, in Hobbes's view, conditional
imperatives: an individual is required to comply with them if, and
only if, he has good reason to expect that the others will also comply.
Before I spell out this claim in more detail I have to say something
about the status of the laws in question. One may lodge two objections to an attempt of elucidating the nature of the realist thesis by
appealing to the Hobbesian laws of nature. First, the realist thesis is
meant to express a principle of political morality while, so the objection may go, the conditions under which the laws of nature cease to
bind are, according to Hobbes, not at all political. Second, the laws
themselves are prudential, not moral. Let me begin with a brief discussion of these objections.

Hobbes links sufficient compliance to the existence of sovereign
power, and he attributes insufficient compliance to the circumstances
characterized by the absence of it. The state in which people are morally permitted to take recourse to any conceivable means to defend
themselves is the state of nature. This seems to imply that, according
to Hobbes, insufficient compliance is a property of a condition prior
to any political struggle for power. If this is true then Hobbes, unlike

Machiavelli, locates the circumstances of insufficient compliance outside the scope of political theory.

Some contractarian authors such as Locke or Rousseau in fact
identify the state of nature with something like a pre-political state of
mankind. Not so Hobbes. He definitely denies that the whole of the
human race ever lived in such a state. And he adds that

> it may be perceived what manner of life there would be, where
> there were no common Power to fear, by the manner of life, which
> men that formerly lived under a peaceful government, used to de-
> generate into, in a civil Warre.[15]

Note that the state of war, for Hobbes, is not a state of continuous military mobilization and confrontation. It is a state where there
are no assurances against the fight starting again at any moment.
Wherever the government is torn apart by power struggles, Hobbes
intimates, the necessary assurances are missing. Only an absolute
sovereign, vested with unlimited and unquestionable power and authority, can save people from the permanent threat of war. In the
absence of unlimited and irrevocable sovereign power the arms may
rest for a while, but the threat of war looms large over society. Everyone must fear everyone else, and the mutual fears sooner or later
bring some of the parties to the conclusion that only a preventive
strike can save them from the attack of others. Speaking about the
state of nature, Hobbes thinks of the Britain of his own times: a
monarchy in ruins, a shaky republic, an uncertain order with much
of the political power divided among many armed political and religious factions.

It is, thus, entirely legitimate to apply Hobbes's analysis of the state
of nature to situations of political struggle similar to those that Machiavelli had in mind: to situations where the struggle for power does
not presuppose the availability of stable coercive institutions but
rather has among its targets the creation of such institutions or their
consolidation if they already exist but are unstable.

Let us now address the second objection. Hobbes famously defines
the concept of the law of nature as

> a Precept, or generall Rule, found out by Reason, by which a man
> is forbidden to do that which is destructive of his life, or taketh

away the means of preserving the same; and to omit that, by which he thinketh it may be best preserved.[16]

This definition strongly suggests that the laws of nature are merely recommendations of prudence as to what people should do in order to reach their self-regarding aims. What they forbid and command seems to mean no more than this: that it is against reason not "to look to the preservation and safeguard of ourselves."[17]

That being said, Hobbes often uses the terms "law of nature" and "moral law" interchangeably.[18] He argues, at one point, that "Justice, Gratitude, Modesty, Equity, Mercy, & the rest of the Laws of Nature ... are Morall Vertues."[19] Elsewhere he states that the laws of nature embody "the natural Duties of one man to another."[20] He apparently thinks that his fundamental laws of nature are instrumental precepts of reason and moral principles at the same time. How can he think this to be the case? A passage of *De Cive* may provide the answer:

Reason declaring peace to be good, it follows by the same reason, that all the necessary means to peace be good also; and therefore that modesty, equity, trust, humanity, mercy (which we demonstrated to be necessary to peace), are good manners or habits, that is, virtues. The law therefore, in the means to peace, commands also good manners, or the practice of virtue; and therefore it is called *moral*.[21]

Hobbes's view of the moral virtues is instrumental: they are means of promoting peace and prosperity. The law of nature is a law of reason because reason tells everyone that peace is good. But it is a moral law at the same time because it commands everyone to act from virtue which is a "necessary means to peace."

The question then is not whether the fundamental laws of nature are of a moral character but why Hobbes thinks it to be important to show that they are at the same time precepts of instrumental reason.

The answer may be found in Hobbes's moral psychology. It was Hobbes's firm conviction that nothing but self-interest is capable of motivating human beings directly, without the support of some further motivating factor: "[O]f the voluntary acts of every man, the object is some Good to himselfe," he insisted.[22] Self-interest is basic for man, he argued, while moral virtue is derivative. Humans are to be argued into morality, they must be shown that to act virtuously does not amount to acting against their own good; that, on the contrary, the acquisition and practice of the moral virtues is conducive to the advancement of their well-being—provided that enough others acquire and act upon the same moral virtues. That is why Hobbes is so eager to show that the laws of nature are "Conclusions or Theorems concerning what conduces to the conservation and defense" of each individual's own life.[23]

Whether or not such an account of the relationship between morality and self-interest is satisfying as a moral theory, it resolves the apparent contradiction in Hobbes's conception of the laws of nature, and allows us to regard these laws as moral laws.

With these preliminaries we can now turn to examining the structure of the laws of nature, as Hobbes outlines it.

The first on the list of the Hobbesian fundamental laws of nature sounds like this:

> That every man ought to endeavour Peace, as farre as he has hope of obtaining it; and when he cannot obtain it, that he may seek, and use, all helps, and advantages of Warre. The first branch of which Rule contains the first, and fundamentall Law of Nature; which is, to seek Peace and follow it. The Second, the summe of the Right of Nature; which is, By all means we can, to defend our selves.[24]

Thus the law is spelled out in the form of an alternative. One can either hope that enough others seek peace on enough occasions, or one cannot. To put it differently, the first branch of the law relies on the assumption of sufficient compliance, while the second is predicated on the assumption of insufficient compliance.

The second branch is presented by Hobbes as a separate principle that he calls the right of nature, i.e.

> the Liberty each man hath, to use his own power, as he will himselfe, for the preservation of his own Nature; that is to say, of his own Life; and consequently, of doing any thing, which in his own Judgement, and Reason, he shall conceive to be the aptest means thereunto.[25]

By thus establishing a right of nature, Hobbes makes a condition where no moral prohibition limits man's liberty to do anything he deems instrumental to preserve his life the default position for normative argument. The fundamental laws of nature are understood by him as principles that impose constraints on this unconditional "liberty to do or to forbeare."[26]

As long as anybody is at liberty to use or not to use the means of war, peace cannot be secured. In other words, to seek peace is to restrict one's own liberty voluntarily. This is made explicit in the second law of nature that prescribes

> That a man be willing, when others are so too, as farre-forth, as for Peace, and defense of himselfe he shall think it necessary, to lay down this right to all things, and be contented with so much liberty against other men, as he would allow other men against himselfe.[27]

Compare the provisos in the two laws. The first law makes the prescription to seek peace conditional on the hope of obtaining it; the second makes the prescription of laying down one's right to all things conditional on the willingness of the others to do the same. Because having a right consists, according to Hobbes, in being free of any obligation, laying down a right must mean accepting an obligation. Therefore, seeking peace amounts to constraining one's action by accepting obligations. The first law of nature expresses an obligation to constrain our action by accepting obligations so that peace may reign among us. This obligation, however, is conditional on having assurance that enough others will satisfy it together with us. It does not bind unless sufficient overall compliance obtains. If sufficient compliance fails to obtain, the second alternative comes into effect, which holds that we are permitted to use every possible means of self-defense.

Hobbes claims that the positive laws made by a powerful sovereign carry with them the necessary assurance. They are not mere commands but commands backed by coercive threats that cancel the advantages from disobedience. Thus, each subject of a successful sovereign has reasonable hope that enough others will comply with the law on enough occasions. Each is bound to comply with the law himself. The laws of nature on their part are not backed by the force of sovereign power. Their requirements always take the form of an alternative: Follow me if sufficient compliance obtains, do whatever you deem necessary for the preservation of your own well-being if sufficient compliance fails to obtain.

3.5 Generalizing Machiavelli's conception

Machiavelli makes the disquieting claim, exemplified by Two Princes–2, that a moral prince must act immorally if he plays with immoral players. Hobbes suggests an even more disquieting possibility. It may be rational for players who are *all* moral to deal immorally with each other.

Clearly, acting morally involves losses in the short run: complying with the fundamental laws of nature involves renouncing unfair advantages and assuming additional sacrifices. Compliance brings its fruits in the long run. Thus, in order to see that complying with the laws is to our advantage, we must be able to compare present sacrifices with future gains without any bias in favor of our present situation. However, according to Hobbes, most men are shortsighted by nature: they nourish in themselves "a perverse desire for present profit," which makes them "very unapt to observe these laws [of nature], although acknowledged by them." This, Hobbes says, is sufficient to maintain the hostilities between such people even if they prefer perpetual peace to an incessant state of war.[28]

Consider d'Agostino and Balducci again.

Two Princes–3. Both d'Agostino and Balducci prefer perpetual peace to an incessant state of war. But Balducci is shortsighted, and d'Agostino knows this.

A shortsighted Balducci is likely to act against his own true order of preferences. He wants perpetual peace with d'Agostino and yet, no matter what d'Agostino is expected to do, he will attack him. As d'Agostino knows this, he will himself attack Balducci, even though he is not biased in favor of "present profit." Shortsightedness of one of the two princes is sufficient to generate an incessant state of war, even if both are moral agents.

We can go even farther by supposing that both princes are impartial as between present and future benefits, and that both are moral, but they do not know this about each other. Hobbes alludes at various points in *Leviathan* to men being insufficiently transparent to each other. The opacity of human intentions and dispositions works in two directions: on the one hand, "reasonable suspicion" makes covenants agreed upon in the state of nature invalid;[29] on the other, a man who breaks a covenant may be received into society "by the errors of other men" who misjudge his character.[30] Based on this assumption, a Hobbesian state of war will reign between people of impeccable virtue and farsightedness:

> *Two Princes–4.* Both d'Agostino and Balducci prefer perpetual peace to an incessant state of war, and both are capable of assessing impartially the value of the long-term gains of peace against the short-term gains of war. However, neither has sufficient evidence of the other's preferences and attitudes to time.

For perpetual peace to prevail, the two princes must be both *farsighted* and *fully transparent* to each other. If one of the two conditions should fail to obtain, d'Agostino and Balducci will be involved in war against each other every year.

Suppose however, that neither of the two princes faces total defeat if the other mounts a unilateral attack on his realm. After moderate initial losses, the aggressor is likely to be pushed back behind his own border. And suppose that one of the princes—say, d'Agostino—is wise enough to reason as follows: The endless series of wars causes a net loss to both of us. What I may gain in one battle I am likely to lose in another, and the same is true about Balducci. Perpetual peace would not deprive us from any net gain, and would allow us to save the costs of military confrontation. Why shouldn't I demonstratively refrain from war preparations now? If Balducci follows suit, we may develop a practice of non-aggression. Should he, rather than following suit, take an unfair advantage of my self-restraint, the damage inflicted on us by his army will be limited, and next time I will punish him for his conduct. The risk is small, the possible benefit is great. Why shouldn't I have a try?

Such a strategy may be called conditional cooperation, because the person who makes the opening move voluntarily restrains himself, but does not continue to display self-restraint unless the other player co-operates. Since both players fare better if neither, rather than both, attacks the other, and since a failed attempt at establishing peace may be followed, at some time in the future, by similar initiatives, a convention of non-aggression has a realistic chance to develop between the parties. Once such a convention is established, both princes can save the costs of mobilizing and attacking at no risk to themselves.[31]

This is an appealing argument, but it does not apply under those assumptions on the purposes of war that were usual at the times of Machiavelli or Hobbes. It would work if wars were waged for the only purpose of expanding power. However, the usual assumptions included a further prize: glory. It may appear that glory is an irrational objective and therefore absent under more modern conditions. This is not the case, however. For what is glory? It is the reputation of military prowess. Princes need this reputation in order to deter their subjects from conspiracy and rebellion against their rule, and potential foreign enemies from aggression against their country. In the absence of full transparency, faithful compliance with a convention of non-aggression may be easily mistaken for evidence that the compliant prince's military virtues have faded and that he is a coward, afraid of the battlefield. Such a perception may be fatal for his rule.

Thus, princes need to maintain their reputation as tough men and courageous warriors. They must also be seen as men who seek military glory. If the one who makes the opening move values both virtues, as he should, he will not make a proposal of perpetual peace. Rather, his choice will convey the message that he is ready to reduce the frequency of wars to reach a compromise between the value of peace and that of glory. Suppose that, up to this time, the two princes have fought a war every summer. He may now attack every fourth summer only. If the response matches the opening move, the two princes will wage war against each other every other year rather than year by year.

The second player's choice is circumscribed by the opening move, but the opening move itself is not circumscribed in this way. The initiator may choose to attack every fifth, or sixth, or seventh year, and so on. There are as many possible equilibria in the relationship of the two princes as there are possible opening moves available to the first player. No matter how virtuous the two princes may be and no matter how clear they may be about the suffering and destruction that wars bring to their subjects: they cannot avoid being involved in periodic wars with each other.

To take stock: strategic decisions are not made on the ground of what *is* true about the individuals who interact with each other. Decision-makers must choose on the ground of what they *believe* to be true, given the information available to them. The fact that the others may *in fact* be entirely virtuous plays no part in the process that leads to the decision. What matters is what the chooser thinks they are. Thus, it may be reasonable, for two people to choose *as though* the other were vicious, even when in fact both are men of impeccable virtue.

In sum, insufficient compliance does not need, for its explanation, Machiavelli's hypothesis that men are, typically, of "evil nature." It is sufficient to suppose that they are not fully transparent to each other as to their true intentions, attitudes and dispositions. This non-moral imperfection is sufficient to yield the moral paradox.

3.6 The thesis of realism

The struggle for power is not a domain of moral indifference. Betraying allies, deceiving followers, misleading the public are not morally permissible means of gaining power, for example. But in a world where too many competitors violate such prohibitions on too many occasions, nobody may succeed to gain power without acting in contravention to the same or similar prohibitions. Suppose no politician who seeks office with the aim of promoting the common cause is ready to commit such morally doubtful acts. Then those in power will never promote the common cause. But it is in the interest of the governed that government power be used in the service of the common cause. It is in their interest that some competitors seek and gain office with the intention of promoting the common cause. If so, then, under the conditions of insufficient compliance, politicians whose aim is to use power for promoting the common cause must be morally permitted to act in contravention of the moral norms of the struggle for power. Acting in contravention to those norms, however, remains morally reprehensible even under the conditions when it is permitted. He who gains power by means of betraying his allies, deceiving his followers, misleading the public gets his hands dirty. Hence the thesis of realism:

Acting with dirty hands is permissible in the context of the struggle for power provided that no competitor can gain power without committing dirty-handed acts, and, that, gaining power enables the agent to do significant good that he intends to do and that he would not be able to do otherwise.

This thesis entails a necessity condition that is clearly spelled out in *The Prince*; we read, for example, that the prince must "not deviate from right conduct if possible, but be capable of entering upon the path of wrongdoing *when this becomes necessary.*"[32] The significant good—or proportionality—condition is implicit in Machiavelli's assumption that the good prince restores the unity and the authority of the state.

The necessity and proportionality conditions restrict the scope of permissible dirty hands but they do not act as constraints on it. An act that violates either of them is less good in terms of its overall effects than it could be. Necessity and proportionality are conditions for maximizing the goodness of the outcome, not limits on the maximization project. What is distinctive about the classical thesis is not whether or not it includes necessity and proportionality but that it does not include any reference to any non-consequentialist constraint. I will call it, thus, the *unconstrained thesis of realism*.

In both of its interpretations, "learning how not to be good" involves, for the good prince, a sacrifice of a moral nature. According to the act-based interpretation, we must understand that sacrifice as a list of dirty-handed acts registered in the moral record of the agent. The fact that he committed these morally awkward acts remains with him throughout his life. An evil queen, Lady Macbeth, asks in horror towards the end of the tragedy: "What, will these hands ne'er be clean?"[33] This is a question a good prince has reason to ask, too. Whatever the overall balance of his life, once he has committed a dirty-handed act, it will remain with him.

When political acts are directly assessed for their moral acceptability, the thesis of realism holds that a dirty-handed act is morally acceptable if, and only if, no acts without any morally objectionable properties could reach its aim, and if the goodness of its effects overcomes the constraint of its moral costs. As we have seen, however, political agents may also be assessed for the moral acceptability of their character, and in this case the claim becomes somewhat different: if it is desirable for the good prince to have a non-ideal character, then some acts that would not be judged as acceptable against a directly act-related standard are re-evaluated as acceptable against an indirect, disposition-based standard. The inevitability of such acts represents the cost the citizenry must pay for having a leader with a non-ideal disposition.

This is a consequence of which Machiavelli was either unaware or to which he remained indifferent. But it is a consequence important enough to be registered by way of proposing an amended version of the realist thesis. What follows is the thesis as stated from the perspective of the necessary character imperfections of the good prince:

> Dirty-handed acts that are not necessary for reaching valuable collective aims, or that involve disproportionate moral costs, are to be accepted if no leader disinclined to commit them has a chance to succeed in the struggle for power, and if the overall balance of the activities of the leader who commits them is significantly better than that of any of his rivals.

I will call this the *necessary character imperfections version* of the (unconstrained) thesis of realism.

Just as the original version of the thesis has some affinity with act-consequentialism but is not reducible to an act-consequentialist thesis, the version involving necessary character imperfections is close to virtue consequentialism without being reducible to a virtue consequentialist-thesis. According to virtue consequentialism, an act is right if a fully virtuous person would be disposed to do it, while virtue is that set of dispositions, attitudes and sensibilities which, if they were shared by all, would give rise to a series of acts whose aggregate consequences are at least as good as those of any alternative set of acts generated by alternative complexes of dispositions, attitudes and sensibilities. The goodness of character is assessed in terms of the outcomes of *sets* of acts rather than in terms of the outcomes of particular acts, a good character being identified as one whose long-run effects are at least as good as those of any alternative character. This allows for the possibility of some particular acts that a fully virtuous person would be prepared to choose being less than optimal. To that extent there is some analogy between the present version of the realist thesis and virtue consequentialism. However, the disanalogies are no less telling than the analogies. Virtue consequentialism identifies the good character traits on the assumption that everybody shares them, and it suggests that a person with such character traits is fully admirable. The character traits that the realist thesis holds desirable in a good leader are based on a different assumption: according to this assumption the rivals, allies and supporters of the leader are far from being admirable characters, and the desirable and necessary character traits of the good leader make him, too, less than fully admirable. Consequently, the realist thesis in its modified version does not argue for the acceptability of wrong acts from the virtuousness of the dispositions, attitudes, and sensibilities that are responsible for them. It argues for their acceptable or permissible nature from the necessity that the good prince's dispositions, attitudes, and sensibilities be less than fully virtuous.

Notice that Machiavelli also reckons with character imperfections that are not necessary for a successful defense of the common interest. He mentions, for example, that the good prince is surrounded by people who "are fickle; it is easy to persuade them about something, but difficult to keep them persuaded."[34] The fickleness of the potential followers of the good prince is certainly no necessary condition of his success. It is a contingent fact, to which he has to adapt his action. As Max Weber, the most important 20th century Machiavellian political theorist, pointed out, the political leader must build up his "apparatus" from people who are of mean and base character, and he must take responsibility for the evil acts these people are inclined to commit:

> The success of the leader is entirely dependent on the functioning of his apparatus. He is therefore dependent on *its* motives, not his own. … [W]hat he actually achieves does not, therefore, lie in his own hands, but is rather prescribed for him by the, in ethical terms predominantly base or common motives prompting the actions of his following.[35]

The good prince is confronted by a choice between refusing the services of the majority of his potential supporters and accepting those people as they are, thus getting his hands dirty vicariously, by what *they* do under *his* supervision and in *his* name. If it is morally permissible to scale political power at all, it must be morally permitted for him to take the second option. If he does so, what he accepts is not a necessary condition of the success of the good cause. The vices of his "apparatus" are not needed for his victory. He could be equally successful—perhaps even more successful—if his followers were not as evil as they are. Because their viciousness is not necessary for the success of the good cause, the acts that flow from their evil intentions are not morally permitted (to them). But it may be morally permitted (to the good prince) to rely on evil people in full knowledge of the fact that they will commit vicious acts in his service.

Interestingly, the same consideration that applies to the decisions of the leader regarding his potential supporters also applies to the potential supporters' decisions regarding their leader. Think of a community of ordinary citizens, or a group of notables or some influential aristocrats contemplating the choice between two aspirants for the prince's position. Imagine one of the contenders—Balducci—as an honest person but a weak leader, unlikely to succeed in securing peace and prosperity for the republic; and his rival—d'Agostino—as a corrupt man but a strong leader who, on the one hand, pursues the enrichment of his family at the expense of the community, but who, on the other hand, can be expected to serve the well-being of his subjects efficiently. The choosers may correctly believe that they would lose more under Balducci's honest but inefficient government than under the highly effective albeit corrupt rule of d'Agostino. In this case, even if d'Agostino is wrong to take advantage of the community's efforts, his supporters may be right in preferring his rule to the honest government of Balducci. D'Agostino's wrongdoings are impermissible, but condoning them may be permissible.[36]

Machiavelli failed to pay attention to this consequence because his intended listener was not the community of subjects, but the prince himself. However, this consequence is of no less importance than what we have seen to follow from the necessary character imperfections of the good prince. It will, therefore, be helpful to restate the realist thesis, this time from the perspective of the contingent character imperfections of the prince:

> Dirty-handed acts that are not necessary for reaching valuable collective aims or that involve disproportionate moral costs may be acceptable even if it is conceivable that a hypothetical leader who is disinclined to perform them would succeed in the struggle for power, pro-

vided that there is no such leader in the actual world, and provided that the overall balance of the activities of the leader who commits the acts in question is significantly better than any of his rivals.

I will call this the *contingent character imperfections version* of the (unconstrained) thesis of realism.

The three versions of the thesis should be read as complementing rather than replacing each other. They reveal slightly different aspects and consequences of the same fundamental problem.

3.7 Transition to the thesis of indirect motivation

In certain respects, Hobbes's theory is more general than Machiavelli's. The conception of *The Prince* was based on the psychological assumption that men are of evil nature. Hobbes did not need such an assumption.

True, his remarks here and there suggest that he endorsed the "evil nature hypothesis." Chapter xvii of *Leviathan* says, for example, that "our naturall Passions ... carry us to partiality, Pride, Revenge, and the like."[37] But this is not Hobbes's last word on the question of human motivation. "The Desires and other Passions of man are in themselves no Sin," he insists elsewhere.[38] Malevolence is no more constitutive of a typical human being's basic psychology than is benevolence. Man is not seen by Hobbes as being born with either good or evil attitudes towards others. He is depicted as simply indifferent towards fellow human beings. All his fundamental desires and passions are self-regarding, Hobbes argues.

This difference between Hobbes's and Machiavelli's anthropology has momentous implications. Genuinely evil people cannot co-operate for mutual advantage, since what is good for the first is by definition bad for the second, and vice versa. Their interaction is reduced to pure conflict. Even a good and successful prince is unable to help them rise above a state in which everybody is the enemy of everybody else.

The relationship among mere egoists is different. Their interests do not exclude co-operation as a matter of conceptual necessity. For such individuals, it is not impossible to find arrangements that are in the long run beneficial to all.

To make short-term sacrifices for the sake of long-term benefits or, what is basically the same according to *Leviathan*, to comply with the "first branch" of the fundamental laws of nature, would be foolish in the state of nature, Hobbes maintains, but he also maintains that it would be foolish not to make such sacrifices once sovereign power is there to secure sufficient overall compliance. So, according to Hobbes, the rise of a sovereign is not a condition for peace and cooperation only. It also serves as a trigger of moral virtue and of the duties entailed by the laws of nature. Morality comes into force with the establishment of sovereign power.

But the sovereign does not bring morality into force by appealing to the moral sense of the subjects. He appeals to their self-interest. By attaching coercive threats to his laws, he changes the balance of their self-regarding preferences. This change makes the demands of virtue coincide with the precepts of self-interest.

Thus Hobbes believes that society can work in accordance with the moral law. But the rule of the moral law is not established by a self-propelled activation of virtue. The moral end must be attained indirectly, through bringing self-interest into harmony with duty. This, in its preliminary formulation, is the second thesis of classical political theory, which I call the thesis of indirect motivation. That thesis will be the topic of the next chapter.

Notes

1 N. Machiavelli: *The Prince*. Ed. by Q. Skinner and R. Price. Cambridge: The University Press, 1988, 82. ("...in order to maintain his power" reads, in the original, "per mantenere lo stato"—in order to maintain *the state* or *the government* rather than *his power*.

2 N. Machiavelli: *Discourses on Livy*. Chicago: The University Press, 1996.

3 *The Prince*, 21.

4 Ibid., 60.

5 Ibid., 54 f.

6 Ibid., 20.

7 Ibid.

8 Ibid, 60.

9 Croce described politics as being *autonomous* with regard to morality. See his *Elementi di politica*. Bari: Giuseppe Laterza & Figli, 1925, 59 ff.

10 N. Machiavelli: *Discourses on Livy*. Chicago: The University Press, 1996, 29.

11 J. G. Fichte: "Über Macchiavelli [sic] als Schriftsteller." In *Fichtes Werke* 11. vol. Berlin: Walter de Gruyter & Co., 1971, 105.

12 *The Prince*, 55. (Italics added.)

13 Ibid., 31.

14 Ibid., 55.

15 T. Hobbes: *Leviathan*. Cambridge: The University Press, 1991, 89.

16 Ibid., 91. Compare this with the following claim: the laws of nature are mere "dictates of Reason ... Conclusions or Theorems concerning what conduces to the conservation and defense" of the individual. Ibid., 111.

17 T. Hobbes: De Cive. In Hobbes: *Man and Citizen*. Indianapolis–Cambridge: Hackett, 1991, 148.

18 *Leviathan*, 199. "the Morall Law (that is to say, ... the Law of Nature)."

19 Ibid., 111.

20 Ibid., 248.

21 De Cive, 151.

22 Ibid., 93. Cf. also 102, 105, 176.

23 The same idea is expressed by Hobbes's celebrated argument against the Foole: "The Foole hath sayd in his heart, there is no such thing as Justice; and sometime also with his tongue; seriously alleaging, that every man's conversation and contentment, being committed to his own care, there could be no reason, why not every man might not do what he thought conduced thereonto: and therefore to make, or not make, keep or not keep Covenants, was not against Reason, when it conduced to one's benefit." Hobbes took great pains to show that this view is not just immoral but also foolish. See *Leviathan*, 101.

24 Ibid., 92.

25 Ibid., 91.

26 Ibid.

27 Ibid., 92.

28 De Cive, 148. See also the following: "[M]en cannot put off his same irrational appetite, whereby they greedily prefer the present good (to which, by strict consequence, many unforeseen evils do adhere) before the future..." Ibid., 151.

29 *Leviathan*, 96.

30 Ibid., 102.

31 This is what Robert Axelrod calls "TIT FOR TAT strategy." See Axelrod: *The Evolution of Cooperation*. New York: Basic Books, 1984.

32 *The Prince*, 55 (italics added).

33 W. Shakespeare, *Macbeth*, Scene V, act 1.

34 *The Prince*, 21.

35 M. Weber: "The Profession and Vocation of Politics." In Weber: *Political Writings*. Cambridge: The University Press, 1994, 365.

36 For a dramatic example, see the decision of leading Bolsheviks—first Zinoviev and Kamenev, then Bukharin—to ally themselves with Stalin against Trotsky in the (mistaken) belief that with all his vices, Stalin would still represent the lesser evil. This case calls our attention to the terrible dangers inherent in such choices.

37 *Leviathan*, 117.

38 Ibid., 89.

CHAPTER FOUR

INDIRECT MOTIVATION: THE NARROW THESIS

4.1 Hume's knave

Hobbes's main question is how mutually disinterested individuals can be brought to cooperate in maintaining peace among themselves. They cannot, so the answer goes, unless they submit to the authority of a sovereign. The sovereign gives his subjects laws and his laws co-ordinate their actions for the purpose of mutual advantage. But how can he motivate them to comply with the law? Not by appealing to their virtuous dispositions but rather by attaching costs to non-compliance so that each individual's personal interests coincide with the public interest. In Hobbes's succinct formulation, "where the publique and the private interests are most closely united, there is the publique most advanced."[1] This is the very idea of indirect motivation.

Hobbes is primarily interested in the question of how the sovereign may influence the choices of the subjects. A secondary question follows from the answer to his main question. Once a person rises to the position of a sovereign, he may use his power to pursue ends other than those of securing peace and prosperity for his subjects. He is supposed to promote the interests of the subjects as a community. But, like everyone else, he has his own personal interests. Thus the question is how the sovereign can be made to do what promotes the public interest. The answer is, again, through indirect motivation.

Rather than relying on the sovereign's dedication to promote the common good, effective institutional arrangements will make his private interests coincide with the public interest. It is with this idea in mind that Hobbes proposes to choose the best form of sovereignty from the conceivable options: monarchy, aristocracy, or democracy. He argues that monarchy is superior to its alternatives because only the one-man sovereign's personal interests in fact coincide with the public interest.

In order to understand this, we do not need to examine whether he succeeded in establishing this claim. What matters for us is the general structure of the argument.

I will try to spell it out in more detail. Suppose that in situation s the sovereign (S) has two alternative courses of action to choose from, a and b. Suppose that the community's (C) ideal ordering gives priority to a over b: $(a > b)_{cc}$.[2] If, for the sake of simplicity, we set aside the possibility that S may be indifferent between a and b, S will prefer either a to b $(a > b)_{ss}$, or b to a $(a < b)_{ss}$. If he prefers a to b, then the contingent fact that his preference happens to match the ideal priority of C will make sure that S does what is best for C in s. There is no need for S to be loyal to C, to feel sympathy for C, or to see himself duty-bound to serve C's interests. In order to be motivated to promote C's good, S does not need to have any preference for C: his self-regarding pursuit of his own preference will have such a side-effect.

The story is very different if S prefers a to b. In that case, S's pursuit of his own interest is likely to cause losses rather than gains to C. Assume that C has an interest that S does not act upon $(a < b)_{ss}$. What can be done in order to change the likely direction of S's action? One possibility that Hobbes explains is unavailable would be to appeal to a different, community-regarding preference of S where the ordering is reversed: $(a > b)_{sc}$. In other words, S may be asked to choose a rather than b, out of loyalty to the community, or out of sympathy for its members, or out of a belief that he is duty-bound to give priority to the common good over his own good. For such an appeal to be successful, two conditions need to obtain. First, S must in fact nourish a community-regarding preference, which is different from his self-regarding preference and which coincides with C's ideal ordering: $(a > b)_{sc}$ as opposed to $(a < b)_{ss}$. Second, S's community-regarding preference must be able to dominate his self-regarding preference, so that S makes his choice on the basis of the former rather than the latter. The second condition does not even come into play unless the first is satisfied. Hobbes's claim is that it is not satisfied. Since men in general are egoists, we have to imagine S to be an egoist, too. We have to imagine him as not responding to any reasons except those that appeal to his self-regarding preferences.

What remains, then, is to change the ranking of S's self-regarding preferences, i.e. to make sure that S actually prefers to do a rather than $b.$. Is such a change conceivable? It is, because the ordering $(a < b)_{ss}$

reflects the advantages and disadvantages arising for S from a and b, respectively. This balance may be changed by attaching disadvantages to b or by removing some of b's advantages, or else by adding new advantages to a or removing some of a's disadvantages. In other words, by manipulating the costs and benefits for s of adopting a or b, the balance of S's reasons may be tipped in favor of $(a > b)_{ss}$. This strategy of changing the self-regarding preferences of the other person by changing the incentives amounts to what I call the strategy of indirect motivation.

Indirect motivation had its heyday in the 18th century. We find it spelled out with particular force in David Hume's essay, "Of the Independency of Parliament," which begins as follows:

> Political writers have established it as a maxim that, in contriving any system of government, and fixing the several checks and controls of the constitution, every man ought to be supposed a *knave*, and to have no other end, in all his actions, than private interest. By this interest we must govern him, and, by means of it, make him, notwithstanding his insatiable avarice and ambition, cooperate to public good.[3]

Hume's advocacy of indirect motivation may come as a surprise because he did not subscribe to the thesis of psychological egoism. Rather, he assumed that man has a capacity for sympathy and benevolence towards other men and that sympathy and benevolence are capable of motivating him directly to do what is good for others. In other words, men, according to Hume, do not always need the incentive of selfish advantage to choose what promotes the good of other people. Even if S (S now standing for any possible individual) should order the alternative between a and b as $(a < b)_{ss}$, he may have a second, other-regarding ranking, $(a > b)_{sc}$ which points in the opposite direction.

Nevertheless, indirect motivation is central in Hume's political thinking, and there is no inconsistency between his recognition that humans are capable of fellow-feeling and his insistence that a good constitution treats people as if they were all knaves, and governs them by appealing to their private interests. For, as we have seen already, the victory of the common good cannot be secured without recourse to indirect motivation, unless two psychological conditions jointly obtain. It is not sufficient that members of a community typically have other-regarding preferences alongside their self-regarding ones. As a second condition, their other-regarding preferences must be capable of dominating their self-regarding ones. Hume maintains that the first condition indeed obtains in human communities, but the second remains unsatisfied.

What do we mean when we assume that the other-regarding preferences of an individual are capable of dominating his self-regarding preferences? We mean, clearly, that there is a reason for the agent not to act on his self-regarding preference if that preference should conflict with his other-regarding preference. But to claim that there is such a reason for the agent is not the same as to claim that the agent is effectively motivated by it. Given his constitution, his normative reason and his psychological motivation may part company.[4]

If people were incapable of sympathy for others, they could not be morally motivated at all, Hume argues. Moral motivation is made possible by our capacity to feel another person's pleasure and pain, to find pleasure in the sight of the pleasure of others, and to suffer from the sight of their suffering.

However, Hume hastens to add, man is a being of "confin'd generosity."[5] And it matters a great deal that we cannot be expected to be infinitely generous. The limitations of human benevolence make this sentiment work in a much less reliable manner than that of self-love. Thus:

'Tis certain, that no affection of the human mind has both a sufficient force, and a proper direction to counter-balance the love of gain... Benevolence to strangers is too weak for this purpose; and as to the other passions, they rather inflame this avidity...[6]

In sum, when benevolence conflicts with self-love, the latter is likely to be the dominant passion. Even if morality has independent psychological sources, the problem Hobbes introduced while denying the existence of any such sources remains. And so does indirect motivation as its solution:

There is no passion, therefore, capable of controlling the interested affection, but the very affection itself, by an alteration of its direction. Now this alteration must necessarily take place upon the least reflection; since 'tis evident, that the passion is much better sat-isfy'd by this restraint, than by its liberty.[7]

In other words, individuals need not be egoists in order for it to be true that he who wants to make them do often and reliably what is impartially good has to appeal to their selfish interests. If an agent's other-regarding preferences cannot, typically, dominate his self-regarding preferences, then it is a change of the latter's direction that seems to remain the only way to make sure that his choices and deeds maximize the good of all. This strategy does not distinguish between the moral person and the knave. It deals with the first as if he were no different from the second. And it succeeds in making even the second, "notwithstanding his insatia-ble avarice and ambition, cooperate to public good." The Hobbesian premises are revised and yet the Hobbesian conclusion remains.

The next steps follow Hobbes's argument. It is up to the institu-tions to ensure that the good of each individual coincides with the common good. Hume's master examples are the institutions of prop-erty and contract. These are beneficial for all and thus they can make sure that people help each other:

> "Were we, therefore, to follow the natural course of our passions and inclinations, we shou'd perform but few actions for the advan-tage of others, from disinterested views; because we are naturally very limited in our kindness and affection: And we shou'd perform as few of that kind, out of a regard to interest; because we cannot depend upon their gratitude," Hume goes on reasoning. Hence "[t]he invention of the law of nature, concerning the *stability* of possession, has render'd men tolerable to each other: that of the *transference* of property and possession by consent has begun to render them mutually advantageous... Hence I learn to do a service to another, without bearing him any real kindness; because I fore-see, that he will return my service..."[8]

4.2 Kant's "nation of devils"

Many others picked up and elaborated Hobbes's and Hume's idea. Bernard Mandeville's fable on private vices becoming public virtues is a famous example. Adam Smith's metaphor of the invisible hand is another. These authors continue the argument of Hobbes and Hume in a most natural manner. It is more surprising that indirect motivation also plays a central role in the political theory of Immanuel Kant.

The idea of indirect motivation seems to be strongly associated with what I called the thesis of realism. Hobbes explicitly held both, Hume and Adam Smith explicitly held the first without denying validity to the second. Kant, however, rejected the thesis of realism both at the level of the general theory of morality and at that of political theory. He claimed that moral duties bind unconditionally, whatever the inclinations and desires of their subjects should be. Circumstances matter for imperatives that are hypothetical, i.e. that depend on the contingent purposes of action. But moral imperatives are categorical, not hypothetical: they are independent of any objective external to the act. One should obey the command of duty not for the sake of the beneficial consequences of the action, but for the sake of acting in accordance with duty.[9]

If this is true then the duties of a particular individual may not vary with the level at which other individuals comply with the correlative duties.

Kant acknowledges that when nobody complies with his duties towards the others nobody does any wrong to anybody else by acting in contravention of the call of duty. "Given the intention to be and to remain in this state of externally lawless freedom, men do *one another* no wrong at all when they feud among themselves; for what holds for one holds also in turn for the other, as if by mutual consent," he maintains.[10] But he hastens to add that when people simultaneously violate their duties towards each other they fail to satisfy the objective requirement of living with each other in a state required by the rights and dignity of rational human beings: "[I]n general they do wrong in the highest degree by wanting to be and to remain in a condition that is not rightful, that is, in which no one is assured of what is his against violence."[11]

It follows that insufficient compliance cannot justify either in general or under the circumstances of politics any failure to satisfy the imperatives of morality.

> True politics cannot take a step without having already paid homage to morals, and although politics by itself is a difficult art, its union with morals is no art at all; for as soon as the two conflict

with each other, morals cut the knot that politics cannot untie. The right of human beings must be held sacred, however great a sacrifice this may cost the ruling power. One cannot compromise here and devise something intermediate, a pragmatically conditioned right (a cross between right and expediency); instead, all politics must bend its knee before right, but in return it can hope to reach, though slowly, the level where it will shine unfailingly.[12]

And so Kant explicitly rejects the thesis of realism: "I can indeed think of a *moral politician*," he insists, "that is, one who takes the principles of political prudence in such a way that they can coexist with morals, but not of a *political moralist*, who frames the morals to suit the statesman's advantage."[13]

If this is true we may suspect that indirect motivation, too, is at variance with Kant's moral philosophy. In fact, Kant starts out from a rejection of the Humean claim that the claims of reason may never overrule the claim of desires. The satisfaction of desires is served better by the instincts, Kant insists, than by reason. Reason has no value as a means to achieve any goals alien to it. Its dignity resides in itself; in other words, it resides in the fact that it sets laws for rational beings and that it demands that they refrain from acting on their maxims (their practical aims or guidelines) unless these can be shown to conform to those laws. If we are to be permitted by the laws of reason to act on a contingent maxim of ours, we must be able to expect *everybody* to accept that maxim and to act on it. Rational beings, Kant goes on to argue, are capable of complying with the moral law for its own sake, rather than for the sake of satisfying a natural inclination, urge, or passion. The moral law, on the other hand, does not merely provide them with information on what would be right for them to do: it is also capable of inducing them to act in certain ways. It may do this without any indirect appeal to inclinations and the like.[14]

Furthermore, in order to be able to attribute moral worth to our acts, it does not suffice that they conform to the moral law. No act is of moral worth unless it is carried out *for the sake of the moral law*.[15] Moral motivation must be independent not only of self-love but of the feeling of love for others as well. The moral law articulates that which we *must* do. And this *must* admits of no restrictions or conditions: performing our duties must not depend on whether doing so promotes the realization of our desire for happiness (whether our own or that of another individual). Moral duties must not depend, for their satisfaction, on any kind of contingent fact concerning our inclinations. As rational beings, we are required to comply with the moral law even if we are moved by our passions and sentiments to act in contravention to it.[16]

It would seem fit, therefore, if Kant were to leave no room in his theory for indirect motivation. But he does. Here is what he says in the First Supplement to "Perpetual Peace":

> The problem of establishing a state, no matter how hard it may sound, is *soluble* even for a nation of devils (if only they have understanding) and goes like this: 'Given a multitude of rational beings all of whom need universal laws for their preservation but each of whom is inclined covertly to exempt himself from them, so to order this multitude and establish their constitution that, although in their private dispositions they strive against one another, these yet so check one another that in the public conduct the result is the same as if they had no such evil dispositions.' Such a problem must be soluble. For the problem is not the moral improvement of human beings but only the mechanism of nature, and what the task requires one to know is how this can be put to use in human beings in order so to arrange the conflict of their unpeacable dispositions within a people that they themselves have to constrain one another to submit to coercive law and so bring about a condition of peace in which laws have force.[17]

Thus, Kant insists that indirect motivation—the strategy of defeating an inclination by means of another inclination, rather than by the call of duty—is both feasible and permissible. It is feasible since a suitable combination of costs and benefits may make the acts of an individual conform to duty without that individual being moved by the intention to comply with duty out of respect for it:

> [I]t certainly conforms with duty that a shopkeeper not overcharge an inexperienced customer, and where there is a good deal of trade a prudent merchant does not overcharge but keeps a fixed general price for everyone, so that a child can buy from him as well as everyone else. People are thus served *honestly*; but this is not nearly enough for us to believe that the merchant acted this

way from duty and basic principles of honesty; his advantage required it...[18]

Furthermore, indirect motivation is a permissible strategy of bringing people to act in conformity with duty even if, according to Kant, it is a general principle of morality that duty is to be carried out for duty's sake rather than for some other reason, external to it. For the realm of duties is divided into two main sub-domains: the *duties of virtue* and the *duties of right*. Duties of virtue are internal to the dispositions and attitudes of the agent. They require us to make their satisfaction the end of our activities. Such duties cannot be satisfied, even imperfectly, by externally conforming to their demands. One cannot act in a benevolent manner, for example, merely by giving due assistance to the needy. In order to act as a benevolent person, one must provide benefits to other people with the aim of being a benevolent person. Furthermore, duties of virtue cannot be provided with support from sources external to the duty-bearer (another person) or the duty itself (some other incentive). Any kind of external support could improve the chances of the agent's acts conforming to duty, but it cannot make those acts comply with duty (i.e. carrying out the agent's intention to do his duty for its own sake).

The duties of right are different. Their requirements apply to the external use of human freedom. Their general principle holds that "Any action is right if it can coexist with everyone's freedom in accordance with a universal law, or if on its maxim the freedom of choice of each can coexist with everyone's freedom in accordance with a universal law."[19] The duties of right stipulate that our acts must not infringe the freedom of others.

It is possible to conform to such duties without doing them for their own sake. And the conformity of action to duty may receive support from the outside. First, it may be made positive law by a person (the legislator) who is external to the agent himself. Second, it may be backed by incentives that are external to the sense of duty. Typically, Kant holds, these incentives are sanctions that attach disadvantages to non-compliance, but there is no general reason why they could not consist in rewards that make compliance advantageous.

Why is providing a duty of right with external support not merely feasible but also morally permissible? Because non-conformity to such a duty is "a hindrance to freedom in accordance with a universal law (i.e. a wrong)"; while coercive interference with non-conformity to duty consists in a "hindering of a hindrance to freedom" and, therefore, is "consistent with freedom in accordance with universal laws, that is, it is right."[20]

As rational beings, humans are capable of doing their duty for its own sake. But complying with duty requires some inner force in beings which are not just rational but also part of nature. As natural beings, humans are subject to the natural power of inclinations, and the latter may push and pull them to act against the call of duty. In order to act morally, they must defeat their inclinations. Virtue is the moral capacity in man to act in conformity to duty even when his inclinations move him in a different direction.

> *Virtue* is the strength of a human being's maxims in fulfilling his duty.—Strength of any kind can be recognized only by the obstacles it can overcome, and in the case of virtue these obstacles are natural inclinations, which can come into conflict with the human being's moral resolution...[21]

Human virtue, however, cannot be assumed to be capable of defeating all the obstacles "that the human being furnishes himself through his inclinations."[22] For if it were of such an unlimited strength man would be incapable of acting in contravention of the imperatives of morality, and his will would be "holy will" rather than ordinary human will. When our inclinations happen to conflict with our duties, we may end up by failing to carry out our duty. This is true of many different kinds of duty we may have. Nevertheless, while the duties of virtue cannot be helped out from external sources, the duties of right can—and such help may not be only possible but also morally permitted or right.

The theory of indirect motivation plays an important role in Kant's theory at two different junctures. First, it constitutes the link between his philosophy of history, his political theory, and his moral philosophy. In Kant's view, rationality requires man to act upon reasons, rather than being pushed and pulled by natural inclinations. But action according to the principles of rationality is not the starting point either for particular individuals or for mankind as a whole. It is rather the (never fully attainable) ultimate end of personal life and collective history. Initially, people are governed by their inclinations. They need education in order to become cultured, civilized, and moral. But what is it that may drive people, locked as they are in their physical inclinations, to the road of culture, civilization, and morality? Given that initially they are driven by instinct, why do they not remain so for ever? Kant's answer is that it is precisely their instincts that steer people towards rationality. As natural beings, people are also social beings; they can live only in society, or at least it is only in society that they can fully develop their inborn capabilities. But they are also "non-social" beings, insofar as their inclinations conflict with the inclinations of others; as they strive for distinction and rank, these aspirations collide with similar aspirations of other people. This inescapable conflict becomes the main driving force behind historical progress. Kant understands the role of the struggle of inclinations in raising mankind to the level of rationality in a teleological manner: it is the purpose of nature that men become worthy of the potentialities latent in them, and this purpose is realized by making the struggle of conflicting passions the instrument of rationalization:

> The means which nature employs to bring about the development of innate capacities is that of antagonism within society, in so far as this antagonism becomes in the long run the cause of a law-governed social order. By antagonism, I mean in this context the *unsocial sociability* of men, that is, their tendency to come together in society, coupled, however, with a continual resistance which constantly threatens to break this society up. ... It is this very resistance which awakens all man's powers and induces him to overcome his tendency to laziness. Through the desire for honour, power and property, it drives him to seek status among his fellows, whom he cannot *bear* yet cannot *bear to leave*.[23]

Second, historical progress never reaches the realm of pure rationality. True, Kant was among the optimistic advocates of the Enlightenment. The imperative of duty tells us, he wrote, that "we *ought* now to be better men," but we can say that we ought to do something only if it is possible for us to do it, therefore "it follows inevitably that we must *be able*"[24] to take the road to perfection. What we are really capable of is, however, not to become perfectly rational and good, but only "to constantly progress from the evil towards the good,"[25] because "nothing straight can be constructed from such a warped wood as that which man is made of."[26]

Therefore, even in the best world attainable for them, humans need a legal system and a state endowed with irresistible power to enforce the law. There will always be cases in which morality will demand that we choose *a* while self-interest prefers *b*, and there will always be people who, even though choosing *a* is an unconditional duty, will tend "to reverse the moral order." But the threat of force makes the choice of *b* undesirable from the point of view of self-interest, and thus everybody may choose *a*, though many do so out of self-love rather than with the aim of complying with duty.

The ultimate goal of the history of mankind, Kant believed, is a civic constitution that combines the greatest equal liberty of individuals with the irresistible power of the state. In such a world the fulfillment of the duties of right is secured by the institutions, while individuals are free to pursue their self-interest.[27]

4.3 Virtue replaced by self-interest

The idea underlying the conception of indirect motivation is that humans are imperfect beings, in politics as well as in any other walk of life. Moral and non-moral interests are, as a rule, not equally strong and reliable motivators of human conduct. Benevolence towards strangers is relatively weak and unstable, while the drive of self-love is typically strong and continuous. When an agent gives priority to benevolence over self-love, he sacrifices some of his self-interest. When he gives priority to self-love over benevolence, he sacrifices some of the interest of others.

There may be a small number of people who, unhesitatingly, choose the good of the others in all such cases of conflict. Other people tend to react to nothing but their own self-interest, or even take pleasure in doing harm to others. Let us suppose with Hume, however, that the great majority do not belong to either of these extreme categories. In other words, most people are prepared to make relatively small sacrifices for the sake of others, but if these others are strangers to them, they are unlikely to make great sacrifices in order to promote their welfare That human altruism is limited is no evidence of its total absence. Human persons have an effective motivation to act out of benevolence. But that motivation has its limits.

The thesis of indirect motivation answers the question as to how political institutions should address this imperfection of human nature. Suppose that agent S faces two courses of action, a and b, and he ranks these from his own point of view as $(a < b)_{ss}$.[28] Suppose that he has another, community-related ranking: $(a > b)_{sc}$. And suppose that his self-regarding ranking dominates his community-related ranking in a particular case of conflict. Even if he had an obligation to give priority to the common good over his own good, and even if he agreed that he has such an obligation, the sacrifice in terms of his own good would be too great for him to be expected to act on his community-related ranking on this occasion. What should the institution-builders do in such cases? In principle, they can explore two strategies. The first reminds S that he has an obligation to give priority to his community-regarding ranking, and exhorts him to live up to that obligation. Such a strategy may be appealing in that it brings politics closer to moral ideals. But it has an irremediable defect. Institutions are doomed to remain ineffective if they expect people to be more virtuous than they are able to become. They cannot reliably secure a sufficiently high degree of compliance with their rules.

The alternative strategy, presented by Hobbes, Hume and Kant, amounts to eliminating the conflict between the demands of morality and those of self-interest. Institutions may have a grip on people if they appeal to their self-interest rather than to their readiness to sacrifice their own good for the sake of the common good. They can do this by attaching sets of rewards and punishments to the alternative courses of action that make what is best from the moral point of view also best from the point of view of the individual agent. Hence the thesis I attribute to Hobbes, Hume and Kant:

> Institutions should be designed in such a way as to make the agents' self-interest coincide with the interests preferred by morality, rather than to appeal to their virtue understood as a readiness to make sacrifices for duty's sake.

This is a special version of a thesis that I call *the thesis of indirect motivation*. It is special in that it takes motivation through moral concerns to be completely replaceable by motivation through self-interest as a means of making people cooperate with institutions. As we will see in Chapter Five (5.2), more general versions would allow for the institutions to rely, to some degree, on moral motivation. Because the thesis as formulated here is restricted to cases where moral motivation or virtue has no role to play, I will call it *the narrow thesis of indirect motivation*.

The question that underlies the realist thesis is what a politician should do, taking for granted a given, insufficiently high level of compliance on the part of the others. The question that underlies the thesis of indirect motivation is what can be done in order to raise the general level of compliance. In its unconstrained version, the thesis of realism insists that under conditions of insufficient overall compliance, a politician is morally permitted to follow the non-compliant conduct of the others, provided that his non-compliant action is necessary for promoting the case of justice and the general good and that the benefits resulting from it are proportional to the moral loss from non-compliance. Indirect motivation insists that insufficient compliance need not be taken for granted: designers of political institutions may make the majority conform better to the rules—but this involves changing the pay-offs of the alternative courses of action.

To illuminate this claim, let me return, for a moment, to the idea of the moral division of labor characteristic of well-ordered societies that I briefly discussed in Chapter Two (2.2). Both indirect motivation and moral division of labor invite institution builders to adopt such rules that secure compliance while letting people pursue their personal ends. But the moral division of labor assumes that individuals comply with the just institutions "for the right reasons," as Rawls puts it, that is, their compliance is directly motivated by a desire to be just. Human beings as they are do not invariably meet this assumption. Therefore, well-ordered societies must comprise institutions that are not only just, Rawls maintains, but capable of generating their own support. In other words, the institutions of a well-ordered society subject its members to a process of "moral learning" in the course of which individual persons acquire a "normally effective sense of justice."[29] Societies that are well-ordered in the Rawlsian sense, are supposed to transform the motivational set-up of ordinary people as we know them rather than taking it for granted.

As Thomas Nagel puts it, the moral division of labor between institutions and individuals consists neither in a complete invasion of the self by social values, nor in the situation of unreconstructed individuals in an institutional context that will make the pursuit of their private aims combine to generate socially desirable results, but in the design of institutions which penetrate and in part reconstruct their individual members, by producing differentiation within the self between public and private roles, and further differentiation subordinate to these.[30]

Indirect motivation does not set such personality-transforming goals; it assumes the motivational set-up of people to be fixed, and proposes to design institutions that are capable of steering social interaction in the desired direction, no matter how defective the motives of the majority may be.

4.4 Difficulties with the classical theory

The unconstrained thesis of realism and the narrow thesis of indirect motivation make up the classical theory of the moral problem of politics. The classical theory offers powerful insights but also gives rise to grave suspicions. To begin with, the realist thesis, in its unconstrained variant, seems to condone any political immorality provided that the general level of compliance is low enough. The thesis of indirect motivation is less opportunistic. After all, it offers a method of raising the level of compliance. Yet it is open to different kinds of objections. Arguably, the method of indirect motivation has a tendency to yield an unjust distribution of social burdens and benefits. That is because it assumes that extra incentives are needed for a human agent to be motivated to promote the common cause. Those in a better position to do this are likely to be recipients of more substantial incentives that tends unjustly to magnify initial inequalities. This undesirable tendency cannot be blocked unless highly unusual initial conditions obtain: unless it is the case, for example, that all the players are perfectly informed at no cost to themselves; that no subjects are able to influence the rules by their conduct; that goods from cooperation cannot be enjoyed without contributing one's fair share to their production; that costs of activities, whether cooperative or not, cannot be shifted unto people who do not enjoy their benefits; and so on. If any of these and similar conditions fail to hold, some of those indirectly motivated may take an unfair advantage of the community's dependence on their doing what is their duty.

Furthermore, indirect motivation may have an adverse impact on human motivation. Indirect motivation leaves the Humean benevolence or Kantian sense of duty behind; it addresses only selfish desires. Such a practice runs the risk of legitimizing selfishness, of reinforcing the priority of self-regarding aims, and of leaving the disposition to respond to the demand of solidarity and justice unused and, in this manner, allowing it to wither away. In other words, indirect motivation runs the risk of bringing human psychology closer to Hobbes's original assumption of psychological egoism. Because the institutions are advised to treat man *as if* he were a pure egoist, he may *actually* become more of an egoist than he originally is.[31]

Next, the classical view of indirect motivation seems to be vulnerable to an objection of infinite regress. It insists on the need to design an appropriate system of rules and incentives. The work of designing, of course, presupposes a designer. And the classical theory fails to ask who the designer will be. We either take this person to be morally superior to the rest of us—an assumption that is in clear conflict with the idea of indirect motivation. Or we accept that the designer is no more virtuous than any other political agent. In that case appropriate rules and incentives will be needed to keep the designer's work on the right track. But, those rules and incentives themselves are, of necessity, the work of a second-order designer who is either morally superior to the first-order designer or is no more virtuous than the latter. The first assumption would be clearly in conflict with the conception of indirect motivation. The second would take us to a third-order designer. And so on, ad infinitum.

The infinite regress charge contains a logical objection, but also expresses a substantive moral concern. Equality insists that a legitimate political regime must include some form of self-government. However, self-government is an empty idea, if the basic rules of political action are made by people who stand above those whose conduct those rules are supposed to guide. Indirect motivation must be made compatible with this idea.

Another objection may be directed against both theses. It starts out from the statement that legitimate political regimes claim the state to be an instrument of self-government in the hands of the political community. Citizens of a state that claims to be self-governing tend to see the holders of public office as their representatives who are subject to special moral responsibilities. They are considered to be bound not to mislead their constituency the truth about their intentions and actions, to serve the public interest faithfully and loyally, and so on. Whenever the office-holders as a class lose the reputation of living up to their responsibilities, the political regime will encounter great difficulties at generating support for itself (see Chapter Seven, 7.6). The classical theory seems to lack the tools for dealing with this problem in an adequate manner. The realist thesis seems to suggest that the moral concerns of the public need not be taken very seriously. The thesis of indirect motivation seems to respond to those concerns, but its response is not adequate. Citizens want their representatives to possess certain virtues: they want them to be honest, trustworthy, loyal, and so on. The thesis proclaims that these character traits do not matter; what matters is that the institutions successfully manipulate the self-interested motives of the office-holders. The recommendation to disregard, in the politicians, the disposition to do the right and the good, may contribute to aggravate the moral alienation of the citizenry from democratic politics.

A final objection follows if we combine the two theses. The unconstrained thesis of realism holds that, since no moral principle can be expected to be sufficiently complied with in the domain of the struggles for power, non-compliance is morally permitted to a participant, provided that his acquisition and retention of power is necessary for the advancement of a valuable collective aim (say, the consolidation of a state over a territory) and that the gains are proportional to the losses from his disregard for the moral principle.

Although the picture of a war of all against all lends some persuasive force to this claim, it is not obviously true even under the circumstances of the state of nature.

Hobbes insists that all men have an unrestricted right (a right of nature) to do anything in their power that they think helps them to protect their life against the threats inherent in this state. According to him, people in the civil condition can be seen as having voluntarily surrendered part of this right by agreeing with each other to comply with the laws of nature. Each individual is bound to comply with the agreement but only if he has a hope that the others will comply, too. The existence of a sovereign gives assurance to all that this hope will come true. Thus, in the civil condition, the natural right of men is constrained by an in-force duty to abide by the laws of nature.

The same relationship between the right of nature and the laws of nature holds in the state prior to the civil condition, Hobbes maintains. But here there is no mutual agreement to restrict one's natural liberty, nor is there a sovereign capable of enforcing the agreement against potential defectors. Therefore, the expectation of noncompliance is general, and nobody is bound to comply with any of the laws of nature. Unrestricted liberty holds.

This conclusion is, however, dependent on the unexamined and undefended assumption that all moral laws are conditional imperatives, that there are no moral laws that would require one to comply with them even if everybody else failed to do so. We have good reasons to believe this assumption to be mistaken. There are moral limits to what people may do to each other even when they cannot expect enough others to keep their action within those limits. If a Hobbesian thinks, for example, that taking civilian hostages, maiming, torturing, or killing these people with the aim of blackmailing the enemy into surrendering is morally permissible provided that the enemy does the same, then he must provide very strong arguments capable of rebutting the presumption to the contrary. Hobbes does not provide any argument to this effect.

There is an absolute moral baseline, a certain moral minimum that constrains political action under all conceivable conditions. There are no circumstances that would make it permissible to promote good aims by all possible bad means. To put it in Hobbesian terms, the laws of nature have a core that constrains the right of nature unconditionally, even in the absence of civil society.

Furthermore, indirect motivation, if successful, raises the overall level of compliance. The rise in the level of compliance, on its part, does not leave the moral baseline unaffected. The more a certain moral requirement is likely to be complied with, the less a particular agent will be morally permitted to disregard it. At each rise to a higher level, the realist thesis submits itself to a more and more narrow constraint. Certain morally objectionable things will become impermissible *at that level*.

Machiavelli and Hobbes identified the struggle for power with a struggle for consolidating the divided and shaky institutions of failed states. Under such conditions, the assumption of generalized insufficient compliance may be simplifying, but it is not completely irrealistic. It becomes irrealistic with the rise of the level of compliance, however. Although we have no reason to believe that the realist thesis ceases to apply in reasonably stable and just political regimes, there are reasons to believe that its application may be more and more constrained in such regimes.

Thus, the classical doctrine is in need of a thoroughgoing revision. One may want to go as far as to reject it altogether and propose a theory of political morality that does not allow for any tension between moral judgment and morally required political sanction. But I do not think such a theory would be applicable within the circumstances of politics. Not even the non-utopian ideal of constitutional democracy can simply eliminate the two classical theses. They rather need to be amended. It is to their amendment that the next chapters will turn. I will call the revised theory to be outlined *neoclassical*.

Notes

1 T. Hobbes: *Leviathan*. Cambridge: The University Press, 1991, 131.

2 The first c in the index stands for the fact that $x < y$ expresses C's priority ordering, while the second c points to the fact that this is the best ordering from C's point of view.

3 D. Hume: "Of the Independency of Parliament." In Hume, *Essays Moral, Political, and Literary*. Liberty Fund: Indianapolis, 1985, 42.

4 Bernard Williams denies that this distinction is meaningful. According to him, r is not a reason for S unless it is capable of motivating S. In other words, the capacity to motivate is an existential condition for reasons. See his "Internal and External Reasons" in Williams: *Moral Luck*. Cambridge: The University Press 1982. I believe that the normativity of reasons cannot be satisfactorily accounted for unless one secures some room for the distinction Williams claims to be meaningless.

5 See D. Hume: *A Treatise on Human Nature*. L. A. Selby Bigge, ed. London: Routledge and Kegan Paul, 1958, 494.

6 *Treatise*, 492.

7 Ibid.

8 Ibid., 520–21.

9 I. Kant: Groundwork of Metaphysics of Morals. In Kant: *Practical Philosophy*. M. J. Gregor ed. and transl. Cambridge: The University Press, 1996, 67.

10 I. Kant: Metaphysics of Morals. In Kant: *Practical Philosophy*. M. J. Gregor ed. and transl. Cambridge: The University Press, 1996, 452.

11 Ibid.

12 I. Kant: Towards Perpetual Peace. In Kant: *Practical Philosophy*. M. J. Gregor ed. and transl. Cambridge: The University Press, 1996, 347.

13 Ibid., 340.

14 See I. Kant: "Religion Within the Boundaries of Mere Reason." In Kant: *Religion and Rational Theology*. Cambridge: The University Press, 1996.

15 "Thus the moral worth of an action does not lie in the effect expected from it and so too does not lie in any principle of action that needs to borrow its motive from its expected effect." *Groundwork*, 56.

16 Ibid.

17 *Perpetual*, 335.

18 *Groundwork*, 53.

19 *Metaphysics*, 387.

20 Ibid., 388.

21 Ibid., 524 f.

22 Ibid., 533.

23 Kant, "Idea for a Universal History," in Kant, *Political Writings*, 44.

24 *Religion*, 46.

25 Ibid.

26 "Universal History," 46.

27 Kant insists that the final aim of universal history is to order all governments according to republican principles (those of constitutional democracy) and to unite them in a universal peace federation. See "Perpetual Peace."

28 As in the previous chapter, the first *s* in the index stands for the subject of the ordering, while the second representing its object (the two being the same in the case of self-regarding preferences).

29 For the distinction between principled agreement and a mere *modus vivendi* see J. Rawls: *Political Liberalism*. New York: Columbia University Press 1993, 141 ff., and Rawls: *The Law of Peoples*. Cambridge–London: Harvard University Press, 1999, 44 f.

30 Thomas Nagel: *Equality and Partiality*. New York–Oxford: Oxford University Press, 1991, 53.

31 See B. S. Frey: "A Constitution for Knaves Crowds Out Civic Virtues." In *Economic Journal* 107 (1997) 1043–1053.

OUTLINES OF A NEOCLASSICAL THEORY

5.1 The thesis of realism constrained

To recapitulate: For Machiavelli and Hobbes, the paradigmatic cases of political struggle are those of civil war, actual or latent. In these conditions there is no single coercive organization in place that could enforce its supremacy over a territory claimed by it as its jurisdiction. There are at least two coercive organizations within the same territory, and their conflict may take one of the following forms: each claims political supremacy and refuses to obey the other; neither claims supremacy; only one claims supremacy but the other does not obey it. As I stated towards the end of the previous chapter, under such conditions of a "war of all against all" the assumption of pervasive insufficient compliance is, perhaps, simplifying but not fully irrealistic, and the unconstrained thesis of realism is as close as possible to obtain.

The thought that politics is not simply applied morality is a lasting contribution of Machiavelli and Hobbes to political theory. They have shown that if a state is to have a legitimate monopoly of coercive power in a territory, it first has to be *de facto* capable of having the last word on the use of coercive power in that territory. They focused on situations where the *de facto* monopoly of control over coercive power is absent. Even in such situations, to assume that the realist thesis holds without any constraints is a great simplification, but if we compare the world of Hobbes and Machiavelli with the one they were striving for, this simplification does not strike us as fully implausible.

However, the struggle for power, which is at the same time a struggle for consolidating the institutions of power, is only a limiting case of political struggles. As I pointed out in Chapter Three (3.7), Hobbes himself believed that the rise of sovereign power is not only a condition for peace and co-operation for mutual advantage; he took it to serve at the same time as a trigger of moral virtue and of the duties entailed by the laws of nature. According to Hobbes, morality comes into force in a territory when a sovereign succeeds in enforcing his rule over everyone in that territory. To the extent that this happens, the justification of non-complying political action on grounds of insufficient compliance ceases to apply. Thus, Hobbes's own theory provides us with a reason for considering a political regime ordered by a legitimate state as one to which the realist thesis applies within ever harder constraints. Hobbes claimed, nevertheless, that in the civil state the sovereign—like everybody in the state of nature—is morally permitted to do whatever he may deem necessary for securing order in his realm. He could not base this claim on the assumption of insufficient compliance, since one of his central ideas was that the rise of a sovereign with an unchallenged monopoly of control over the use of force raises the overall compliance to a level of sufficiency. His explanation for the unlimited liberty of the sovereign was different.

Hobbes was conscious that the sovereign, like any other person, is morally "bound ... to observe the laws of Nature."[1] He agreed that if the subjects comply with those laws, the ruler is required to comply, too. But he maintained that the laws of nature bound the ruler to his own conscience (or, as he put it, to God), not to the individuals affected by his action. That David killed Uriah was against the law of nature, "yet it was not an injurie to Uriah but to God."[2] In other words, although David got his hands dirty by killing Uriah, he was not accountable to his victim for his dirty-handed act but solely to his own conscience.

Leviathan provides many converging explanations as to why the sovereign should not be viewed as politically accountable to his subjects. First, the sovereign power issues from a covenant that the subjects have made with each other and not with the ruler; as the sovereign himself is no party to the covenant, he can do nothing that would count as a breach of it.[3] Second, the sovereign is the representative of his subjects; he acts in their name; it is the subjects themselves who act through him and, therefore, he cannot injure them because they themselves are the authors of the injury.[4] Third, whoever makes laws for another holds authority over him; if the sovereign were restricted by law, the maker of that law would be the sovereign, and not the sovereign himself.[5] Finally, and most importantly, Hobbes argues as follows: In the state of nature, everybody is judge of his own acts and of the acts of everybody else insofar as these affect him. There is no superior judge whose impartial judgment everybody would be required to recognize and accept. One service that the sovereign may provide for his subjects is issuing laws that bind all and adjudicating conflicts in the light of those laws. But he can do so only if the subjects waive their right to be judge in matters of conflict among themselves. If they fail to do so, one of them may support a ruling of the sovereign that the other disagrees with. The result will be the collapse of sovereign power and a return to the state of nature.

> [I]f any one, or more of them, pretend a breach of the Covenant made by the Sovereigne at his institution; and others, or one other of his Subjects, or himselfe alone, pretend there was no such breach, there is in this case, no Judge to decide the controversie: it returns therefore to the Sword again; and every man recovers the right of Protecting himselfe by his own strength, contrary to the designe they had in the Institution. ... The opinion that any Monarch receives his Power by Covenant, that is to say on Condition, proceedeth from want of understanding this easie truth, that Covenants being but words, and breath, have no force to oblige, contain, constrain, or protect any man, but what it has from the publique Sword; that is, from the untied hands of that Man, or Assembly of men that hath the Sovereignty...[6]

Hobbes's arguments seem to split the domain of political theory into a kind of moral dualism. On the one hand, once sovereign power is established, it is subject to moral appraisal, and is not morally acceptable unless it meets the moral standards applying to it. On the other hand, no such judgment has any force against the sovereign himself. On the one hand, it requires politics to be moral. On the other, it leaves politics free of moral sanctions.

But the Hobbesian arguments are notoriously defective. The claim that the sovereign cannot break the contract as he is no party to it is question-begging. Hobbes wants the sovereign to stand above the contract in order to make him incapable of breaking it. The relationship between a person who represents another and the person represented by the former is not one of identical intentions but rather one of accountability of the representative to the represented, whose intentions he is supposed to serve. The limits of sovereign power need not be determined by subjecting the sovereign to restrictive rules. Suppose that the sovereign receives his powers from a constitution-maker ("the people" or a constituent assembly acting on behalf of the people): the fact that he has powers explicitly conferred on him by the constitution limits those powers because he will have no powers not laid down in the constitution. However, this does not necessarily mean that the constitution-maker imposes restrictive rules on the sovereign and, thus, is sovereign over him. Finally, it is a great mistake to believe that limited governments cannot be stable. Actually, constitutional democracies tend to be more stable in the long run than any of their alternatives.

If Hobbes is mistaken, then the rise of a state capable of monopolizing the decisions concerning the use of coercive force imposes constraints on the thesis of realism. Those constraints are not merely standards of the sovereign's private consciousness but *public standards*. On such a view, the politician might act wrongly even if he were not inhibited by his own conscience in carrying out the act in question.

I said above that once sovereign power is established, it is subject to moral appraisal, and it is not acceptable or legitimate unless it meets the moral standards that apply to it. In the last paragraphs of Chapter Four I made the assertion that there are certain core principles that constrain the right of nature unconditionally, even in the absence of general compliance. These core principles set an absolute moral baseline that even sovereigns are prohibited to transgress whatever their subjects may do. They are not predicated on the moral features of the political relationship between representatives and the people represented by them. We tend to refer to them as the basic human rights. There are further core requirements that express the special relationship that holds, in a state, between representatives and represented.

In Chapter Two (2.1), I offered a rough outline of this idea. To remind, states claim for their office-holders the authority to issue and enforce binding directives within their jurisdiction. Such a claim is at odds with the fundamental principle of the equal moral standing of human beings, because the relationship between the wielders and the subjects of state authority is asymmetrical. Thus, the claims of authority need to be defended against the charge that they are incompatible with moral equality. The conditions of compatibility include a requirement that those occupying positions of authority should receive their authorization from the people who are subject to their authority and whom they should serve. The special moral status of the holders of public office is that of agents, the citizenry being the principal.

Let us focus on a single aspect of the principal-agent relationship in order to gain a preliminary understanding of why the idea of categorical prohibitions—beyond those entailed by the idea of human rights—is not meaningless in the domain of political action.

As principals in general, citizens have a right to demand information on whatever is done in their name, and this right involves a correlative duty of providing the information demanded. Moreover, authorities have an obligation to make their activities transparent to the citizens, i.e., to make all relevant information publicly accessible even in the absence of a special demand, and in a way that makes that information comprehensible and manageable for ordinary citizens. The authorities may be subjected to special inquiries to account for their actions. They must accept public criticism, and bear the consequences of public dissatisfaction with their activities. In other words, those in authority must be accountable to the subjects of authority. Accountability is, thus, a necessary condition for the legitimacy of an institutional system of power and authority.

Now imagine a polity where all conceivable political practices are morally permitted. In such a polity, the conditions of legitimacy cannot obtain. If politicians were allowed and able to mislead the public,[7] it would mean that they are totally unaccountable. Accountability presupposes that the epistemic and moral distinction between sincere and deliberately misleading statements is upheld. If it is not upheld, elected officials cease to be representatives of the community in all but name because representation entails the representative's accountability to those whom he represents.[8] Thus, if political deception is tolerable without limits, the legitimacy of the entire institutional system is compromised. No regime can be legitimate unless there are certain moral constraints on lies, misleading statements, suppressing of relevant information, and so on, and unless the community successfully imposes those constraints on its representatives.

In Chapter Two, I suggested that we should not read the claims of legitimacy as all-or-nothing statements. Legitimacy admits of dimensions and degrees. And so do the violations of the constraints on permissible political action. A situation in which all prohibitions are completely disregarded is a limiting case. Typically, only some of the prohibitions are disregarded, and they are disregarded only to some degree. In such cases the institutional system is *pro tanto* more legitimate than it would be if it were unable to generate any degree of compliance, and it is *pro tanto* less legitimate than it would be if strict compliance were to obtain.

If, however, legitimacy is a matter of degree, then the assertion that deception in politics cannot be fully tolerable expresses a vague requirement. It would be clear and sharp if a single tolerated lie completely delegitimized an otherwise morally attractive regime. This not being the case, the requirement of truthfulness needs interpreting in order to draw a line between politically tolerable and politically intolerable lies and misleading statements or concealments. The main body of the next chapter will be dedicated to the question how the abstract principles that mark out the limits of the realist thesis are translated into more specific constraints. Here we can rest contented with the general statement that if a political regime is to satisfy the conditions of legitimacy to an acceptable degree, it must enable the community to keep the actions of holders of public office within certain moral limits.

To say that an act is prohibited at a given level of compliance is not to predict that the politician found guilty of committing it will quit or be required to quit his office. The fact of violation is neither a necessary nor a sufficient condition for such a prediction to come true. It is not necessary because a politician may find upon consulting his conscience that the only honest response to what has been revealed about him is to resign from office, even if the revelation were not be a sufficient reason, in the eyes of the public, for demanding that he resign. We may admire such a politician for his moral courage without agreeing that a minimal condition for staying in office has been in fact violated. Nor is it a sufficient condition because often the revealed facts are so grave that the only appropriate response on the part of the politician would be to leave, but he is neither tempted by the idea of resignation, nor seriously pressured to go. We may note the cynicism of the politician and the indifference of the general public and maintain, at the same time, that a minimal condition for staying in office has been violated.[9]

I will now try to restate the thesis of realism with the claim of this section incorporated in it. To remind, the thesis holds, in its unconstrained version, that acting with dirty hands is permissible in the context of the struggle for power provided that no competitor can gain power without committing dirty-handed acts and, that, gaining power enables the agent to do significant good that he intends to do and that he would not be able to do otherwise. The argument of this section allows us to add the following clause to the thesis:

> The thesis of realism is constrained, first, by the absolute moral baseline of the fundamental human rights. Second, it is constrained by the moral requirements characteristic of the relationship between the subjects of a state and the political officials as the representatives of the former. Where a state of reasonable legitimacy succeeds in consolidating itself, the levels of overall compliance are likely to rise, and their rise results in the emergence of new and more demanding moral minima that no participant of the power struggles may permissibly disregard. The acts that violate those minima must not be performed, and if they are nevertheless, they make the agent liable to political sanctions.

I will call this the *constrained thesis of realism.*

The term "moral minima" is shorthand for a structured set of principles that would generate a list of prohibitions. Thus, unlike the unrestricted realist thesis, the constrained thesis provides us only with a template for the analysis of particular controversies in political morality. While the unconstrained thesis has a determinate practical conclusion for all cases of political action (the moral condemnation of a political act should never entail practical consequences if that act satisfies the conditions spelled out by the thesis), the constrained thesis provides us only with some general guidance in the search for a determinate conclusion. In order to yield more specific results, concrete cases are needed. That work cannot be accomplished once and for all, as I will argue in later chapters of this book. But it does not follow that the constrained thesis is empty or useless.

5.2 Indirect motivation extended

In Chapter Four (4.1), I quoted Hume as saying that a well-designed political regime is capable of putting even the "insatiable avarice and ambition" of a knave in the service of the common good, and Kant as saying that the task of state-building is feasible even for "a nation of devils," provided that they are sufficiently rational. These provocative assertions were meant to illuminate the claim that good institutions do their job without relying on moral motivation—for even completely amoral beings can be directed towards promoting the common good by appealing to their self-interest.

We have seen that these assertions are deeply rooted in Hume's and Kant's moral and political theory. And yet, the reference to knaves and rational devils cannot be their last word on the matter. In this section I will explain why neither Hume nor Kant could stop at their claim that the designers of institutions should treat all the people as if they were knaves or intelligent devils. The next section will be dedicated to the examination of a further reason why Kant ought to have been troubled by the assumption that a nation of devils can form a republican community.

The figure of the knave returns once more in Hume, in his *Enquiry Concerning the Principles of Morals*, where it is accompanied by much less optimistic expectations than in "Of the Independency of Parliament":

> "And though it is allowed," Hume contends here, "that, without a regard to property, no society could subsist; yet according to the imperfect way in which human affairs are conducted, a sensible knave, in particular incidents, may think that an act of iniquity or infidelity will make a considerable addition to his fortune, without causing any considerable breach in the social union and confederacy. That *honesty is the best policy*, may be a good general rule, but is liable to many exceptions; and he, it may perhaps be thought, conducts himself with most wisdom, who observes the general rule, and takes advantage of all the exceptions."[10]

If "human affairs" were not conducted in an "imperfect way," the "sensible knave" would never be in a position to think that "an act of iniquity or infidelity will make a considerable addition to his fortune, without causing any considerable breach in the social union and confederacy." A society with perfect institutional arrangements could consist of "sensible knaves" only—and they would still behave exactly as though each of them were linked to everyone else by strong feelings of sympathy.

However, institutions are man-made artifices, and given the natural imperfections of man, his works are also doomed to be imperfect. No society consisting of "sensible knaves" alone could function in a morally acceptable fashion.

Without the original impulse of self-love, cooperation and society would never have emerged in the first place, according to Hume. "[A] regard to public interest, or a strong extensive benevolence, is not our first and original motive for observation of the rules of justice," he insists in the *Treatise*.[11] Somewhat later he adds:

To the imposition then, and the observance of these rules, both in general, and in every particular instance, they are at first mov'd only by a regard to interest; and this motive, on the first formation of society, is sufficiently strong and forcible.[12]

But the convergence of interests, even if it may be sufficient to initiate cooperation, is insufficient to maintain it, Hume would argue. With the progress of cooperation, the number of persons involved increases, and the effects of individual contribution to the benefits produced by collective effort become negligible:

[W]hen society becomes numerous, ... this interest is more remote" that is, it is not so self-evident that it is in the individuals' interest to comply with the institutional rules, "nor do men so readily perceive, that disorder and confusion follow upon every breach of these rules, as in a more narrow and concentrated society.[13]

It may not make any difference, under such conditions, whether or not a particular individual contributes his share to the cooperative effort: the outcome remains the same, provided that the others continue to cooperate. If the benefits are such that the individual who fails to contribute his share cannot be denied access to them, then a "sensible knave" may indeed think that "an act of iniquity or infidelity will make a considerable addition to his fortune, without causing any considerable breach in the social union and confederacy."

True, it is better for everyone if everyone fully complies with the cooperative rules than if no one cooperates at all. It is even better for everyone if one defects while everyone else cooperates. But if all were to pursue only their selfish interests, cooperation would not be sustainable. On the other hand, if sufficiently large numbers disregarded the advantages of non-compliance and continued conscientiously to comply, cooperation would be sustained, but its burdens would be unjustly distributed.[14]

Thus, for cooperation among humans to be sustainable, and for the distribution of its burdens and benefits to be fair, a sufficiently large part of the community must not be motivated by self-interest alone. Fortunately, according to Hume, the "cofin'd generosity" built into human nature is a sufficient material for institutions to work with to generate in us the virtues necessary for sustaining them (these are what he calls the *artificial virtues*):

> But tho' in our own actions we may frequently lose sight of that interest, which we have in maintaining order, and may follow a lesser and more present interest, we never fail to observe the prejudice we receive, either mediately or immediately, from the injustice of others; as not being in that case either blinded by passion, or byass'd by any contrary temptation. Nay when the injustice is so distant from us, as no way to affect our interest, it still displeases us; because we consider it as prejudicial to human society, and pernicious to every one that approaches the person guilty of it. We partake of their uneasiness by *sympathy*; and as every thing, which gives uneasiness in human actions, upon the general survey, is call'd Vice, and whatever produces satisfaction. In the same manner, is denominated Virtue; this is the reason why the sense of moral good and evil follows upon justice and injustice.[15]

Hume's idea is, thus, that in large-scale societies where an individual can defect from cooperation and still enjoy the benefits of it, there is a gap between the demands of the institutions and the motivation provided by self-interest, and this gap is to be filled by the (artificial) virtues.

This train of thought is not alien to Kant. Man, he writes,

> certainly abuses his freedom in relation to others of his own kind. And even although, as a rational creature, he desires a law to im-

pose limits on the freedom of all, he is still misled by his self-seeking animal inclinations into exempting himself from the law where he can.[16]

Kant believes that such a conduct is not rational. According to his practical philosophy, reason commands us to act morally, and so whenever a man violates his duty, the non-compliant action is not guided by rational principles: rather, it is caused by "animal inclinations." Hume would not agree, and nor do the contemporary collective-choice analysts of the phenomenon of free-riding. But insofar as the possibility and pervasiveness of that phenomenon is concerned, Kant takes it very seriously, whatever explanation he finds for it. And once it is conceded that man has an inclination for "exempting himself from the law where he can," the way is open towards the claim that human institutions cannot do without effective moral motivation. Thus, Kant has no less reason to find the idea of a republic designed for "the nation of devils" disturbing than Hume had on recognizing that a "sensible knave" may find it advantageous to defect while the others cooperate. Like Hume, he had to arrive at the idea that virtue is indispensable for political institutions to work.

But how could we conceive of virtue doing its job?

Better than Hume, Kant helps us to understand this. Remember his definition of virtue. "*Virtue* is the strength of a human being's maxims in fulfilling his duty," he says in *Metaphysics of Morals*. "Strength of any kind can be recognized only by the obstacles it can overcome," he continues, "and in the case of virtue these obstacles are natural inclinations, which can come into conflict with the human being's moral resolution."[17] If a person's virtue is not strong enough to overcome the resistance of a particular inclination, it remains ineffective. Inclination wins and virtue lies defeated. It remains ineffective for a different reason if the vector of the inclinations is changed so that it pulls in the same direction as duty itself. In that case, it is not virtue that moves a person to act in accordance with duty but his inclinations. Virtue may, however, be made effective—and it may be effective in two different ways. It either gains additional strength so as to overcome the same obstacle or the obstacle is diminished so that the same moral force becomes sufficient to overcome it.

According to Kant, human beings are morally required to make the perfection of their virtue their goal.[18] But this requirement, he insists, is addressed to their internal forum; it cannot be enforced legally or politically.[19]

The other method, however, is accessible for institutional action. Suppose that the obstacles to duty-abiding action are reduced to a level where virtue is capable of overcoming them. At this level, the agent's self-regarding ranking of priorities, $(a<b)_{ss}$, remains different from his community-regarding ranking, $(a>b)_{sc}$, but the relationship of dominance is reversed. Because the personal advantages from b are lessened (by attaching additional costs to this alternative) or the personal advantages from a are enhanced (by attaching additional benefits to it) the personal sacrifice involved in the choice of doing a rather than b is diminished, and so is the obstacle that virtue is supposed to overcome. The reduction is of a magnitude that allows the community-regarding ranking of the individual to dominate his self-regarding preference.

The availability of such less radical methods of indirect motivation invites us to revise the thesis as it was spelled out in Chapter Four. To remind, the thesis holds that

> Institutions should be designed in such a way as to make the agents' self-interest coincide with the interests preferred by morality, rather than to appeal to their virtue understood as a readiness to make sacrifices for duty's sake.

In the light of the present argument this appears to be merely a special case. In general, indirect motivation does not cause the agent's self-regarding ordering of preferences to coincide with that demanded by morality, nor does it totally dispense with the appeal to the moral sense of the agent. Therefore, it seems more appropriate to formulate the thesis as follows:

> Institutions should be designed in such a way as to reduce the losses, in terms of the agents' self-regarding priorities, to the level where their moral judgment becomes capable of dominating their self-regarding priorities. In the limiting case, the losses are fully eliminated, so that the self-regarding priorities coincide with the priorities demanded by moral judgment. In this, but only in this, case the institutions can dispense with the appeal to the agent's virtue altogether. In all other cases, the success of indirect motivation

depends on the costs of acting on the individual's moral reasons becoming small enough, so that the moral reasons are capable to decide the choice.

Rather than suggesting that institutions should eliminate virtue from the motivational set-up to which they appeal, this version of the thesis invites the institution-builder only to economize on virtue. I call it, therefore, *the wide thesis of indirect motivation* or, perhaps, *the thesis of indirect motivation as economizing on virtue*.

I do not claim that the wide thesis restates Hume's or Kant's idea. To my knowledge, they nowhere speak about institutions merely *reducing* rather than *eliminating* the losses the individual incurs through compliance with moral reasons, or about the moral preferences becoming dominant. I was not being unfaithful to either of them when, in Chapter Four, I introduced the thesis in a variant restricted to the limiting case of the total replacement of virtue by self-interest. I believe, nevertheless, that the extended variant provides us with a good interpretation of Hume and Kant in that it makes their insistence on indirect motivation compatible with their other claims—e.g., with Hume's claim that for an institutional arrangement to work, the agents must be endowed with at least some "confin'd generosity," and with Kant's claim that virtue must be measured by the size of the obstacle it has to overcome.

The non-extreme methods of indirect motivation do not work with agents who are incapable of being morally motivated. And their effects are not the same with regard to Hume's men of "confin'd generosity" or to Kant's men of limited virtue, as they are with regard to Hobbes's egoists. They have a chance to succeed with the first two but not with the third. Moderate altruists or moderately duty-inspired people can be brought to make sacrifices for the sake of others, provided those sacrifices are not prohibitively great. Egoists cannot.

In its narrow reading, the thesis of indirect motivation insists that institutions must deal with people as if they were all rational egoists. The wide reading rests on a more complex assumption. People can be arranged on a scale between pure egoists and moral saints. Presumably, the egoists far outnumber the saints, but they, in their turn, are outnumbered by those who have other-regarding preferences and are ready to act on them, provided that the sacrifice demanded is moderate. Indirect motivation succeeds if it sufficiently reduces the personal costs of compliance, so that a critical mass of moderately altruistic or moderately duty-inspired individuals choose to comply. Once this group begins to go along with the institutions, their conduct may reduce the costs of compliance and increase its benefits for another group whose altruism or inspiration by duty is weaker but still genuine, so that they also may choose cooperation. And so on, until even pure egoists may find it rational to cooperate. As a limiting case, everybody—moral saints, moderate altruists, and rational egoists alike—will find it better to comply with the institutions rather than disobeying. This is, of course, a limiting case that no institutional regime is likely ever to attain. But it is the way the logic of cooperation ideally works on the assumptions of the wide account.[20]

What about the relationship of wide indirect motivation to moral division of labor? In Chapter Four (4.3) I mentioned Rawls' distinction between complying with just institutions on the basis of a desire to be just and compliance as mere *modus vivendi*. The moral division of labor characteristic of well-ordered societies relies, I said there, on a principled agreement that just institutions should be complied with, while indirect motivation (narrowly understood) amounts to no more than a *modus vivendi*. Wide indirect motivation seems to lie somewhere in-between. It creates something more than an unprincipled *modus vivendi*, since it engages the agents' sense of justice and their moral sense in general. But what it sets in motion is less than cooperation maintained "for the right reasons" alone, since it assumes that, normally, the moral reasons need additional support from non-moral reasons of personal advantage to ensure sufficient compliance.

The implications of the difference between the narrow and the wide account are momentous. First, if indirect motivation is capable of working with a combination of moral and non-moral motives, it is less likely to result in unjust allocations of burdens and benefits when it combines non-moral motives with moral ones, than when it treats its subjects as if they were morally cool egoists. This is because the appeal to the moral sense, if effective, motivates people not to take unfair advantage of the cooperative efforts of others.

Second, indirect motivation, combining non-moral incentives with moral reasons, does not make the moral sense inert, and so it is less likely to crowd out moral virtue from society than it is on the narrow account. Finally, whatever its side effects on justice and the education of the moral sense, wide indirect motivation certainly cannot be divorced from moral controversy and deliberation. The moral sense does not report on internal states of mind that bear no relation to the external world. It responds to the belief that certain human acts are right or wrong, that certain human attitudes or dispositions are laudable or deplorable. Its reactions are inseparable from judgments that are capable of being true or false. Whether a moral reaction is adequate depends on whether the judgments on which it rests are true. Therefore, moral reactions can be challenged for being based on mistaken beliefs. Whenever an institution confronts a person with a demand to act in a certain way, it may be asked whether failing to act in that way is *really* wrong. Once such a question is asked, the moral expectations on which an institution relies for the efficacy of its rules need to be justified to the subjects of those expectations. Indirect motivation does not replace common deliberation, but is intimately linked to it.

5.3 "...to publicly let his opinion be known"

In the previous section, I argued for a moral thesis of indirect motivation, and in so doing I relied on certain empirical assumptions made by Hume: on the assumption of the imperfection of man-made institutions and on the related assumption of an ever-present opportunity for "sensible knaves" to take advantage of the cooperative efforts of others. It is the incapacity of a society's institutions to fully close the gap between the public interest and the private interest of the individuals that explains, according to this Humean argument, why moral dispositions, limited as they may be, are indispensable for politics. But once they are there, disagreement and debate about moral matters are there, too.

As we have seen, this train of thought is not alien to Kant. But Kant sees a further reason that would make the idea of a republic designed for "the nation of devils" disturbing, even if such a republic could successfully eliminate all opportunities for free-riding. He illuminates that further reason from two different perspectives.

The first is of an epistemic nature. According to Kant, reason cannot work as a faculty of isolated individuals. Men, left to their own devices, could never attain knowledge, he insists. Knowledge is possible only because our thoughts are public: they are made accessible to others and, thus, they are open to criticism. Free and impartial discussion is the only guarantee that an erroneous belief will be identified as such and eliminated, and that knowledge will advance towards the never fully attainable truth. As the *Critique of Pure Reason* puts it:

> [F]or the voice of reason is not that of a dictatorial and despotic power, it is rather like the vote of the citizen of a free state, every member of which must have the privilege of giving free expression to his doubts, and possess even the right of *veto*.[21]

The epistemic claim is general, and therefore it naturally also applies to political beliefs. The mere fact that a political regime exists, that the office-holders approve of it and the subjects go along with its directives does not in itself justify the claim that the regime is legitimate and worthy of support. Its legitimacy is not warranted unless it withstands the test of free criticism. Kant draws the conclusion that "[t]he public use of man's reason must always be free."[22] Freedom of the public use of reason makes sure that the deficiencies of the existing order may come to light, and "by general consent ... a proposal could be submitted to the crown"[23] about the need for change.

Freedom of opinion does not do its job unless the citizenry is enlightened, i.e. able and willing to think "without the guidance of another."[24] Only individuals capable of and prepared for the independent use of their reason may form a critical public opinion. At the same time, Kant believes that freedom of opinion is also the best means of enlightenment. Any community may become enlightened out of its own effort, provided that the public use of reason is free, because "there will always be a few who think for themselves," and who "once they have themselves thrown off the yoke of immaturity, will disseminate the spirit of rational respect for personal value and for the duty of all men to think for themselves."[25]

Thus, Kant presents his idea of the free public use of reason as naturally applying to politics. But this idea is not specifically political. Kant's second argument is. Here is how he formulates it:

> [T]he citizen must, with the approval of the ruler, be entitled to make public his opinion on whatever of the ruler's measures seem to him to constitute an injustice against the commonwealth. For to assume that the head of state can neither make mistakes nor be ignorant of anything would be to imply that he receives divine inspiration and is more than a human being.[26]

This passage shares a point with the epistemic argument: the head of state is not infallible, Kant maintains, and thus his beliefs need to be tested against public criticism. But the statements cited here make a further and more specific point. From the point of view of knowledge, the free use of the public reason is of instrumental value. From the point of view of the citizen, the entitlement "to make public his opinion on … an injustice against the commonwealth" is of intrinsic, rather than instrumental, value. The question, whether "the ruler's measures" are just or unjust does not raise a purely theoretical problem for the citizen. He is affected by those measures, directly or as a member of the commonwealth. If those measures are unfair, injustice is committed against a particular citizen, a group of citizens, or citizenry at large. The entitlement of each citizen to make his opinion on unjust government public is not merely a means of uncovering the fact of injustice, of restraining the ruler, and of obtaining redress for the grievances suffered. It is also a way of affirming the status of the humblest subject as equal to the ruler, a status the ruler is obliged to respect.

Contesting an official measure as unjust is an adversarial act. It points to a conflict of interest between the agent (the state or its officeholders) and those negatively affected by his action. By taking the side of the latter it aims to obtain reparation for their grievances. What we are talking about here is, nevertheless, very different from the measures of indirect motivation. Indirect motivation is a strategic move: A wants B to do x rather than y, and he provides B with an incentive to change his preference from $y > x$ to $x > y$. A does not appeal to anything like a community of interest between him and B: he simply uses an interest of B as a means of reversing his preferences in the desired direction. Voicing a judgment of injustice, no matter how adversarial, presupposes that *A* and *B* are connected by a shared interest: it assumes the relationship to be ordered by the principles of justice that they both have good reasons to strive to identify and to uphold. This shared interest creates what Gerald A. Cohen calls a justificatory community between the two persons. If *A* makes a charge of injustice against *B*, *B* is required to respond.[27]

The celebrated second formula of the categorical imperative prescribes: "So act that you use humanity, whether in your own person or in the person of any other, always at the same time as an end, never merely as a means."[28] Applying this formula to the case of false promises, Kant makes it clear that treating another person's humanity as an end involves not doing anything to him with which he "cannot possibly agree."[29] But this implies that the agent, if he does not treat the person who is affected by his acts as a mere means, must be prepared to justify his acts to that person. And the claim that one is prepared to give such a justification is not intelligible unless one recognizes that the other has a right to demand it. In other words, the second formula of the categorical imperative assumes that human beings as rational persons constitute a justificatory community.

The passage quoted from "Theory and Practice" applies this general idea to the relationship between the state and the persons who are subjected to its power and authority. It intimates that the policies of a government are not legitimate unless they can be justified to those whose interests they affect. This claim is not about the good consequences of freedom of opinion for the collective enterprise that aims to attain the truth, but about the conditions of the acceptability of political authority exercised over individual persons. Freedom of opinion appears, in this perspective, as constitutive of a relationship between the ruler and the ruled, where the former treats the latter as they ought to be treated, given that they are free and equal persons.

The ruler subjects the ruled to his coercive power. He makes them cooperate with his aims by giving them laws backed by force. This cannot be morally permissible unless he can show them that they have no reasonable complaint against the resulting acts and outcomes. Even if their subjection to the law may not be voluntarily assumed, they must be able to take responsibility for their conduct as if they complied with laws that they have given to themselves. They must be able to see themselves as co-authors of the law. So the law and its enforcement must be justified, and the people subjected to it must have the right to ask for justification and to protest if it is denied to them or if they find it unsatisfactory. The state must not treat its citizens as though they were intelligent devils—it must treat them as moral agents, as bearers of dignity.

This explains why citizens must possess the freedom to voice their personal grievances. But Kant goes farther than this: he speaks about the right of people to let their opinion on the wrongs done by the government be known *publicly*. Why *publicly*? Arguing for the moral significance of the freedom of opinion, Kant speaks about the injustices inflicted on the *commonwealth* rather than on this or that particular individual. This does not mean that the victims of injustice should not be particular individuals or that the injustice should not be seen as being inflicted on the commonwealth unless it has many individual victims. The violation of the rights of a single individual is an injustice inflicted on the commonwealth. It diminishes the moral standing of the whole community, and thus it is the business of the whole community. Therefore, each citizen as a member of the community must have the right to object to official measures, no matter who may be personally affected by them, and each citizen must have the right to know the objections raised by any fellow citizen. The issues of political justice are not issues between the government and the governed one by one: they are matters involving the whole citizenry.

Because the constrained thesis of realism, as it was spelled out in Section 1 of this chapter, includes a reference to moral minima of political action, its practical application depends on moral judgment. The wide thesis of indirect motivation, formulated in Section 2, also grants a certain role for moral judgment and for a disposition to act on it by inducing the political agents to comply with the institutions. Kant's thesis on the right of the citizens to let their opinion be publicly known moves the argument a step further. It shows that where moral judgment is at stake, the issue is never limited to reaching practical conclusions and acting according to these. Moral judgments are inseparable from public justification, and the debate to which the need for public justification gives rise is a constitutive part of the more general debate on what the citizens of a state together should do, and what the officials of that state are required and permitted to do as powerful servants of this common venture. This process is called common deliberation. It is called *deliberation* because it seeks to find out what is the best aim the community may decide to reach; and it is called *common* because it assumes that the participants are moved by a shared intention to identify common aims and to distribute the burdens and benefits of their common action in a just manner. Common deliberation, however, does not presuppose an absence of disagreement or conflict of interest. It may—and it does, typically—take adversarial forms where the antagonist is criticized as an enemy of justice and the general good. It is *common* deliberation nevertheless in that it rests on a shared acceptance that the adversaries owe justification to each other for their acts and their claims.

5.4 Summary

The neoclassical theory of political action departs from the classical one as I reconstructed it in the previous chapters in three important directions. First, it constrains the thesis of realism by what I called the moral minima of political action. In other words, it incorporates into the realist thesis a rider stating that at each level of overall compliance there are moral prohibitions that no consequences can lift (at that level). Once this constraint is identified, the impact of the thesis of indirect motivation on the content of the realist thesis can be presented in a new form: a successful regime of indirect motivation shifts certain types of acts from the main part of the thesis to its constraint.

Second, the neoclassical theory relies on a conception of indirect motivation that does not eliminate the moral dispositions from its motivational basis: rather than fully displacing virtue as a motivating factor, it only aims at economizing on it. And, third, moral concerns do not figure in the neoclassical theory merely as attitudes on which strategic influencing can and must rely, but also as objects of public controversy and common deliberation. Agents do not treat each other as equal moral persons unless they recognize that they form a justificatory community whose members have the right to ask for, and the duty to supply, justification of their acts that adversely affect (or are believed so to affect) others.

In Chapter Three (3.5) we found that, in Machiavelli's account, the virtuous prince faces two paradoxical demands. First, he has to commit dirty-handed acts that a virtuous man would be reluctant to perform. Second, in order to be able to do this, he has to unlearn the dispositions of a virtuous man. Unless he becomes as little repelled by dirty-handed acts as possible *ex ante*, and unless he becomes as little haunted by remorse for having committed them *ex post*, he cannot succeed in his struggle for promoting the common good.

This claim is fully supported by the unconstrained thesis of realism. In that version, the realist thesis does not expect the political leader to have any concerns about the moral nature of his action. The unconstrained thesis recommends that the leader "not be troubled about becoming notorious for those vices without which it is difficult to preserve one's power." The constrained thesis makes more complicated recommendations. On the one hand, it continues to support the claim that prudent participants in the struggle for power assume their rivals to be unscrupulous. It acknowledges that unscrupulous people have the strategic advantage of being free of moral concerns, so that they are capable of acting without hesitation. It concludes that if the good leader allows himself the luxury of being too tormented by moral doubts, he risks losing the struggle for power even before it has begun. Like the unconstrained thesis, its constrained counterpart advises the good leader to learn "how not to be good." But the constrained thesis adds a caveat. Citizens have no reason to want the good leader completely to lose his sensitivity for the moral awkwardness of the politically best choices and acts. It matters to them whether the leader of their preference takes the constraints on permissible political action seriously. The capacity of acting resolutely does not provide, in itself, good leadership. The good leader is perhaps not maximally sensitive for the problem of dirty hands but he is certainly not maximally indifferent towards it. His character represents an optimum compromise between the two extremes. Only so can he be sufficiently determined when it comes to acting and sufficiently responsive to the constraints of political action at the same time.

This calls for an amendment to the second variant of the realist thesis, as formulated from the perspective of the necessary character imperfections of the good leader:

Dirty-handed acts that are not necessary for reaching valuable collective aims or that involve disproportionate moral costs must be accepted if no leader disinclined to perform them has a chance to succeed in the struggle for power, and if a leader with a "politically optimal" character (neither maximally sensitive for the problem of dirty hands nor maximally indifferent towards it) would be ready to commit them.

The third variant, formulated from the perspective of the contingent character imperfections of the best of the actually available leaders, must also be amended:

> Dirty-handed acts that are not necessary for reaching valuable collective aims or that involve disproportionate moral costs must be accepted even if it is conceivable that a hypothetical leader who is disinclined to perform them would succeed in the struggle for power, provided that there is no such leader in the actual world, and provided that the overall balance of the activities of the leader who commits the acts in question is significantly better than that of any of his rivals. This thesis does not apply to acts that are prohibited by the minimal moral requirements of political leadership.

In addition to these amendments, the neoclassical theory raises new questions.

First, we have to flesh out the very rough idea of the moral minima that has been presented in this chapter. We have to show that this idea is not empty or impressionistic, but capable of giving structure to genuine political arguments with practical consequences. This brings us to a second task. In Chapter Two, I argued that no politics is separable from strategy. The present chapter came to the conclusion that no legitimate politics is separable from common deliberation. But is there a way for common deliberation and strategic interaction to combine? Does strategic interaction leave any room for good-faith common deliberation?

Human beings are rational: they act on reasons. For an agent who acts on reasons, the properties of his environment are reasons, and so are the properties of other agents who belong to that environment. However, the latter present him with a special category of reasons. They, too, are rational, and their reasons enter into the set of reasons that an agent takes into consideration when he tries to find out what he has most reason to do. He must also take into consideration that they, for their part, take *his* acting on reasons into consideration.

There are two ways to respond to this circumstance. The first is the strategic way. From the alternative courses of action open to him, the agent has to choose the one with the most favorable outcome, given what the others can be expected to do on the basis of what he knows about their reasons. The choice must respond to his assessment of the likely reactions of the others to the alternative courses of action he may adopt. In other words, when an agent deals strategically with other agents, he treats their rationality in an instrumental manner, "merely as a means."

The second way to respond to the rationality of fellow human beings is to treat them as parties to common deliberation. That is what an individual does when he expresses his readiness to justify his action to others, or when he asks for a justification of what they are doing, and when he and they adapt their plans and conduct to the outcome of the examination of the reasons presented. An agent who is ready to deal with others deliberatively, does not treat their rationality "merely as a means." He recognizes that, as rational persons, they are not simply beings whom he must not subject to unnecessary or disproportionate harm—rather, they are beings who have a right to insist that they are not harmed, and to ask for a justification of any action that they deem harmful.

The unconstrained thesis of realism, combined with the narrow thesis of indirect motivation, implies that, in politics, it is permissible to treat others strategically, and only strategically, that is, "merely as means." This is, first of all, unappealing. It is unappealing because the claim of an equal moral standing of human beings as persons implies that humans have a right to ask for justification whenever they believe that harm is done to them or that their liberty is constrained. Political rules and practices restrict the liberty of the subjects and impose other kinds of disadvantages on them. Consequently, the subjects have a right to expect that those rules and practices are justified to them. No politics that deals with the subjects strategically, and only strategically, satisfies the principle of moral equality.

This is a Kant-based argument against the classical theory. We have found another argument with roots in both Hume and Kant. If people are invariably egoists, their interaction cannot be steered towards the common good, at least not under the circumstances of human imperfection and the rough equality of human capabilities. Strategic interaction cannot work towards the common good unless it is allowed to build on reliable moral expectations. Moral expectations are, on their part, different from expectations based on personal advantage. They presuppose a willingness to seek shared principles in terms capable of justifying them to the person to whom they are directed. Politics among humans cannot be completely free of strategic interaction, but neither can it eliminate common deliberation.

Chapter Six will discuss the consequences of constraining the realist thesis. Chapter Seven will be dedicated to the question how politics according to the wide thesis of indirect motivation is different from politics according to the narrow thesis. The contents of the two chapters will be interdependent in a way the contents of Chapter Three and Four were not. The classical theory kept the theses of realism and of indirect motivation separate from, and standing in an external, additive relationship, with, each other. For the aims of the neoclassical theory, they are interlocking and mutually illuminating. They are united by their moral components, which cannot be given for the two theses separately. The constraint on the realist thesis and the moral element in indirect motivation both invite argument on principle and on judgment, and that argument is the same for the aims of both contexts; it yields twin answers to different but related questions.

Notes

1 T. Hobbes: *Leviathan*. Cambridge: The University Press 1991, 148.
2 Ibid.
3 Ibid., 122.
4 Ibid., 114, 124.
5 Ibid., 184.
6 Ibid., 123.
7 There is nothing special in the second, empirical part of this assumption. Agents are in general much better informed on the details of their activities than their principals, and this is particularly true about politicians who oversee complex organizations and deal with complex issues. For the informational asymmetry between the holders of public office and the citizenry at large, see R. Hardin: "Representing Ignorance," in E. F. Paul, F. D. Miller, Jr., and J. Paul, eds.: *Morality and Politics*. Cambridge: The University Press, 2004.
8 See H. F. Pitkin: *The Concept of Representation*. Berkeley–Los Angeles–London: University of California Press, 1967.
9 In April 1982, the Argentinian army occupied the Falkland Islands, which were under British authority but had long been claimed by Argentina. The United Kingdom declared war on the aggressor, and issued a statement that it would

attack any alien ship within 200 miles of the islands. On May 2, the Argentinian cruiser General Belgrano, with a 1093 strong crew on board, was heading away from the forbidden zone. Nevertheless, the British submarine HMS Conqueror launched an attack and sank the cruiser. 322 members of the crew died. The action had been personally authorized by Prime Minister Margaret Thatcher. Not long before the incident, the Peruvian president had attempted to mediate a truce between the warring parties. His services were accepted by both sides, but the sinking of the General Belgrano put an abrupt end to the talks. In London's official position, the Argentinian warship was located in, or at least heading for, the forbidden zone. Thatcher denied any personal involvement with the order to fire. In 1984, the speaker of the House of Commons barred Labour MP Tam Dalyell from the plenary sessions for claiming that the Admiralty had been instructed by the prime minister to sink the Belgrano deliberately in order to stall the Peruvian peace effort. In 1985, the undersecretary of state for defense, Clyve Ponting, walked out of the ministry with the documents of a secret investigation into the case and handed them over to Dalyell. The records showed beyond any doubt that Thatcher had lied. At the time of the strike, the cruiser was outside the forbidden zone and departing; the order was given with the knowledge and approval of the prime minister. However, the Iron Lady refused to apologize. Instead, she took legal action against Ponting under the Official Secrets Acts of 1911, and it took the jury two weeks to clear the accused civil servant of the charges. By the time the verdict about Ponting's innocence was handed out, the story had outlived itself.

10 *An Enquiry Concerning the Principles of Morals*, 282–283.

11 Hume: *A Treatise of Human Nature*, 495.

12 Ibid., 499.

13 Ibid.

14 Adam Smith shared this view. While he certainly assumed that natural sympathy and benevolence were weaker than self-love, he rejected the belief that people might be led to the service of others by their self-love alone. He attributed the latter view to Mandeville and Hobbes, with whom he was engaged in an extended polemic on this matter. See A. Smith: *The Theory of Moral Sentiments*. Oxford: The University Press, 1976, 306–317.

15 *Treatise*, 499.

16 "The Idea for a Universal History with a Cosmopolitan Purpose," in Kant, *Political Writings*. Cambridge: The University Press, 1991, 46.

17 See Chapter Four at fn 19.

18 See *Metaphysics*, 517 ff.

19 Ibid.

20 Cf. M. Taylor: *The Possibility of Cooperation*. Cambridge: The University Press, 1987, 109.

21 I. Kant: *The Critique of Pure Reason*. New York: Prometheus Books, 1990, 415.

22 I. Kant: "An Answer to the Question: What is Enlightenment?" In Kant: *Political Writings*. H. Reiss, ed. Cambridge: The University Press, 1970, 55.

23 Ibid., 57.

24 Ibid., 54.

25 Ibid., 55.

26 I. Kant: "On the Common Saying: 'This May Be True In Theory But It Does Not Apply In Practice.'" In *Political Writings*, 84.

27 See G. A. Cohen: "Incentives, Inequality, and Community." In S. Darwall, ed.: *Equal Freedom*. Ann Arbor: The University of Michigan Press, 1995.

28 I. Kant: "Groundwork of the Metaphysics of Morals." In Kant: *Practical Philosophy*. M. J. Gregor, trans. and ed. Cambridge: The University Press, 1996, 80.

29 Ibid.

CHAPTER SIX

REALISM: THE CONSTRAINED THESIS

6.1 The ethics of responsibility limited by the ethics of conscience

Let me introduce the problem of this chapter by way of a rough outline of the theory of the ethics of political leadership developed by Max Weber, a late follower of Machiavelli.

There are several ultimate values, Weber asserts, and since they are all ultimate, they are also mutually independent. Things, states of affairs or acts may be evaluated from innumerable points of view—e.g. as beautiful, holy, pleasurable or useful—including the moral. These different evaluations are not united under one single overarching value: "It is possible that there are such ultimate evaluations that are in principle and inescapably *divergent*."[1]

The plurality and mutual independence of ultimate values have two important implications. First, the adoption of an ultimate value cannot rely on reasons. It cannot rely on statements of fact since no conjunction of statements of fact may imply an evaluative statement, or so Weber argues. Nor can it rely on evaluative statements since no ultimate evaluation has any other, "more ultimate evaluations" behind it. Therefore, Weber concludes, ultimate values must be adopted by something like a blind choice. Call this his *value decisionism claim*. Second, the clash of ultimate values does not allow for compromises. One does not do justice to their demands by trying to satisfy each value to some limited degree. To do so is "to evade our duty of basic intellectual honesty" and to "lack the courage to face our ultimate stands."[2] Call this Weber's *radical choice claim*.

It is not possible to realize all the valuable options in a single society, or in a single individual life, let alone in a single choice. This claim has a weak reading that most philosophers would accept. In this reading, Weber's statement affirms the impossibility of simultaneously satisfying all the evaluative rankings that apply to the choices facing an individual or a group of individuals. The impossibility is due to the contingent features of the world: plurality of values, scarcity of resources, limited human capabilities and the like. The weak reading entails that in order to realize a certain set of values in our lives we may be forced to resign from pursuing some others. It does not entail that when we opt for one of two or more conflicting values we implicitly declare that the value that is not going to be realized by us is unappealing or positively repellent.

The weak reading attributes the conflicts of value to contingent facts about the world, rather than to necessary relations between the conflicting values. There is nothing in what makes the career of a concert pianist and that of a scientific researcher valuable that would make it impossible for the same person to dedicate his life to both at the same time. The reason why one has to choose between the two kinds of career is that time and other resources necessary for the pursuit of either are available in scarce supply.

Weber rejects this view as shallow. In a celebrated passage of "Science as a Vocation" he maintains that the conflicts of value are of a non-contingent character:

> Something may be holy, ... because and insofar as it is *not* beautiful; ... and something may be beautiful ... in what it is *not* good ..., and it is common knowledge that something may be true notwithstanding and because of its *not* being beautiful, holy, and good.[3]

He does not mean to say that the holy is *always* ugly, or that ugliness is *always* a reason for something to be holy. His idea is that the conflicts between beauty and holiness would not be possible if our ultimate evaluations were not *indifferent* with respect to each other's standpoint. As all of them are ultimate, each is independent of the rest. The value of the sacred and that of the beautiful, for example, are not determined in relation to each other, so that each would implicitly recognize that the other is valuable. Therefore, valuing sacred things allows for beauty being worthless or even contrary to value. We need not value beauty in order to be able to value the sacred.

Furthermore, each value demands unconditional dedication from those who appreciate it. The only adequate way to appreciate a value, Weber believes, is to pursue it unconditionally, with no regard to the conflicting claims of other values. From the standpoint of beauty, there is nothing intrinsically valuable in leading a holy life; therefore, whatever I may do with the aim of participating in holiness is a loss to the cause of the arts—a sacrifice that cannot be justified from the point of view of the aesthetic value. Conversely, from the standpoint of the sacred, it is the attention dedicated to the aesthetic values that appears to involve an unjustifiable diminishment of the holiness of one's life. As none of the ultimate values acknowledges the others, both the arts and the sacred make an unconditional, unrestrained claim to our loyalty.

Thus, Weber believes that the conflicts of value are essential and radical: "Values do not merely present alternatives to us," he insists, "they are involved in an irreconcilable and deadly fight with each other, like 'God' with 'Devil'. There is no intermediary position, there is no compromise here."[4]

In their ordinary lives, most people tend to make unprincipled compromises between conflicting values. Like the ancient polytheists, they try to worship many different gods at the same time. This is not appropriate to the ideal of a responsible man, though. "Life in itself and as long as it is interpreted from within does not know but an eternal fight among those gods," and we must face the "necessity of *choosing* among them."[5]

Such an irreconcilable and deadly fight goes on between the value of ethical goodness and the other values such as beauty, holiness, knowledge, pleasure, national greatness, and so on. Ethics, moreover, is an internally divided domain of value, or so Weber believes. It confronts us with demands that are impossible to satisfy simultaneously. It sets intrinsic standards for our action that we ought not to violate whatever the consequences—and, at the same time, it requires us to act so as to make the consequences of our acts as good as possible. The first set of standards prescribes that we should never kill an innocent, non-threatening person, for example; the second prescribes that we should do whatever we can in order to minimize the occurrence of such killings.

Suppose we are told that unless we kill one innocent, non-threatening person, an evil man will kill two, but if we kill the one, he will refrain from killing the two. If Weber is right, the first type of standards will prohibit us to kill the one, while the second will require us to do so. He distinguishes these two types of ethical standards as *Gesinnungsethik* (the ethics of conscience) and *Verantwortungsethik* (the ethics of responsibility). The ethics of conscience tells us that certain acts are intrinsically wrong and that we should refrain from performing intrinsically wrong acts, regardless of the consequences. "Putting it in religious terms: The Christian does what is right and places the outcome in God's hands."[6] The ethics of responsibility, on the other hand, requires us to face up to the consequences of our acts and omissions, irrespective of their intrinsic goodness or badness.

According to the ethics of conscience, there is a categorical difference between doing harm and allowing harm to be done by other people. We are morally responsible for what we do, while what others do is their moral responsibility. If I do not kill an innocent person, and an evil man kills two others, *he* gets his hands dirty, while *my* hands remain clean. According to the ethics of responsibility, keeping my hands clean cannot be my priority. I bear responsibility for not allowing harm to be done to innocent, non-threatening persons whom I am able to protect against aggression.

Given his conception of the essential and radical incompatibility of the ultimate values, it is no surprise that Weber sees the conflict between the ethics of conscience and the ethics of responsibility to be sharp, systematic, and unbridgeable. There is no way to combine the two attitudes under a single moral theory. These are "ultimate *Weltanschauungen* [that] collide, and one has *to choose* between them."[7]

Weber's substantive characterization of the ethics of conscience provides further support to his view that the conflict is sharp and irreconcilable. He does not rest contented with defining the ethics of conscience as an aspiration to avoid violating the intrinsic moral constraints of action, no matter what the price of complying with them would be. He identifies its requirements as almost impossible to abide by.

On the one hand, the ethics of conscience declares all use of force to be wrong, even if it would be necessary for self-defence or for the defence of innocent third parties. "Resist not evil with force" is a categorical, exceptionless command of the ethics of conscience, as Weber characterizes this ethical stance. On the other hand, the ethics of conscience makes it impermissible to pursue any self-regarding aim so long as there are others who are worse-off than ourselves. "Give out that you hast"—give out everything, absolutely, the ethics of conscience commands, according to Weber. What he has in mind when he identifies the content of *Gesinnungsethik* is the Sermon on the

Mount, "the absolute ethics of the Gospel."[8] There is no midway between living according to its stringent demands and completely rejecting it. "[W]e must accept it in its entirety or leave it entirely alone," Weber insists.[9]

The ethics of conscience is an ethics for those people who "seek their own salvation and the salvation of others."[10] Accepting its aspirations comes at a serious price. Only those who give up their this-worldly responsibilities—monks and hermits—can lead their lives according to its canon. The rest of us remain subject to the command to take responsibility for the consequences of our acts and omissions. This is particularly true about the politician whose job it is to lead his community towards certain collective ends: security, social protection for the needy, national greatness for the fatherland, and the like. The political leader's maxim cannot be "Resist not evil with force"; it is rather "You *shall* resist evil with force, for if you do not, you are *responsible* for the spread of evil."[11]

Someone with less extreme views on value pluralism could have taken the incompatibility of living up to the stringent commands of the ethics of conscience with discharging one's this-worldly responsibilities as evidence that "the absolute ethics of the Gospel" cannot give a correct account of the content of the moral constraints the ethics of conscience is supposed to set for us. Weber took it as evidence that the ethics of conscience and the ethics of responsibility embody valid but incompatible moral aspirations: both may give proper guidance to human life but they cannot be united in the life of the same person. We have to choose, and a mature, responsible, intellectually honest person would not try to bring them together by way of an unprincipled compromise. Faced with the ethics of conscience and the ethics of responsibility, we must adopt one and give up the other completely.

This incompatibility, together with the characterization of the ethics of conscience as an ethics of clean hands, implies a particular conception of the ethics of responsibility. Like Machiavelli's ethics for princes, Weber's *Verantwortungsethik* has a consequentialist aspect in that it identifies the right action as the one the consequences of which are at least as good as those of any of its alternatives. And like Machiavelli's ethics, it is non-consequentialist in that sometimes it demands, or at least permits acts that Weber characterizes as "morally suspect."

Weber's ethics of responsibility wants to make room for the possibility of an agent getting his hands dirty by performing an act that is right. It wants to make us aware that by pursuing consequentialist values, we often cannot avoid incurring a sacrifice of a moral nature. Weber's view is that we cannot do what our this-worldly responsibilities demand of us and keep our hands impeccably clean at the same time.

This is particularly true about political action. "[A]nyone who gets involved with politics, which is to say with the means of power and violence, is making a pact with diabolical powers," Weber maintains.[12] The means to which a politician may be forced to resort are "morally suspect," and the fact that they are employed in the service of good ends does not make them any less "dangerous." Taking responsibility for the consequences of one's choices involves taking responsibility for getting one's hands dirty.

So far, Weber may appear as deploying a new argument in support of an old conclusion. His argument, however, has a further implication, of which his predecessors remained unaware. *Gesinnungsethik* and *Verantwortungsethik*, as presented by Weber, are mutually excluding alternatives, but their relationship is not symmetrical. The ethics of conscience requires us to ignore the consequences of our acts and omissions completely. It allows for one, and only one, concern that its follower must pursue single-mindedly: a concern for keeping our hands clean. An adherent to the ethics of responsibility is supposed to give up this concern. He must accept that, unavoidably, his moral record will become tainted. But we should not imagine that—at least as long as he is not "inwardly dead"[13]—he takes the fact that some of his acts are "morally suspect" lightly. He must be alert to the gravity of the moral costs of his action. He must take responsibility for acting with dirty hands. If he does, then at some point he may find a permissible act so abominable as to make him unable to carry it out. On such occasions, he will say with Luther: "Here I stand, I can do no other."[14]

"In this sense, Weber continues, the ethics of conscience and the ethics of responsibility are not absolute opposites. They are complementary to one another, and only in combination do they produce the true human being who is *capable* of having a vocation for politics."[15] It is with this proviso that he declares the ethics of responsibility to be the proper ethics for political leaders. If we interpret Weber's ethics of responsibility, as we should, as a variation on the theme of the thesis of realism, then we find that, according to Weber, that thesis is not without constraints. There are acts that would maximize the good of the community, but that the political leader may find himself prohibited to carry out by his own moral convictions.

To take stock, Machiavelli's conception differs from act-consequentialism on one account only: it tries to accommodate the phenomenon of dirty hands. Weber's conception is non-consequentialist on two accounts: it has room for acts that are dirty-handed and morally required at the same time, and it has room for acts that the agents rightly refuse to carry out even though they may be required by the ethics of responsibility, the ruling ethics of political leadership.

Weber believes at the same time that the constraints on the pursuit of the ethics of responsibility are internal to the political leader's private conscience. It is the leader's personal incapacity to do certain things that deprives him of the ability "to do other."

Sometimes politicians refuse to get their hands dirty or they take responsibility for having done so even if nobody else agrees that they should not commit the act in question or that they should bear out the consequences if they have already committed it.[16] Weber believes that this is always the case when a political leader decides that he "cannot do other." His decisionism concerning value adoption rules out the very possibility for subjecting the ultimate choices of any person— politician or not—to external criticism.[17]

6.2 A principle of accountability

Weber held that the political leader faces the ultimate choice between the two ethical attitudes as a lonely hero, whose choice takes place in the internal forum of his soul:

> [W]hether one *ought* to act on the basis of an ethics of conscience or one of responsibility, and *when* one should do the one or the other, these are not things about which one can give instructions to anybody.[18]

According to "Politics as a Vocation," the question of which attitude should be given priority and when is purely personal. A serious politician is fully conscious of the burdens of choosing either way. But he takes this problem to be one of his personal attitudes and dispositions. Weber's question is whether *the politician himself*, given his ethical character, is capable of carrying out a particular act. The right question is, I maintain against Weber, whether the *public standards* of political morality permit the politician to carry out that act.

The contention that political action is subject to public standards has two aspects. It entails, first, that the standards of political morality are independent of the personal attitudes and dispositions of the agent. It is not up to his contingent attitudes and dispositions to decide whether it is appropriate, in a particular situation, to adopt a certain course of action; it is up to the standards to decide whether those attitudes and dispositions are at all appropriate. Second, the claim of public standards entails that the political leaders are accountable to the public for satisfying or violating those standards. This section will be devoted to the accountability aspect of the public character of the standards of political action. The question of how they are independent from the attitudes and dispositions of the political agents will be addressed later in the chapter.

There is a sense in which the very idea of moral responsibility—a central idea for Weber—is inseparable from that of accountability. We owe explanation to those negatively affected by our acts and to third parties. But accountability entails a stronger claim, too. Others may be entitled to react to our own acts in certain ways, and we may be expected to bear out the consequences. They may blame us or express blame-related attitudes such as resentment, anger, scorn, indignation, and the like. They may decide to avoid us, to break with us, they may demand compensation, they may forgive us, etc. For the aims of my book, it is this consequential aspect of accountability that will matter most. Unless explicitly stated otherwise, "accountability" will be understood as liability to practical consequences. In his celebrated essay "Freedom and Resentment" Peter Strawson argued that responsibility is to be understood as having done something to which others have reason to react by expressing anger, scorn, resentment, indignation, etc. When we hold someone responsible for an act, we want to say that such blame-related reactions (or praise-related reactions, at the other end of the spectrum) are in place.[19] On this account, responsibility is identified with accountability. If such a reductionist view is correct, then Weber's conception is not simply mistaken: it is incoherent. The politician's readiness or reluctance to get his hands dirty cannot be a matter of his private attitude. No one can be both morally re-

sponsible for his choices and immune to other people's reactive attitudes and their expression, for it is these attitudes and reactions that
constitute his moral responsibility.

But even if we take the judgment that S is responsible for a wrong to
be conceptually different from and prior to the judgment that S is a
proper target of blame-related attitudes,[20] Weber's view still remains
unacceptable. It is unacceptable on substantive moral grounds rather
than on grounds of logical inconsistency. When an individual does
something wrong, his action changes his moral status in relation to
other persons: it makes him a proper object of certain judgmental and
emotional responses. The facts of his responsibility for the wrong make
him liable to blame and to blaming-related reactive attitudes. Furthermore, whether he can recover his moral status antecedent to the offense
depends to a large extent on the will of the offended person. Without a
change in the victim's attitude from resentment to forgiveness (or some
functional equivalent of forgiveness, such as condonation, oblivion, and
the like) the perpetrator would have little hope of advancing beyond his
present status in the interpersonal relationship as a blameworthy person. The victim tends to have a margin of discretion to decide whether
or not to forgive, whether to forgive unconditionally or on condition of
a serious change of heart in the offender, whether to inflict some punishment on the offender and forgive him only after he has suffered, or to
refrain from punishing him on the ground that he has suffered enough
already, and so on.

Sometimes the margin of discretion shrinks to zero, as when, for
example, sincere repentance of a relatively minor offense makes it a
duty for the offended person to forgive. But no matter how wide or
narrow the margin of his discretion, the dynamics of accountability
relations are determined by interactions between punishing or forgiving on the one hand, and suffering or repenting on the other.

The reactive attitudes and their changes may, but need not, remain
internal to the reacting person. Blaming, reproaching, asking for apology and/or compensation, for example, are all external communicative acts. Anger, scorn, indignation may also be publicly expressed.
Forgiveness may be asked for and granted in as many words. Thus,
moral responsibility involves the responsible agent in interactions of
accountability.

A theory which denies the tools of holding an offender accountable to the offended person and other people sympathetic to the plight

of the latter is seriously flawed as a theory of morality. We have reason to reject it on the ground that it categorically disconnects responsibility from accountability.

This brings us to Weber's radical value decisionism. The thesis that the limits of the dictates of the ethics of responsibility are of a private nature is an application of a more general thesis of how ultimate values are adopted. If, as Weber believes, the adoption of an ultimate value is merely a work of blind choice, individuals cannot be held accountable for the kind of ultimate values they pursue in their lives. The reasons for rejecting a theory which categorically disconnects responsibility from accountability are also reasons for rejecting value decisionism.

There are also specifically political reasons why it is appropriate for holders of elected office (and for those running for such office) to see themselves as accountable to the citizens. Remember what was said in Chapter Two (2.1) about self-government: no government can be legitimate unless it qualifies as self-government, and one of the conditions of government to qualify as self-government is that it should be accountable to those who are subject to it.

While as persons we are all morally accountable to other persons, and at the same time in a position to hold any other person morally accountable, politicians are accountable not merely as persons but more specifically in their capacity as elected officials, and the largest group of individuals to whom they are accountable is the citizenry. Let us call this political accountability.

Moral accountability is symmetrical: A can hold B morally answerable for his acts, but this right is conditional on B having the right to hold A morally answerable. Political accountability is asymmetrical. An elected official is answerable to the citizenry for what he does in his official capacity,[21] but citizens are not answerable to the elected official for what they do in their capacity as citizens. They are not required to provide him with an explanation of why they vote him out of office, or why they refuse to support his policy proposal. As their agent, he is supposed to act in their interest, but as his principals, they are not supposed to act in his interest. Moral accountability is related to responsibility for past action; political accountability, while clearly having such a backward-looking dimension, has also forward-looking aspects. Citizens as principals have a right to hold a bearer of elected office to account on non-moral grounds—for example, on the basis of his prospective chances, based on skills and competence, to serve them well.[22]

This book focuses on the *moral* answerability of politicians to the citizenry—a subcategory within the wider concept of political accountability. Since there is no need to discuss here the other—non-moral—cases of political accountability, I reserve this term for those cases where politicians are being held publicly accountable for the moral defects of their relevant acts.

Political accountability has institutional aspects that further distinguish it from general moral accountability. First of all, it entails a specific transparency requirement. In a limited sense, we as persons are required to make ourselves transparent with regard to the acts for which we are being held to moral account (we should not lie about the harm we caused to someone, for example, nor should we cover up the relevant facts in other ways); in this sense, transparency is a general moral requirement. Insofar as we have such a moral obligation, that obligation is symmetrical. The transparency requirement characteristic of political accountability is stronger, and it is asymmetrically distributed: holders of elected office are required to disclose to the citizenry (almost) all the relevant information about their official activities, but citizens have no similar obligation to the holders of elected office with regard to their activities as citizens.

Finally, and most importantly, political accountability brings with it a specific set of sanctions. The moral practices of holding a person to accounts are also equipped with a wide variety of sanctions. Blaming someone or expressing scorn, anger, indignation, resentment in reaction to his conduct works in itself as a kind of sanction. Depending on how close or how loose the relationships, ranging from great intimacy to complete anonymity, between the people concerned may be, a large panoply of further reactions can be mobilized between them. When it comes to a conflict between old friends or lovers, for example, the richness of their relationship allows for many alternative sanctions: quarrel, silence, temporary avoidance, break, etc. Most of these sanctions would be grossly inappropriate, or would not make any sense at all, in occasional encounters between strangers. Thus, moral sanctions are variable and relation-specific.

When a political office-holder is held publicly accountable for his conduct, the difference between closely related people and strangers shrinks to zero: the relationship between citizens and office-holders is typically anonymous. This makes the set of political reactions much less rich in forms. It is further simplified by the fact that, as an institutional practice, holding elected officials to accounts becomes, to a large degree, standardized over time. On the other hand, political accountability has a sanction that is quite atypical as compared with those of general moral accountability. The person who is held to account politically is dealt with as a bearer of a role. He is politically accountable because he occupies that role, and one way to punish him for his objectionable conduct is to remove him from his office or to call for his resignation.

There is an obvious way in which political accountability entails the possibility that the politician found guilty of a serious offense gets removed from his office. In a democracy, the succession in office is determined by periodic elections. Elections are the occasions when incumbents are held accountable in the sense that the citizenry chooses between keeping them in, and dismissing them from, office. These are the occasions when the voters make an all-things-considered judgment on a representative's or a party's performance, and translate this judgment into a practical decision. When a government loses a general election, the press is often tempted to say that it was punished by the electorate.

But this is a very imprecise way of putting the matter. First of all, elections are not just occasions for expressing the voters' judgment on the moral conduct of the incumbents. Nor are they occasions merely to express judgment on their general performance. Such retrospective judgments are only one among the many types of considerations that affect the choices of the individual voters and the collective decision aggregated from those choices. The judgment about the past activities of the government competes with other judgments, including those related to its electoral promises for the next cycle. Thus, backward-looking judgments mix with forward-looking hopes and fears in the deliberations that lead to the voters' choice in the ballot box.

Furthermore, the choice voters make is never simply one between confirming and dismissing an incumbent—it is always a choice between an incumbent and his rival(s). The voters make a comparative assessment between the incumbent and his potential replacement(s), and the decision will reflect an overall view of the many advantages and disadvantages attributed to the competitors. The moral judgment the electorate may pass on the deeds of the incumbent is only one component of this complex picture. Even when a voter strongly condemns the incumbent, all things considered, he may want him to stay rather than be replaced by his main rival (although he would perhaps be glad to see him replaced by a better alternative). Such a preference may not be morally reprehensible, as the contingent character imperfections version of the realist thesis insists.[23]

In sum, the moral judgment about an incumbent's deeds tends to compete with too many other considerations to be typically decisive for the outcome of an election.

But there are occasions when such a judgment may indeed become decisive. These are occasions when a scandal erupts between two elections, raising the question whether a politician who has disgraced himself should be allowed to stay in office until the end of his term. That question is raised not merely because a strategically decisive part of the electorate may now want to see him removed from his post although, as we will see in Chapter Seven (7.5), this desire acts as the final regulator of the process that leads towards his dismissal. Rather, it is raised because the voters who want to see the disgraced politician removed from his post have a reason for wanting to see this outcome, and it is that reason that justifies asking the question. The role held by an elected office-holder is constituted in part by norms of proper conduct for its occupier. Should this person disgrace himself, he does not compromise himself alone but the office as well. If so, there is reason to dismiss him or to pressure him into resignation because it may not be possible to salvage the integrity of the office unless it is separated from the disgraced person who held it.

Our discussion will focus on this sanction of separating the elected official from his office between two elections, rather than as part of the normal electoral contest.

Removal or resignation from office is an ultimate political sanction. The departure of the official conveys the judgment that what he has done was no ordinary moral mistake; that it does not allow a return to business as usual. If such ultimate sanctions were not available, the claim that certain things are incompatible with the integrity of public offices would be vacuous. The public expressions of regret and apology are often sufficient to rectify a morally awkward act. But in the absence of a serious possibility of losing office as an ultimate penalty, they would ring hollow. Instead of meaning, "I take responsibility," they would rather come to mean, "I *don't* take responsibility." Admitting one's fault would simply immunize one from being held to account.

To take stock: According to Max Weber, the permissiveness of the ethics of responsibility has certain limits; it ends where the dominance of the ethics of conscience begins. At the same time, Weber believes that the boundary between the domains of the two ethics is marked out by the moral personality of the political leader who at some point comes forward and makes the solemn statement, "Here I stand, I can do no other." I have tried to show in this section that Weber was right in his first claim, and wrong in the second. The realist thesis is subject to a constraint, and the constraint embodies a principle of accountability. Rather than speaking to the private conscience of the politician, it addresses both him and the community. It equips the participants in politics with tools to subject political action to moral criticism and to press for practical consequences.

Politics as a moral problem is not simply a problem of how the politicians themselves should deal, in their hearts, with morally reprehensible acts they may feel required to carry out. It is, first and foremost, a problem of how *the political community* should deal with such acts. The central question of political morality is not how politicians should see their own actions, but rather how the community should see, and react to, them. This question, however, has no practical reality outside a specific—democratic—type of political organization. The fact that no early modern advocates of the realist thesis had any thoughts about its constrained character may be closely related to the fact that they had no experience of democracy. The fact that Weber presented the constraint as fully internal to the personal character of the political leader may be related to his ambiguous attitude towards democracy.

6.3 The constraint: its content and scope

In Chapter Five (5.1), I claimed that at each level of overall compliance there are certain moral minima that constrain political action at that level. Most of these minima are not the same at all levels. In this sense, the constraint is relative to the levels of compliance. But the levels of compliance do not determine the content of the standards people ought to comply with provided that enough others comply as well. What they determine is whether a particular person ought to comply, at the given level of overall compliance, with a standard that he would certainly be required to comply with at the level of what John Rawls calls strict compliance.[24] In order to be able to characterize the content of the constraint, we must look for information about something other than the overall levels of compliance. In Chapter Five I suggested that the moral minima making up the constraint are rooted in the principles of political legitimacy. In this section, I will continue elaborating this theme.

To remind: if a political regime is to satisfy the conditions of legitimacy to an acceptable degree, it must enable the community to keep the action of the holders of public office within certain limits. Those limits make up the content of the constraint. A look at the conditions of legitimacy may help us form a rough idea of the relevant limits.

It is a background assumption of the theory developed in this book that legitimate political regimes respect the principles of human rights, of self-government, and of the rule of law (see Chapter Two, 2.1). Human rights insist that the equal moral standing of persons is inviolable and that the authorities must defer to that inviolability by refraining from arbitrarily killing or detaining people, from subjecting them to cruel and humiliating treatment, from curtailing their liberties, from invading their privacy, and so on. Self-government means that because human beings are each other's moral equals, political authority must be mandated by, and wielded in the service of, those over whom it is exercised, and to whom its holders must be accountable. The rule of law may be understood as a corollary to the first two principles: citizens have a right to expect that political authority is not applied to them arbitrarily but rather under the constraints of general, impartially administered, prospective, stable, and public laws.

We have already agreed that legitimacy admits of degrees. Regimes satisfy the conditions set by human rights, self-government, and the rule of law to different degrees and thus they command legitimacy to different degrees.

Suppose that a political regime commands legitimacy to an acceptable degree. I maintain that in a consolidated state any political action under such a regime will be subjected to a set of moral requirements that constrain the realist thesis. The outline of the legitimizing principles given above does not suffice to generate a systematic account of these constraints (perhaps no definitive account could be generated in any case) but it may serve to provide illuminating examples.

Human rights and the rule of law exclude naked violence from the permissible arsenal of the struggle for power. The principle of accountability condemns all acts that count as deliberately misleading the public. In particular, it prohibits office-holders to conceal information of public interest in order to shield political activities from criticism; it prohibits lying to the legislature, especially when the lie affects a legislative decision, or covers up illegal acts. The fact that the resources controlled by a political office-holder belong to the community makes it a betrayal of his mandate to channel such resources into a private firm (unless the expenditure is the market price for a service to public welfare). For the same reason, the politician is unfaithful to his mandate if he promotes policies that are biased towards special interests; the bias is particularly invidious if it is related to a transaction where official influence is sold for private money. The rule of law prohibits exceeding the limits of one's office, exercising power without legal authorization, usurping or ignoring the powers allocated to other offices, and so on. The equal moral standing of all makes discrimination suspect, and it puts any talk about the inferiority of a class of citizens, and any advocacy of discrimination or segregation, beyond the pale of permissible political strategy.

The items on this list are not defined with any precision. One may suspect that some instances of misleading the public, for example, or of exceeding the powers attached to an office call for resignation or dismissal, while others do not. The separation of those that do from those that do not is a task that depends for its solution on, among other things, the actual level of overall compliance. Or at least this is the case with the variable component of the moral constraint on permissible political strategy. But the argument has an aspect that is not relative to the given level of compliance. The principles mobilized by it are those of political legitimacy. As such, they are of an abstract and general nature, and can be appealed to at all compliance levels. The actual level of compliance may, then, determine the way the general principles apply in particular circumstances.

The same type of argument applies to the question of the scope of the constraint. That question is raised by the fact that the political offices are filled with persons who occupy and act in many roles, most of which are private rather than official or public: they may be members of a family and parts of a kinship network, they may be the owners of economic assets, they may be affiliated to a religious community or a professional association, they may sit on various boards, and so on. The question of the scope asks in which of his roles the political office-holder is subject to the constraint? Clearly, public vices may justify the claim that he ought to leave his office. But what about his private vices? Legal offenses, whether public or private, are obvious reasons to go. But can a private moral offense that is not also a legal offense serve as such a reason?

If the moral minima are related to the conditions of political legitimacy in the way I have suggested in Chapter Five and in the present section, the answer seems to be no. After all, legitimacy is a normative property of public institutions. I argued that no state can command legitimacy to a sufficient degree unless it provides the political community with powers to keep the way the holders of public office make it work within certain moral limits. The acts performed in the role-bearer's official capacity are clearly relevant to the way he makes his office work. His private acts are typically irrelevant to this. The love affair of a married cabinet minister with a married woman may reverberate through the tabloid press, but it should not weaken his position as member of the government, since it is a completely private matter. It would be an oversimplification, though, to state in a general form that no acts committed in the office-holder's private capacity matter in relation to his activities as office-holder. The same politician may legitimately come under fire when the story of how he has fast-tracked the procedure of granting permanent residence to his lover's nanny—a foreign national—is revealed to the public. Such an intervention amounts to the abuse of an official position to obtain private advantage.[25]

Shall we say, then, that the scope of the constraint extends to private acts in so far as they are relevant to the moral assessment of what an office-holder does in his official capacity?

One may endorse this formula and claim at the same time that it fails to limit the scope of private acts that matter in connection with political accountability. *All* private vices are relevant to the moral assessment of performance in public office. For moral conservatives, they are certainly relevant because, in their view, politics properly understood, must promote correct standards of conduct in all domains of life, including the private. Liberals would deny this; they argue that individuals have a moral right to pursue their own conception of the good life and that this right requires the state to draw a sharp line between matters of public concern and matters that are the business of none but the persons involved.[26]

The liberal view is my view. But there is an argument in support of the political relevance of the private conduct of public office holders that seems to be neutral with regard to the liberal-conservative controversy. This argument relies on the observation that voters are typically ill-prepared to judge the official acts of their representatives because they have no personal experience of the way political institutions work. But they have ample experience of private life, which makes them competent to judge the character of a politician when it comes to his conduct towards his family and friends. Marital infidelity, for example, may serve, for them, as evidence of a disposition to be unfaithful in general. For the American voter, one could say, the fact that Hillary had reason not to trust Bill as her husband was evidence that the community had reason not to trust William Jefferson Clinton as their president.[27]

This does not seem accurate. One effect of the institutional system, and of the multiplicity of distinct roles we occupy as participants in it, is that human character becomes compartmentalized; it is grossly misleading to try to judge someone's conduct in one of his roles on the basis of his conduct in another, very distant, role. If President Kennedy's extra-marital adventures had been generally known, it would have been a great mistake on the part of American voters to deny him their trust as their loyal servant on the ground of his private infidelities.

But let us accept, against the evidence to the contrary, that such extensions of judgment are warranted. Then, informed citizens would be correct to think that the husband who betrayed his wife might, in the future, betray the confidence of his electorate. That would be a legitimate concern. Citizens have good reasons for trying to make judgments on the moral character of their elected representatives. They may not know enough about the particular policy options in order always to be able to judge whether a politician stands for the right choice. Nor can they rely on the political institutions providing the politician with incentives that make his interests fully coincide with those of his constituency. Therefore, information on the moral dispositions of the politician is an important cue for the voter when he makes up his mind about whom to elect. A politician with a proven disposition to deceive his wife would be a bad choice, provided that this trait would be just a particular instance of his general disposition to deceive anybody with whom he may interact. In any case, as we have seen in Chapter Three (3.6), political communities have an interest not only in the moral properties of what their leaders do but also in those of their character.

But this interest is essentially forward-looking. When a voter refuses to vote for a candidate on the ground of a character trait, she does not punish him for what he did in the past. She tries to keep him away from an official position in which he seems likely to do undesirable things in the future.

The concern we are dealing with in this chapter is backward-looking. One is not held morally accountable for what one may do in the times ahead; moral accountability is attached to what one has done in the past, or is doing in the present. For the aims of holding a politician to account for what he is morally (retrospectively) responsible the fact that certain private wrongs may serve as evidence for predicting public wrongs not yet committed is irrelevant. And so is the expectation based on past private wrongs, whether correct or not, that the wrongdoer will commit—unspecified—public wrongs in the future.

I conclude that private vices in themselves are not within the scope of political accountability. It is not the private vice itself for which an official could be held politically accountable. He is accountable for something that he does in his official capacity and that acquires a special significance against the background of his private conduct. The latter matters only because of the light it sheds on the *political acts* of the office-holder,[28] or the consequences it may have for his ability to carry out the duties of his office.[29]

6.4 Institutional rules

Typically, non-compliance is attributed to opportunities to free-ride on the cooperative efforts of others or to the hope of resolving conflicts by force or fraud, to the absence of any assurance that others will comply, to lack of co-ordination, to the perception that the scheme of cooperation in force is unfair to some of the participants, or to disagreement on the content of principles the parties are supposed to abide by, and to whether a particular principle applies under particular circumstances. In order to raise the level of compliance, such shortcomings need to be remedied. The prime remedy is the law itself. The legislature provides a unique set of authoritative rules for a society that is deeply divided on what kind of rules its members ought to follow; the judiciary provides unique authoritative decisions on particular issues where the application of the rules is controversial; laws give salience to one among the many available alternatives and, in so doing, facilitate co-ordination; they are equipped with sanctions that give assurance to those willing to comply that enough others will be deterred from free-riding or using force or fraud; the procedures of legislation and adjudication may ensure that the law is designed and administered with a sufficient degree of impartiality, and so on.

No large-scale and complex society can do without a legal system. Some of the moral minima constraining political strategy themselves find their best institutional vehicle in the law. Appropriate legislation on conflicts of interest or on party finances, for example, is a must for attempts to raise the level of compliance in these domains. Other requirements, however, are not well served by legislation.

Institutions, whether legal or non-legal, are always less than perfect means of bringing social interaction in harmony with the requirements of morality. Even the best designed system of rules is likely to encounter future situations that it is incapable of dealing with adequately because the designers could not foresee them. In such situations, the moral standards that usually require the same conduct as the institutional rules in force may exclude action that is permitted by those rules. The rule of law demands that in such cases the legal provisions be given priority over the commands of morality. However, as we have seen in Chapter One (1.2), this principle does not necessarily apply to political (as distinct from legal) accountability. The imperfections of law leave room, in the public domain, for moral reactions that are permitted but not required by law, and that do not follow legally designed procedures.

Arguably, such imperfections lend themselves to corrections, once they are discovered, and so the moral issues that are not being taken care of by the law at a certain point in time sooner or later come under proper legal regulation. But, and this is my more important point, there is a vide variety of issues of public morality that under no circumstances can be satisfactorily dealt with by the law.

I will not embark on an exhaustive account of them here. But I would like to mention three such types of issues, in order to convey a sense of their nature and diversity.

Consider, first, the norm that prohibits political office-holders to express racist views or any opinions that offend the principle of moral equality in some other way. Suppose that this norm is formulated as a law. In that case, losing office is a legal sanction attached to such an offense. A legal provision to this effect would conflict with the very principle it is supposed to protect, i.e. the principle of moral equality.

Moral equality entails that all persons have the same fundamental rights and duties. This status is not acquired in virtue of meritorious acts; it is part of what it means to be a person. Its possession is not to be understood as being conditional on the value of someone's conduct. The right to express one's views is one of the rights human beings have as persons. The possession of this right cannot be made conditional on the value of those views. Speech ought not to be restricted on the basis of its content, no matter how wrong or despicable it may be.

One could object that political office-holders do not speak in their general capacity as persons. Even if freedom of expression rules out content-based restraints on speech in ordinary contexts, it may not rule out imposing such restraints where the speaker is a political office-holder. Holding a public office depends on a voluntary agreement. If someone agrees to become an elected official, by the same token he agrees to abide by the norms of the office. Respect for the equal moral standing of human individuals is part of the norms that apply to public office in a democracy. Why should the law of a democratic community refrain from stating this among the requirements it applies to political office-holders?

The reason, I think, is as follows. Politicians run for elected office. Their aim is to be representatives of the citizenry. If a candidate who expresses racist views has a chance to be elected, it is because there are enough voters who see themselves as adequately represented if, and only if, they have the opportunity to vote for a racist.

Unlike the role of the political office-holder, the role of the citizen is typically a non-voluntary one. Political communities are not voluntary associations of the like-minded. The duty to obey the state that is incumbent on their members does not depend on consent or on any other act that counts as voluntarily undertaking an obligation.[30]

Should a citizen be hostile to the basic principles that inform the constitutional order of the republic, those who want to uphold these principles cannot tell him: We are a community of equals, and we do not allow you to try to change our constitutional system.

Equality demands that everybody have the right to express his views on how members of the republic should be related to each other, and to try to convince his fellow-citizens that they should change the constitutional order accordingly. This right is violated if those citizens who want to be represented by a racist are prevented by law from electing a representative of their own preference. It is the equal standing of all citizens that protects the freedom of anti-egalitarian discourse for political office-holders, irrespective of the content of their political views.

To put it briefly, equality requires the law to provide room for political forces that refuse to endorse equality.[31] A republic of equals is supposed to guarantee the freedom of assembly, association, and speech not only to those who approve of equality but also to those who reject it. Democrats, i.e. citizens who agree that their community is one of equals, must confront and defeat such adversaries in the political arena, not in the courts.[32]

If this is true, then equality does not allow racist political discourse to be legally banned. But racist discourse is still *morally* banned. A politician who professes the inferiority of a social group identified by the criteria of race, and who advocates their exclusion and subordination, does something that political morality does not permit a holder of, or a contender for, public office to do. It is a legitimate demand that a politician who claims in public that a certain race group is inferior to the majority and/or advocates exclusionary and discriminatory measures against this group leave his office.

Let us now turn to a second type of reason why certain moral minima may not be laid down as law. In a constitutional democracy, the different branches of government are expected to refrain from interfering with each other's domain. Some boundaries separating the jurisdictions of different powers are fixed by the constitution or by ordinary laws. Other boundaries, however, do not lend themselves to formal definition, whether legal or non-legal. Consider the powers of presidents with regard to legislation. In parliamentary regimes the president of the republic is usually elected by the legislature, but even if he is not, his powers are limited. But how narrowly limited they are?

Typically, it is the president who ratifies and promulgates the laws adopted by the legislature. If he disagrees with a law or with a provision of it, he may refer it, along with his comments, back to the legislature for reconsideration.

The constitutions I know of are silent on *how often* a president elected by the legislature may veto a duly adopted law. He would not find himself in conflict with the letter of the basic law if he vetoed *all* the laws, without exception.[33] However, such a practice would effectively obstruct the process of legislation, and obstructing legislation would count as an abuse of presidential powers—a grave offence that may even trigger the process of impeachment.

Thus, there must be some limits to the use of the presidential veto. But there is no legal way to fix these limits. The presidential veto is devised as an ultimate guarantee that the legislature does not decide a matter of great importance without serious consideration. This guarantee cannot work unless the president himself gives serious thought to the legislative material. When he chooses a piece of legislation to refer back to the legislature, he must exercise judgment. He must decide whether the importance of the issue and the magnitude of any mistakes in the law justify his intervention. His assessment of how important the issue is and how great the mistakes are will, of course, depend on how he feels about the frequency with which he, as the president of the republic, may veto the decision of the legislature. But he will not make his judgment about the invisible limit to the frequency of presidential interventions independently of his judgments about the importance of the issues and the magnitude of the mistakes, as if the frequency norm were an external parameter of his deliberations. Rather, he will make these judgments simultaneously, adjusting the different considerations to each other.

To put it briefly: the president cannot do his job as guardian of the quality of legislation unless he exercises judgment on the merits of the successive cases; he cannot exercise judgment on the merits of the various different cases unless he also exercises judgment on the desirable frequency of his interventions; and he cannot exercise judgment on the frequency of his interventions if it is subject to a formal limit. Thus, the limit on the frequency of presidential vetoes resists formalization; it must take shape in a process of interaction between the president and the legislature.

The judgment dependence of the proper use of presidential veto makes this practice inaccessible to formal regulation, legal or non-legal (the same reasons that rule out its regulation by law exclude its regulation by a code of ethics, for example). Some other issues, however, while resisting regulation by legal codes, lend themselves very naturally to regulation by ethical codes. Here is an example.

Combating corruption is a job for the law in the first place. But the law is unlikely to do this job effectively if it is not aided by a set of non-legal rules and procedures. In order to deal with corruption with the hope of success, the law needs to be supported by a workable distinction between mere gifts and bribes. Such a distinction is needed because gift-giving is an innocent act of courtesy that cannot and should not be legally prosecuted or morally condemned. The boundary between innocent gift-giving and bribery is fuzzy, though. Suppose that a politician is given a bookmark by an admirer for his birthday: we interpret this as gift-giving. If the same politician is offered, and accepts, a valuable package of securities, we speak about bribery. Where does the range of innocuous presents end, and the range of bribes begin? The difference between gift-giving and bribery is one of degree, not of kind. On the other hand, it is a sociologists' commonplace that gift-giving is embedded in practices of reciprocal favors. So the mere fact that a bribe is handed over in the expectation of some return (whether or not explicitly stated) does not separate it from a gift. Nor is it sharply distinguished by the value of the donation. It is not the case that a thing of, or below, a certain value would still count as a gift, while any donation of a slightly greater value would count as a bribe. We have no reason to think that if we knew something that we do not know at this moment we would come into possession of an objective limit that would unmistakeably separate innocent gifts from bribes. The right answer to the question of political corruption will remain underdetermined until agreement is reached about some (morally acceptable) dividing line.

Now suppose that the line is drawn by the law. If the legislature draws it too high, many doubtful transactions will be made legally permissible. If it draws it too low, many innocent transactions will become liable to legal prosecution.

There is a further difficulty. Wherever the line may be drawn, the difference in value between what is punishable and what is not will be insignificant. On the assumption that politicians are no better than ordinary human individuals, it seems likely that the value of the gifts they are prepared to accept will converge on this fine line between gifts and bribes. In other words, if the dividing line is set by the law, the practice of gift-giving and gift-taking will be likely to verge on criminality. Typical transactions will be separated from acts of corruption by the smallest possible margin. However, incorruptibility, the virtue we want to flourish among our politicians, is not separated from corruptness by a fine line. They are diametrical opposites.

Where the difference between innocent gift-taking and acceptance of a bribe is negligible, the choice between crossing the divide or remaining on the right side is likely to be determined by dispositions such as risk-aversion or risk-seeking, caution or carelessness, and so on. Even if a politician is risk-averse and cautious enough never to cross that fatal line, he will not act out of the virtue of incorruptibility. An incorruptible politician does not weigh the costs and benefits of refusing a bribe against those of accepting it. He does not even consider the option of selling official influence for economic gain. By allowing the line between permissible giving and taking of gifts, on the one hand, and punishable bribery, on the other, to shrink towards insignificance, the rule-maker harms the morality of the political class. If the ethos of incorruptibility is to flourish among politicians, a wide zone needs to be established between typical practice and criminal practice.

These difficulties can be handled if there are non-legal rules that set the upper limit of the value of gifts a politician may accept far below the lower limit of what is defined as a bribe by the law. The existence of such rules allows the legislator to avoid the error of prosecuting innocent gift-giving, while it provides the politicians with a strong incentive to avoid the situations where their transactions become hard to distinguish from criminal proceedings.

Codes of ethics are suitable for setting such upper limits to permissible gift-taking. Their great advantages are, first, a relative precision in drawing the relevant boundaries and, second, easiness of attaching enforcement procedures to violations. Such codes may set the maximum value of a gift a politician may accept at any one time. They may set a maximum for the total value of gifts the same politician may accept from the same person or firm over a period of time. They may set a maximum price for his dinner consumption paid for by a lobbyist and the number of dinner invitations he may accept from the same lobbyist or his firm within a period of time. They may prohibit politicians to travel at a lobbyist's expense, require them to submit a statement about all the presents they have received, and so on.

The argument from the necessity of keeping the gap between morally and the legally permitted conduct wide has an interesting corollary. If we contemplate the constraint from a certain distance, it may seem obvious that the gravity of a moral transgression and the eligibility of the act for justifying political sanctions are positively related. The more outrageous the act, we may think, the greater the likelihood that it will call for the perpetrator's removal or resignation from office. But consider a community where the moral constraints on political leadership are specified by elaborate institutional rules, written or unwritten. As we have seen, such rules may prohibit acts that, even if immoral, are only trivially so, and revelations about their infringement may involve the departure of the politician from office. A politician in a democratic country may be made to resign over a relatively small offense.[34]

6.5 Willy Brandt's resignation

To conclude this chapter with an example that I hope makes its claims vivid, I will tell a real-life political story: that of Willy Brand giving up his office as chancellor.

On April 24, 1974, the national security agencies of the Federal Republic of Germany arrested the East German spy Günter Guillaume. Guillaume worked at the chancellor's office as one of his three personal aides. In June 1973 the agency warned Brandt that Guillaume was suspected of being a spy, but they advised him to keep Guillaume until they had investigated the case. Brandt not only followed the advice, but he even took Guillaume with him on his holiday in Norway and entrusted him with taking care of his top secret messenger mails. On April 26, he told the Bundestag that Guillaume had no access to classified documents. Perhaps he had forgotten the Norway episode, but in any case it was soon discovered that his statement was not true. Then, on May 4 Brandt was given to understand by his minister of the interior that his "woman affairs" are under investigation, reasoning that Guillaume, who probably knew about those affairs, might have used them in the past or try to use them during his trial. The next day Brandt composed his letter of resignation, on May 6 he submitted it to the president, and on May 7 he told the SPD parliamentary group about his move.

Brandt did not take his decision under pressure; he resigned out of his own initiative. His primary adversary within the party, Herbert Wehner, assured him that he had his full backing, no matter what he might do.[35] His only possible rival for the position of chancellor, Helmut Schmidt, sharply opposed his resignation.[36] The SPD parliamentary party did not understand why he should quit.[37]

The chancellor himself justified his move by moral reasons. "I take responsibility for my carelessness about the spy affair," he wrote in his letter to the federal president.[38] Thus, voluntary acceptance of responsibility played a key role in Brandt's resignation. Other politicians with a weaker sense of the moral stakes would not have left so easily. This does not mean, however, that Brandt departed for reasons of personal morality alone. There was general agreement that *someone* had to go as a consequence of the Guillaume affair, but Brandt was not the obvious candidate. The fact that Guillaume had been able to infiltrate the chancellor's immediate circles, and stay there even after suspicions about him had arisen, was first and foremost the fault of the national security agencies. Political responsibility rested not with a single person but with all those who were supposed to supervise counter-intelligence and the activities of the chancellery: the undersecretary for the interior in charge, the minister of the interior, the chancellor's chief of staff and only at the end of the line the chancellor himself. In such cases, when responsibility is shared by a number of persons, it need not be the most senior of those affected who should quit, and quite often it is not clear at first which of them will actually do so. Initially, it appeared that one of the undersecretaries for the interior would be dismissed. It was Brandt himself who decided that the credibility crisis could only be ended by his own resignation.

He did this with an eye on how his position was likely to change in the weeks ahead. He did not make his decision at the moment the scandal broke. The arrest of Guillaume shook the chancellor's office, but it did not occur to Brandt that he should resign. Shortly afterwards it transpired that his statement before the Bundestag had not been true, yet he still did not resign. About ten days after the eruption of the scandal he learned that the counterintelligence was after his "woman affairs." The next day he wrote his letter. Why now if not earlier?

He certainly did not think that his fleeting affairs would put the country at risk. Moreover, it was his firm conviction that the public had nothing to do with his private life. Nevertheless, he had to consider that should he stay on, his relationships would be in the spotlight, and he would be forced to explain and defend himself. "They will pursue you, and force you to resign in six to eight weeks," he was advised by his confidant, Egon Bahr, "but as for now, you are still able to set the course of events."[39]

As Brandt told the SPD caucus, "my resignation was necessitated by my experience in office, by my views about the unwritten norms of democracy, and the protection of my personal and political integrity."[40] The reference to his experiences in office is vacuous. As for the unwritten norms of democracy, the chancellor's views about them did not emerge in the days between the beginning of the scandal and his resignation, and they surely hardly changed during that period. But the protection of "personal and political integrity" was a new component. Brandt was probably concerned to avoid compromising his reputation under the attacks of the press, an outcome that he believed would not have been worth the attempt to deflect the charges. He may not have had much trust that he would succeed in any case. Much like Bahr, he might have thought that, with his reputation in ruins, he would become a liability for his own party. And if that was what he thought, he had to accept that the options before him were being reduced to a single choice: whether to leave immediately, at his own initiative, or to be forced to leave by others later on.

Notes

1 "Der Sinn der 'Wertfreiheit' der soziologischen und ökonomischen Wissenschaften." In M. Weber: *Gesammelte Aufsätze zur Wissenschaftslehre*. Tübingen: J. C. B. Mohr (Paul Siebeck), 1922. Weber says "it is possible", but his reasoning is based on the assumption that this is in fact the case.

2 "Wissenschaft als Beruf." In M. Weber: *Gesammelte Aufsätze zur Wissenschaftslehre*. Tübingen: J. C. B. Mohr (Paul Siebeck), 1922.

3 Wissenschaft.

4 Wertfreiheit.

5 Wissenschaft.

6 Ibid, 359.
7 "Politics as a Vocation." In M. Weber: *Political Writings*. Cambridge: The University Press, 1994, 355.
8 Ibid., 357.
9 Ibid., 358.
10 Ibid., 360.
11 Ibid., 358.
12 Ibid., 362.
13 Ibid., 368.
14 Ibid., 367.
15 Ibid., 368.
16 In the summer of 1995, the Bosnian-Serbian army launched an attack on the city of Srebrenica, which had at that time been declared a safe haven for refugees by the United Nations and placed under the protection of a tiny peacekeeping unit of Dutch nationality. The commander of the unit asked for reinforcement, but to no avail. Finally, the Dutch soldiers departed without as much as a shot being fired, leaving the Muslim population to its fate. The invading Serbs slaughtered more than seven thousand men and boys. A Dutch private organization called War Documentation Institute issued a report about the incident in the summer of 2002, pointing out, among other things, the failures of the then Dutch government. A few days later, Prime Minister Wim Kok and his whole cabinet submitted their resignation. By this time, Bosnia had been living in peace for years, and the Netherlands had long been governed by a completely different cabinet than the one in office during the Bosnian war. The massacre in Srebrenica presented the Netherlands with only one duty: to come to terms with the past. The Kok cabinet, not unlike its predecessor, failed to investigate the affair, and it was suspected that officials in the ministry of defense even attempted to cover up the responsibility of the government in charge at the time of Srebrenica. Consequently, the minister of defense and a colleague of his decided to resign, come what may; and the other members of the cabinet concluded that under the ensuing circumstances they had no other choice but to follow suit. They clearly thought that the resignation of the cabinet was an appropriate—perhaps the only appropriate—way of expressing guilt for the failure to investigate the case. This judgment was not shared by the general community. Wim Kok was the most popular Dutch politician of the time; the scandal did not harm his credibility. Neither the opposition nor the press demanded his and his cabinet's departure, and the resignation was received as a shock.
17 This claim needs qualification. According to Weber, whatever we may choose, we have to take responsibility for our ultimate decisions. An agent may be criticised for taking this responsibility lightly.
18 Weber: "Politics", 367.
19 See P. Strawson: "Freedom and Resentment", in *Proceedings of the British Academy* 48 (1962) 1–25.

20 See G. Watson: "Responsibility and the Limits of Evil", in Watson: *Agency and Answerability*. Oxford: Clarendon, 2004.

21 I will say more on the scope of political accountability in the next section. Acts performed in the agent's official capacity clearly fall within this scope, and this much will suffice for the time being.

22 A party leader may resign because his senior colleagues have lost their confidence that he is able to win the coming elections. Suppose they visit him as deputation to tell him that he should go. The call for resignation is a consequence of what he has done in the past. But the only way in which his past performance counts in this case is as evidence that he lacks the capacity to lead the party to victory. He may leave amidst expressions of sympathy and pity on the part of his party and the public. Nobody claims that he must go because that is the appropriate way for him to take responsibility for the morally awkward character of his past deeds.

23 See Chapter Three, 3.6. In the first round of the presidential elections in France in 2002, Lionel Jospin, the socialist candidate, came third behind Jacques Chirac, the right-wing incumbent, and the openly racist Jean-Marie Le Pen. Charges of political corruption had been lodged against Chirac, whom the left wanted to see out of his office so that he could be indicted and tried. But once the run-off had been reduced to a choice between Chirac and Le Pen—"le voleur et le fasciste"—the socialist voters had no other option but to vote for Chirac. Some held their noses with a clip when they entered the voting booth, while others conspicuously washed their hands when they left.

24 Strom Thurmond had once been a "Southern Democrat," an ardent proponent of racial segregation. When Harry Truman called upon the Democratic Party in 1948 to endorse the cause of civil rights, Thurmond with other splinter "Southern Democrats" established a new party by the name of States' Rights Democratic Party, and he ran for president as the nominee of this obscure formation, on a racist platform. "All the laws of Washington and all the bayonets of the army cannot force the Negro into our homes, our schools, our churches," he declared in the campaign. During the 1950s and 1960s he was in the forefront of the fight against the Civil Rights Act, this time once again as a Democrat. In 1956, he initiated the Southern Manifesto against the anti-segregationist rulings of the Supreme Court. In 1964, he endorsed the far-right presidential bid of Barry Goldwater, and switched to the Republicans. Thurmond celebrated his hundredth birthday in December, 2002. Trent Lott, at the time leader of the Senate Republicans, thought it appropriate to praise him for his racist past in his laudation speech. "When Strom Thurmond ran for president, we voted for him. We're proud of it. And if the rest of the country had followed our lead, we wouldn't have had all these problems over all these years, either," Lott was quoted by the press as having said. (See R. Toner: "Ugly Echoes." In *The New York Times*, December 15, 2002, WK 5.) His words caused immense outrage. Jesse Jackson, Al Gore, Bill Clinton took turns to denounce the senator; the press went on to un-

cover his speeches with a racist sting. His fellow senators began to distance themselves from him. President Bush, too, condemned the ominous words. ("Every statement to the effect that the segregationist past was acceptable or positive is offensive and wrong", he said. See K. Anderson: "Republicans Divide Over Lott." *BBC News Online*. December 16, 2002.) Lott was forced to resign from his position as leader of the Senate Republicans.—When Thurmond had ventilated his views that Lott saw it appropriate to praise half a century later, he was able to avoid Lott's misfortune. After the short-lived adventure with his openly racist splinter party, he was readmitted by the Democrats. When he broke with them for good, the Republicans had no qualms about embracing him. But they punished him when he extolled the virtues of Thurmond's racist past. (See P. Applebaum: "Lott's Walk Near the Incendiary Edge of Southern History." In *The New York Times*, December 13, 2002, A36.)

25 This is, in a nutshell, the story of the first fall of David Blunkett, then minister of labor in the government of Tony Blair, in December 2004. Until the information on fast-tracking the residence permit to Leoncia Casalme, a young Philippino woman, surfaced, Michael Howard, then leader of the Conservative parliamentary group, told his colleagues to leave Blunkett alone. But they went on the attack as soon as the case of the residence permit became public.

26 See T. Nagel: "The Shredding of Public Privacy." In Nagel: *Concealment & Exposure*. Oxford–New York: Oxford University Press, 2002.

27 Another argument is based on the assumed relevance of a somewhat different relationship between public and private in the lives of public figures: ordinary people learn what moral norms are and how to order our lives according to those norms from role models. Public figures are eminent candidates for serving as role models for the others. Thus, they cannot legitimately object to a lowering of the threshold of protection of their privacy. See J. Haldane: "A Subject of Distaste, An Object of Judgment." In E. F. Paul, F. D. Miller, Jr., and J. Paul, eds.: *Morality and Politics*. Cambridge: The University Press, 2004.

28 Mark Foley, a member of the US Congress, had to resign, in October 2006, upon revelations that he had sent sexually explicit e-mails to pages employed on Capitol Hill. Foley was a champion of conservative values, and for some time, head of the House Committee on Abandoned Children.

29 In 1970, Lord Lambton, a defense minister in Edward Heath's government resigned over a sex scandal. The Diplock Commission appointed by the prime minister to investigate security issues related to his involvement with prostitutes found no security breaches, but said that he had made himself vulnerable to blackmail. In 1963, John Profumo, secretary of defense in the government of Harold MacMillan, was revealed to have been involved with Christine Keeler, a call girl who was also having intimate relationships with the naval attaché of the Soviet Union in London. The security issue was clearly part of the reason why both Profumo and, ultimately, MacMillan himself had to resign.

30 States claim the authority to issue binding directives to anyone staying on their territory whether or not that person agreed to obey. Voluntaristic theories of political obligation try to show that if this claim is justified, some kind of implicit agreement must lurk in the background. But such theories are notorious about their failure to establish their thesis. If the claim of authority is defensible, the requirement to obey must express a duty that does not depend, for its force, on consent.

31 Typically, it is objected to this view that it tries to make freedom of expression unlimited. This is not the case, though. The principle spelled out above denies the existence of content-based limits to the freedom of expression, but it is not incompatible with limitations based on the dangers that may be generated by speech. Its advocates tend to agree that speech can be restricted and prosecuted if it is associated with a clear and present danger of violent action.

32 See R. Dworkin: "The Unbearable Cost of Liberty," in *Index on Censorship*, May–June, 1995.

33 The Polish president Lech Kaczyński is said to have warned Donald Tusk, the leader of the major opposition party at the time of their conversation, that he should not press for early elections because in case his party happens to come to government, he will veto all the laws of to be adopted by Sejm, the Polish Parliament.

34 Gregor Gysi, the leader of the Bundestag members of the Party of Democratic Socialism resigned, in the summer of 2002, over a Lufthansa offer of free tickets to passengers who had travelled a certain number of kilometers at their own cost: Gysi (like many other members of the Bundestag) asked the company to take his official travels into account and so derived a relatively modest private benefit from them.

35 Willy Brandt: *Erinnerungen.* Frankfurt/Main: Propyläen, Zurich: Ferenczy Verlag AG, 1989, 323. Cf. P. Merseburg: *Willy Brandt 1913–1992. Visionär und Realist.* Stuttgart–München: Deutsche Verlags-Anstalt, 2002, 736.

36 G. Schollgen: *Willy Brandt. Die Biographie.* Frankfurt/Main: Propyläen, 2001, 206.

37 *Erinnerungen*, 324.

38 Ibid.

39 E. Bahr: *Zu meiner Zeit.* München: Karl Blessing Verlag, 1996, 458.

40 Ibid., 324.

CHAPTER SEVEN

INDIRECT MOTIVATION: THE WIDE THESIS

7.1 Common deliberation and strategic interaction

The narrow thesis of indirect motivation disregards the possibility that the motivator and the motivated may share common objectives. It attributes community-regarding aims to the motivator but not to the motivated. Under this assumption indirect motivation appears as pure strategic action.

The choice situation and the act chosen in it are strategic when the outcomes are evaluated by the parties on the basis of their separate and, therefore, possibly conflicting interests. In such situations, the preferences of different individuals may or may not converge. For example, A and B may cooperate either to produce x or to produce y. They either rank these alternatives similarly (both preferring x to y or y to x), or differently (A preferring x to y and B preferring y to x or vice versa). If their preference orderings diverge, they are incapable of cooperating. If they are to be able to cooperate, the preferences of either A or B must change. The problem of indirect motivation is how to change the preference ordering of the potential partner. This problem is independent of the nature of the participants' preferences. A may try to change the balance of the costs and benefits of doing x or y for B in order to make it possible for the two of them to cooperate for an outcome that A values in terms of his self-regarding preferences, or he may try to change B's preference ordering in order to promote the cause of justice and the common good. The political thesis of indirect motivation is interested in the latter type of cases. In its narrow version it insists that A should not assume B to be motivated by public concerns. Rather, he should change the costs and benefits of the alternative choices open to B so that B comes to prefer, in terms of his self-regarding aims, the alternative that is preferable from the point of view of the political community.

The wide thesis does not completely dismiss this idea; rather, it amends it. It assumes human agents to have community-regarding preferences alongside their self-regarding preferences. It assumes, furthermore, that in many situations they find it too costly, in terms of their self-regarding preferences, to act in conformity with the requirements of their community-regarding preferences. In order to make the latter effective, indirect motivation must reduce the self-regarding losses that an agent suffers when acting for reasons of justice and the common good, so the thesis goes.

Thus, the wide thesis describes indirect motivation as belonging to two different domains at the same time. It assumes that the motivator and the motivated have, on the one hand, a set of separate aims and that, on the other hand, they have certain aims in common. Their separate aims motivate them to act strategically. Their shared objectives allow them to deliberate with each other on how to promote those objectives. The purpose of strategic action is, ideally, to facilitate convergence between separate and mutually independent aims. The objective of common deliberation is to reach a consensus on what the shared aims really consist in, and what those aims really require from the agents.

In his *Theory of Communicative Action*, Jürgen Habermas drives a categorical wedge between strategic action, where the participants provide each other with, and react to, incentives, and communicative action, in which the participants aim to convince each other of the truth of their claims about their shared world.[1] This distinction seems to me overstated for two interrelated reasons. First, as Habermas himself notes, strategic action has a communicative aspect of its own: it includes attempts to influence the opinions and views of the partner in a direction favorable to the agent's own interests. He hastens to add, however, that only communicative action aims directly at a shared understanding of the world people inhabit together.[2] He fails to consider that even if the aim of the communication is strategic, it includes statements about the world that claim to be true. Second, since different people may have both separate and shared aims at the same time, the same communicative act may lend itself to be interpreted both strategically and deliberatively.

Suppose a community agrees in the objective of establishing a health care system that determines the expenditures on health care in function of the individuals' preferences, allocates those expenditures efficiently, and provides a just basic coverage to those unable to buy insurance themselves. Suppose this community is deeply divided on what kind of system would best promote this objective. Some believe the best system would be a centralized social security system. Others believe a system based on competing private insurance companies would be the best one. Still others believe in a mixed system. These three conceptions mutually exclude each other. It is not possible to act on a combination of them. There is no conceivable compromise solution that would be centralized, competitive, and mixed at the same time. The community must choose either a centralized, or a competitive, or a mixed system. Each party must try to persuade the others on the superiority of their proposal. They must deliberate in common. But suppose common deliberation predictably will not conclude in a consensus before the date when the decision is due to be taken. Then, the parties must select the conception on which to act on the basis of bargaining. Each group must consider the two alternatives to its own conception in order to find out which one they may accept as the second-best. From the perspective of each of them, it is better if its conception is adopted as second-best, than if a different conception is adopted as second-best. Thus, they must try to conduct the communicative process so that their conception is chosen as second-best by the others. They must communicate strategically, rather than in a merely deliberative manner.[3]

Such combination of common deliberation with strategic interaction allows for the same communicative act to have a strategic and a deliberative aspect at the same time. Its manifest content may refer to an issue up for common deliberation, and it may convey, implicitly, some meaning of strategic value. Or its manifest content may be of a strategic nature, while its latent meaning may relate to an issue up for common deliberation. An example for the first type of cases is when the father tells his pugnacious son that it is not nice to hurt the weak. The statement expresses a moral judgment that, if true, involves a duty. But by uttering it the father commits himself to intervene whenever his son would hurt a weaker child again and, in this manner, he informs the boy that the costs of misusing his superior force are increased. An example for the second type is when a man promises his neighbor to help him to clean the rubble from his courtyard on condition that the neighbor helps him to dig up his garden. The manifest content of the utterance spells out the conditions for a bargaining deal. Latent to it, however, is a judgment according to which it is good for the neighbor to get rid of the rubble in his courtyard. "You should not be indifferent towards the state of your courtyard," the proposal communicates. Furthermore, it conveys the claim that it is not too much to ask that the man digs up half of his neighbor's garden in exchange for getting half of the rubble cleared from his courtyard. "It is not too much," does not mean here that given his preferences, the neighbor will not find the costs too great as compared to the benefit. Rather, it means that the relationship between the cost-benefit balances of the two neighbors is not unfair. The claim of fairness implicit in the offer is a moral judgment that, if true, must carry the consent of both parties. Its truth may be questioned, of course. The neighbor may respond that he is being asked to do too much in exchange for too little, meaning not that the benefits are not worth the costs but rather that the distribution of costs and benefits between him and his partner would not be fair. His objection, however, is evidence for the offer implying a claim of fairness. That the parties disagree on whether a particular distribution of burdens and benefits is fair does not make the issue any less of an object of common deliberation. The terms of a bargaining deal are a matter of trade-offs; its fairness is a matter of argument.

Common deliberation may combine with strategic bargaining in more complex ways. Suppose the father tells his son that it is not nice to hurt the weak when they arrive in the kindergarten, and the guardians are there watching the scene. The intended listener is still the boy; the instruction is directed to him. The audience is larger, however, since it now includes the guardians as well. The presence of the latter may be a contingent fact about the situation in which the statement is made or it may be calculated by the father. But whether it is contingent or calculated, it affects the latent information conveyed to the boy. It may be that no guardian utters a word, and yet their conduct—their silence—may express their agreement with what the father says. Given the circumstances, the father's judgment commits not only him but the guardians as well to intervene if the boy should beat up a weaker child. The boy may not see the moral force of the judgment communicated to him. But he learns that the guardians agree with his father, and this information may change the balance of the costs and benefits of his acts as he expects it to be.

The split of the audience into an intended listener (or a group of intended listeners) and a wider group of hearers, readers or watchers is the normal case at the level of large-scale, public political speech. Public speech differs from the father instructing his child in the presence of other adults in that its audience is anonymous. Any particular member of a large-scale public has personal knowledge only of a tiny fraction of the other members. And none of them receives the message in the presence of all the other members. Nevertheless, they all are aware that they are part of a communication process involving a multitude of people, and they see themselves as belonging to that multitude. In a passage of his book about the rise of nationalism, Benedict Anderson provides a vivid picture of this:

> Hegel observed that newspapers serve modern man as a substitute for morning prayers. ... [Newspaper reading] is performed in silent privacy, in the lair of the skull. Yet each communicant is well aware that the ceremony he performs is being replicated simultaneously by thousands (or millions) of others of whose existence he is confident, yet of whose identity he has not the slightest notion. Furthermore, this ceremony is incessantly repeated at daily or half-daily intervals throughout the calendar. What more vivid figure for the secular, historically clocked, imagined community can be envisioned? At the same time, the newspaper reader, observing exact replicas of his own paper being consumed by his subway, barbershop, or residential neighbours, is continually reassured that the imagined world is visibly rooted in everyday life.[4]

Every reader (listener, viewer, internet browser) perceives himself as receiving the conveyed facts and arguments together with many others who receive the information more or less simultaneously with him. When he understands what the speaker wants to persuade him about, he becomes aware at the same time of what the speaker wants to persuade the *others* about—and thus he receives information that helps him assess what shape the others' conduct may take with respect to the issue under consideration.

This provides the speaker with an opportunity to influence the intended listeners indirectly, through the way other segments of the audience may be expected to respond to his speech. The intended listeners may or may not be sensitive to the manifest content of his speech. But even if it leaves them perfectly cold, there may be others in the audience who are gripped by it. Furthermore, the intended listeners may have goals that depend for their successful realization on the conduct of those members of the audience who are highly sensitive to the manifest content of the communication, and the intended listeners may be aware of this. If so, the public speech may cause the intended listeners to change their conduct according to the intentions of the speaker even if they do not respond to the speech's manifest content.

To sum up, the same communicative act may have an aspect of common deliberation and an aspect of strategic influencing simultaneously, and sometimes its strategic impact helps it reach its deliberative aims.

At the same time, however, the strategic aspect of the communicative acts seems to have a potential to subvert and frustrate common deliberation. Common deliberation holds truth and truthfulness as its supreme values. It assumes that the parties sincerely state what they believe to be true about the matter under discussion. Strategic communication, in contrast, seems to be hostile to truthfulness. When parties are bargaining for mutual advantage, they have an interest in concealing their true preferences. Furthermore, they have an interest in concealing any fact about the world that would make the other side withdraw its preference from the proposed cooperative venture if they became known.

Suppose that A wants B to do x rather than y. Suppose further that A correctly believes that if he tells B that p is the case, then B will not do x. Suppose, finally, that A also believes that p is true. One may believe that A has an interest in concealing or distorting the truth if, and only if, he is pursuing some self-regarding aim. This is not the case, however. Let A stand for a policy-maker, B for the majority of an electorate, x and y for alternative schooling policies, and p for the claim that the career opportunities of a disadvantaged minority group, C, would be raised by x but not by y. Because A knows that the Bs are unfavorably biased towards the Cs, he also knows that the Bs would not support x if they were to learn that the Cs are the intended beneficiaries of x. In the context of common deliberation, A has a reason for straightforwardly telling B that p is the case. In the strategic context, though, he has a reason to remain silent on p or, perhaps, to claim that the case is non-p.

A may not necessarily be conscious of strategically manipulating the information available to B. The predisposition for cognitive biases has a prominent place on the list of human imperfections. We know much more about our own interests than about those of others, and we tend to interpret the interests of the others in analogy to our understanding of our own interests. Furthermore, we tend to be more sensitive to the losses suffered by ourselves than to those incurred by others. When it comes to comparing our burdens and benefits with those of someone else, the meaning and weight given to the interests we assess against each other are likely to reflect these spontaneous prejudices. We need not be biased in favor of our advantage, but we may perceive the advantages that we want others to enjoy in a biased manner.

Our interests may influence us in less subtle ways as well. We may not want to see ourselves to be misleading the others. At the same time, we may have an interest in their not seeing the true reasons that apply to their choice. If we do not spontaneously misperceive the situation in our own favor, we may deceive ourselves about the truth of the matter. Because the evidence that could decide a political disagreement is often insufficient and controversial, there is room for genuine self-deception. We may allow ourselves to be convinced by an inconclusive argument that a false proposition is true. Or we may interpret the available evidence in such a way that it ceases to count against that proposition.

In sum, we may bend our judgments of fairness to strengthen our case without necessarily becoming conscious of this. If we are not, then we engage in deliberative communication with each other in good faith, although our communicative acts bear a latent strategic meaning for the listener, since the spontaneous biases of the two persons pull in opposite directions. As a consequence, both parties may be sincere deliberators with each believing that the other is not.

If such phenomena are general enough, the strategic aspect of communication is an enemy rather than a friend of its deliberative aspect. The distorting effects are indeed widely believed to be a pervasive fact of politics. Important political thinkers tend to claim that truth and politics are mutually incompatible.[5]

It seems to follow that on its wide account indirect motivation is an inconsistent idea. It cannot do without its strategic component, nor can it do without its common-deliberation component, but the two components are incompatible. Strategic communication subverts and frustrates common deliberation.

One may be tempted to conclude that if no legitimate polity can do without robust processes of common deliberation, then, in order to command legitimacy, a polity must separate common deliberation from strategic interaction, leaving no room at all for the latter. To put it briefly, legitimate polities are purely deliberative democracies.

I would like to argue against this view. The next section will be dedicated to the argument that the ideal of common deliberation is more limited than that embodied by deliberative democracy. Strategic action seems to limit it from outside. It is, however, also limited internally by the very moral principle on which it is said to rest. Section 7.3 will try to show that although strategic choice situations may indeed encourage the chooser to conceal or distort the truth, indirect motivation is able, if not to undo, at least to counteract this incentive. It will discuss how modern democracy is designed to restrain that undesirable incentive latent in strategic choice situations.

7.2 Deliberative democracy: internal limits

Deliberative democracy insists that if human beings are each other's moral equals no official directive can be binding and enforceable against disobedience unless it issues from common deliberation, structured in a certain way. Each member of the community must have an equal opportunity to make a contribution to the public debate; participation in the debate and acceptance of the views put forward by others must be free of coercion; the social position of the participants must have no impact on the outcome of the controversy: all claims must be weighed impersonally; the better argument (rather than the argument made by a better placed person) must win, and so on. States command legitimacy to the extent that their decisions emerge from such an egalitarian, unforced, and impartial deliberation process.[6]

I maintain that this conception of deliberative communication, where the views supported by the better argument always emerge as victorious, provides a mistaken and ultimately unappealing account of public discourse in a democratic polity.

Of course equal freedom for all to participate in the public communicative process is a highly important condition of legitimacy, and so is good quality common deliberation not distorted by built-in biases. But, although not unrelated, the two requirements are not identical, and they tend to clash. Equal freedom of expression contravenes the ideal of common deliberation, where the better argument is destined to win. This may sound implausible. However, it only appears to be implausible owing to a lack of distinction between the way political communities discuss the best course of collective action with the aim of reaching a practical decision (the purpose of deliberation) and the way scientific communities discuss alternative theoretical explanations for particular problems with the aim of establishing the truth about the matter (the purpose of scientific inquiry).

Scientific communities are special-purpose voluntary associations. Their purpose is objective knowledge, and they impose strict norms on their members in order to facilitate the growth of such knowledge. They demand, for example, that theoretical claims be supported by appropriate evidence; the evidence must be available to all, the experiments must be repeatable in principle. No theories that have been falsified in the past are permitted to be cited as true unless new evidence or a new argument is brought up in their defense. It is forbidden to present the results already published by others as new findings of one's own. Those who fail to comply with such standards, exclude themselves from the scientific community, and this is as it should be, given that they joined it voluntarily and were sufficiently informed about its rules and norms. Norm enforcement makes sure that, in scientific debates, the better argument has a fair chance to win.

Political communities, on the other hand, are not voluntary associations. Rather than being created and adhered to with some particular purpose in mind, a political community provides a framework for an open-ended set of pursuits to a multitude of individuals, most of whom find themselves belonging to it as a matter of birth, not choice. This difference has two important consequences.

First, since the choice is not open to most inhabitants of a country, their membership in that country's political community cannot be made conditional on acquired qualifications such as those on which membership in a scientific may depend. Citizenship cannot be limited to those with an expertise in political, social or economic matters. All permanent inhabitants of the country should have all the rights entailed by it. Furthermore, all citizens must have an equal right to express themselves publicly on any issue of public concern. People to whom the option to choose their role in the community is unavailable have a moral interest in having a voice. This interest has a deliberative

component: having an opportunity to make one's voice heard increases the chances of one's preferences and views being voiced as
loudly as possible. But it has a more fundamental, symbolic component: having an opportunity to make one's voice heard secures one the
status of an equal member. This component is fundamental and cannot be denied to a person without declaring him to be unworthy of the
concern and respect due equally to all those with the moral standing
of a human person.

But as we saw in Chapter Six (6.4), the right of expression cannot
be made dependent on the content of the speech. No communicative
act can be banned on the ground that it hinders rather than promotes
the discovery of truth in matters of collective action, that its content is
false, unsupported by evidence, that there is nothing new to it, that it
is biased, and so on. Even when the speaker claims novelty, impartiality, testability or truth for his statement the absence of such features is
not a good ground for prohibition. Very often, however, the speech act
is unrelated to such claims. Rather, what it communicates is an expression of personal commitment, an expression of what the speaker
stands for.

Think of a person who walks the streets wearing a cross round his
neck, a hammer-and-sickle badge on his jacket, or a red ribbon in his
buttonhole. He is not making a statement or putting forward an argument. Rather, he conveys the message that he belongs to a community
of faith, is a member of a political movement, or identifies with a
specific social group. Such messages do not claim to add anything to
the clarification of controversial issues, for example, whether there is a
god, whether socialism is worthy of support, or how people with
HIV/AIDS should be treated. They are valuable, nevertheless, and
their value is rooted in the opportunity they provide for the agent to
take sides in an issue that divides the community. There are many
different reasons why freedom of expression must enjoy a privileged
protection, but the first and strongest reason is symbolic rather than
deliberative.[7]

It follows that freedom of expression as a political right cannot be
made conditional on conforming to a set of norms that aim to secure
an argument of high quality. The public space of a political community is full of redundancies, long-refuted claims, false proofs and poor
arguments. A scientist who warms up an old theory that the scientific
community has good reasons to believe to be false, and who asserts

that it is true while refusing to provide any new evidence in its defence, excludes himself from the scientific debate. But a citizen cannot forfeit his right to participate in the public arena by warming up views that are seen as falsified by the rest of the community. Inability or unwillingness to provide new evidence for those views is not a reason for exclusion.

Among the theories of deliberative democracy equality appears to be a more fundamental principle than the expectation that the better argument should win. And if equality requires political arrangements that are not ideally favorable to the victory of the better argument, then an egalitarian polity cannot be an ideal deliberative democracy.

One may object that freedom of expression is not incompatible with the upholding of strict standards of common deliberation. Free speech does not entail the right of access for everybody to every means of mass communication. The press is supposed to sift valuable ideas and credible information from worthless rubbish, or a well-argued case from cheap demagoguery, not unlike a scientific review that is supposed to sift new research results supported by the required evidence from plagiarism or hoax. A polity with a high-quality press may be able to combine freedom of expression with high-level public deliberation, so the argument goes.

I think this objection has something to recommend it, but its force is limited. The main audience of a scientific review is the scientific community itself, a group of experts in the field covered by it. The main audience of a newspaper or a magazine is the political community (or a segment of it), a group of people who, typically, are not experts in matters of political interest. They take the ultimate decisions on the fate of candidates as voters, and they take the ultimate decisions on the fate of the media as readers, viewers and listeners. What, in the last resort, determines the quality of the ideas, news, and arguments filling the public sphere is not a group of experts but groups of non-expert people who find it hard to draw a clear line between the roles the media plays in their lives as a source of political information and as means of entertainment.

This is not to argue that the rise of the tabloid press to preeminence or the demise, in the realm of the internet, of the distinction between a serious newspaper willing and able to filter ideas and information and a website where anyone may place any text without checking it for reliability or novelty is to be accepted as the ineluctable destiny of the public sphere in technically advanced democracies. The search for institutional and political means to improve and consolidate the standards of public discourse should never stop. But if the relevant audience is the citizenry, those standards cannot be expected to be as strict as the standards applied to the scientific debate.

In sum, the egalitarian principle does not support the ideal of deliberative democracy, according to which the best argument has the best chance to win. The ideal of common deliberation that civic equality does support is more modest; it allows for imperfections in dealing with the truth on condition that those imperfections are kept under control. If so, it may not rule out strategic action, provided that the distorting effects of strategy on truth and truthfulness can be counteracted and limited.

In the next section I will try to show that it can indeed be. One of the functions fulfilled by the institutions of modern democracy is to make truth and truthfulness relatively safe against the effects of strategy.

7.3 Truth and democracy

In the previous section I made an unqualified statement to the effect that strategic choice situations make the parties inclined to conceal or to falsify the truth as far as they can. I added that the holders of political power are generally believed to be not only inclined but also able to do so. Whether consciously and guided by self-interest or not, they regularly distort the picture of reality that is available to the political community as a material of common deliberation.

These statements must be qualified. Strategic choice situations indeed hold out incentives to conceal or to falsify the truth, provided that the speaker's interests are different from those of the listener and that the listener is not in a position to monitor the speaker's veracity and to punish any misleading communication. However, if the speaker's interests coincide with those of the listener, he does not derive any advantage from concealing or lying about the truth. Nor is it to his advantage to make misleading statements if the listener can detect and punish the lies or concealments with relative ease.[8]

Modern democracies bring the interests of the political leaders closer to those of the electorate and, in particular, they subject their statements to various kinds of reliability checks. Let me say something about these claims.

We cherish democracy first of all for its intrinsic value. Democracy is the political system which comes closest to the ideal of a state treating all its subjects as moral equals of the officials and of each other. It is because in a democratic regime binding decisions are made by the elected representatives of those who are bound by them; it is because virtually each subject of the state has a vote; it is because everybody's vote is equal to that of everybody else; it is because virtually every subject of the state, but only of the state in question, can run for elected office; it is because the official decisions are supposed to give equal consideration to each subject's interests; it is because the official decisions must claim to be good for the community and fair to each member of it; and it is because this claim can be defended in open political debate, from which no citizen can be excluded: it is for all these reasons that democracy is intrinsically valuable.

Nevertheless, democracy also has instrumental value. Primarily, of all known political systems, it regulates power struggles best. It is a common view that power struggles easily degenerate into internal wars. The founders of modern political theory, Machiavelli and Hobbes, were haunted by the specter of the struggle for power bringing down the state. Democracy does not eliminate political power, and as a consequence it cannot eliminate the struggle for power. But it significantly reduces the destructive potential of that struggle.

Periodic elections give the participants a predominant interest in the peaceful transfer of power, and they marginalize those tempted by the possibility of obtaining or retaining power by means of unlawful violence.[9] In a system where offices are redistributed every four years, the gains and losses from the political game are neither absolute nor definitive. The winner does not hold the office for good: if he wants to keep it, he will have to run again in the not so distant future, and he will have to run in a more or less open contest, which being the incumbent does not insure him against the possibility of losing. This also means that the loser does not lose the prospect of coming to government for good: he will have a fair opportunity to try again in the not so distant future. Nor does the winner take all: the victorious party obtains the majority of the seats in the legislature, but it is highly unlikely to obtain all the seats. The defeated party has its own seats, so that the legislative power is not monopolized by the winner but is shared with the defeated rival(s). In other words, the losers do not lose everything: they lose or fail to win the majority needed for coming into, or remaining in, power, but they are partly compensated for this loss by minority positions in the legislature. For the loser obtaining these positions is both an advantage in itself and a means to be used in the next round of the bid for power. While the costs of an attempt to subvert the legitimate outcome of an election by violence are relatively high, the benefits to be expected from it are relatively low. Winners and losers alike have an interest in playing by the rules. This is true about both the contenders for power and the electorate at large. While rebelling against the winner would carry a high risk for the supporters of the loser, the costs of acquiescing in the defeat are moderate: no large electoral bloc remains without representation, nor are its members deprived of the hope of having their party in government in the foreseeable future.[10]

The democratic way of securing peaceful succession in office has two further advantages. First, as was discovered by Jeremy Bentham early in the 19th century, the competition for the votes of the electorate helps to adjust the policy offers and governmental performance to the desires and expectations of the "greatest number," provided that the electoral process is arranged in accordance with the principle of universal equal ballot.[11] With all its weaknesses, democracy is more likely to make governmental action dependent on the interests of the governed than any of its alternatives. Second, by distributing the parliamentary seats between a majority and a minority, democracy transforms the struggle for power into a means of improving the quality of public deliberation and of keeping the incumbent under permanent control. It is this second consequence to which I want to turn now.

In most modern democracies, the legislative minority is not a junior partner of the majority. The two sides typically do not govern together. The majority forms the government, and the minority goes into opposition. The opposition's job is not that of supporting and helping the government but criticizing it, pointing out the undesirable consequences of its policies, revealing the special interests at work behind its policy choices, exposing ministerial lies, revealing conflicts of interest, confronting the government with its failures and proposing alternatives to its projects and practices. It is by acting as a relentless critic of the government that the opposition can improve its chances of success at the next election.

The intrinsic value of democracy—democracy as political equality—cannot be upheld without the institution of free and fair periodic elections, universal equal ballot and the like, but it does not require as a matter of principle that the legislature be divided into a majority in government and a minority in opposition, nor does it require that the political process take an agonistic shape.[12] However, the instrumental value of securing peaceful succession in office demands that the defeated party, if it commands a modicum of electoral support, should not remain without parliamentary seats, and it ensures that the best way for the minority to become the majority at the next elections is to serve as the government's opposition rather than its support. This helps to keep the avenues of public political debate open.

The claim made above needs further support. We have learnt from Machiavelli and Hobbes that the contenders for power may find it rational from their own particular point of view to make a choice that is irrational from the point of view of the community. Their teaching also applies to the way the contest between government and opposition affects the fate of truth. I said a moment ago that the opposition had an interest, determined by its institutional role, in revealing the truth the government may try to suppress. But consider the following story. Dean and DeLuca are democratic politicians competing for elected office. Their competition includes a third agency: the electorate.

Two politicians–1. Suppose that Dean is the incumbent, and he faces a serious budget deficit. One-and-a-half year before the elections, he is told by his economic advisors that unless he immediately submits an austerity package to the legislature, the country will run into a deep financial crisis after the elections. DeLuca receives the expert advice, given the seriousness of the situation, not to oppose the much needed restrictive measures if Dean has the courage to introduce them. However, the electorate is unlikely to tolerate sharp cuts in government expenditures. Perhaps it has no grasp of the gravity of the problem, or even if it has, its economic subgroups fiercely resist any cuts that would affect them specifically, so that although everybody agrees that cuts are unavoidable, everybody wants to shift the burden onto the others. Consequently, no particular scheme of budgetary restrictions can be advanced without running the risk of alienating some important electoral group or other.

Under such conditions, DeLuca may decide against all expert advice to mount a fierce attack on the austerity package to be announced by Dean. Correctly anticipating DeLuca's demagogic reaction, Dean decides to postpone the austerity measures till after the elections.

However, as we have seen it, the gains and losses in any particular electoral contest are limited, and each competitor has the opportunity to repeat the bid for government at regular intervals. It is appropriate, thus, to insert the above story into an open-ended series of electoral games. Once we do this, the priorities of the competitors change.

Two politicians–2. If Dean and DeLuca make false promises of roughly the same dimensions, they will have exactly the same likelihood of winning as they would if they both refrained from making any false promises. Thus, in the long run, none of the contenders derives any advantage from adhering to the false promise game. But they suffer disadvantages from making false promises. Whichever should win, he will face a choice between engaging in dangerous fiscal policies that would, in the longer run, ruin the economy and destroy his reputation, and doing the opposite of what he promised during the campaign, and thereby provoking an immediate crisis of confidence.

Given the limited nature of the ordinary losses and the periodic repetition of elections, either of the two contenders may decide to abandon the strategy of false promises, and the other find it prudent to follow suit. A convention of truthfulness may be consolidated between Dean and DeLuca as they both find themselves better off overall if they go along with such a convention rather than defecting from it.

This may not be the end of the story, though. For the winner may carry out some of his promises and set aside the rest for later times. By skillfully maneuvering between the promises and the realities, he may succeed in avoiding both the Scylla of a financial crisis and the Charybdis of a confidence crisis.

Two politicians–3. Suppose the winner pursues such an intermediary strategy. Even if he avoids running into either a financial crisis or a confidence crisis, his spending policies exert a heavy pressure on the budget, and the citizenry ends up worse off than it would if a convention of truthfulness and restraint had prevailed. The voters, however, are not in a position to compare the real outcomes with the hypothetical outcomes of fiscal sincerity and reasonable budgetary policies. The carrying out of some of the promises may convince them that the party on government does everything it can to live up to its commitments, and they may become accustomed to the fact that not all promises are fulfilled immediately.

Under such circumstances many different conventions may form, from unbridled competition between false promises to unexceptionable fiscal sincerity. The two contenders may agree to lie all the time but to tell big lies only on even-numbered occasions, while keeping their lies within limits on the odd-numbered occasions. Alternatively, they may agree not to lie at all on the odd-numbered occasions, and to lie on even-numbered occasions, and so on.

The two politicians may run the risk of a third contender descending into the political arena with the claim that the other two are lying and therefore unworthy of the trust of the electorate. Paradoxically, however, such an attack may not necessarily threaten the stability of their game. This is because the voters may come to believe that all politicians are professional liars, including the one who pretends to be sincere; therefore, they may not expect any benefit from the victory of a new contender.

So far we have tacitly assumed that the contenders for office have no priorities other than that of maximizing their own long-term electoral success. However, we have already abandoned the Hobbesian assumption of human motivation. We have, thus, to ascribe some preference for the good of the community to Dean and DeLuca. Such an ascription changes the picture again:

Two politicians–4. No matter how weak it may be, the preference for the good of the community could have an enormous impact on the outcome of the story. We have found that the two contenders are neutral, from their own point of view, with regard to the different conventions between unexceptionable truthfulness and unbridled lying. If they rank all these equally against their self-regarding preferences, then the weakest community-regarding preference will be able to decide their choice. And if they find that, from the point of view of the community, unexceptionable truthfulness is the best alternative, then it will be rational for them to settle for it.

However, this optimistic scenario fails to take into account the fact of disagreement, one of the rock-solid circumstances of politics. Suppose that DeLuca favors generous spending policies because he believes in the Keynesian theory that economic growth is constrained by insufficient consumer demand. And suppose that Dean is against deficit financing because he believes in the post-Keynesian macroeconomic orthodoxy, according to which economic growth is constrained by insufficient private investment. DeLuca sincerely believes that more government spending helps economic growth, while Dean sincerely believes that whenever the government engages in a policy of deficit financing, it becomes a competitor of private firms for credit, restricting private investment and the opportunities for economic expansion. Suppose, finally, that there is no conclusive evidence to rule out either of the two positions as mistaken under the particular conditions of the country. Then, we may have the following story:

> *Two politicians–5.* Both contenders are honest believers in the economic policies they want to implement. DeLuca, however, has the advantage that his sincerely held views are capable of generating popular support if straightforwardly presented. Dean's sincerely held views, on the other hand, are not easy to get accepted by the popular segments of the electorate. Dean is convinced that DeLuca's policy platform is one of dangerous fiscal irresponsibility: it risks pushing the economy into a deep crisis and bringing a great deal of suffering to large groups of the population.

Dean faces a dilemma. If he tells the truth about his program, he will be honest with the electorate, but he is certain to lose the elections and, thus, to allow DeLuca to inflict great harm on the same voters who vote him into power. If he misleads the public about his true platform, he will have a chance of saving the country from the curse of DeLuca's fiscal policies—at the cost of being dishonest with the electorate.

Dean's decision may be unpredictable. But this much can be established: if the fact of disagreement obtains, and if the perceived dangers of the rival's policies are great enough, then the claim that the preference for the common good will tip the balance in favor of truthfulness cannot be generally correct. We have no reason to assume that the division of the legislative branch into government and opposition, in itself, will ensure that truthfulness becomes the ruling convention.

To remind, we assumed that, for various reasons, the electorate is likely to punish politicians who propose austerity measures. And we have seen that under such conditions the game of false promises is unlikely to be stopped by the division of the legislature into a majority in government and a minority in opposition.

This model is incomplete. First, some important agents are missing from it. We have considered three actors so far: two contenders for elected power and the electorate. That picture disregards the various intermediary players who occupy the public space between the contenders for office and the public at large: communications experts, media pundits, journalists, reporters, analysts, commentators, public intellectuals, pollsters, advocacy groups, social movements, and many others with a role in the political process other than that of participants in the struggle for power.

Second, when I spoke about the conduct of the electorate, I ignored an important dimension of the way voters assess the alternatives open for choice. I said that voters may reject austerity policies either because of ignorance or because of a desire to shift the burdens onto others. Such a description takes the voters to be guided by self-regarding preferences alone. A more complex picture would include an account of how their moral judgments affect their preference orderings. In particular, it would include an account of how their attitudes and reactions are affected by their judgment about the morality of the political establishment: its trustworthiness, honesty, and reliability. Since the questions of this book are determined by the assumption that the ethics of political leadership belongs to the province of the politicians' accountability to the citizenry, the latter consideration is of special relevance for us. To put it simply: Dean and DeLuca may both tell the truth and command the firm support of their constituencies, provided that they are judged as trustworthy, honest, and reliable. And they are likely to be swept away by a new contender who breaks into the political arena, if their attempts to cooperate in the interest of economic stabilization are not backed by a high moral reputation. I will address this second point later in this

chapter. Here, I turn to the first issue, that of the intermediary players.

I claimed in 7.1 that political speech always has a strategic aspect.
Its strategic ends are typically related to influencing government decisions and/or to the struggle for power. The speaker himself may not
run for office or speak on behalf of someone who does. This is only a
negative characterization of the intermediary players. It would be far-
fetched to claim that the activities of all these people help to improve
the quality of democratic deliberation. The invasion of politics by the
language of advertising, the predilection towards sensationalism, and
the frequent attempts at subliminal influencing, etc. suggest that many
of the intermediary players actually contribute to the degradation of
political discourse. Yet there is a category, smaller or larger as the case
may be, of investigative reporters and columnists, professional analysts, public intellectuals, and citizens' groups, whose activities serve
to clarify, explain, and criticize the political practices and the statements made by the politicians. Let us call them the *critics*.

In a well-designed democratic public sphere, critics do well—are
likely to succeed—if they gain a reputation of objectivity and impartiality. Objectivity and impartiality cannot mean that a critic should
have no political ideals and principles or that he can have only such
ideals and principles that are neutral as between the ideological profiles of the competing parties. Nor can objectivity and impartiality
mean that what they have to say should never be favorable to one of
the rivals. Rather, it means that in doing his job, a critic must not consider which of the parties will be advantaged by his fact-finding or
commentary. It would be wildly implausible to expect a critic not to
wish the evidence uncovered and the arguments made by him to serve
the victory of his own favorite. What objectivity and impartiality demand is that he should seriously try to apply the same standards to
both the party of his preference and its rival and that he should not be
deterred from making the truth public even if "his" party is disadvantaged by it.

Objectivity and impartiality are demanding virtues. Am I suggesting that, ultimately, public deliberation of good quality is possible
only if the critics are unusually excellent? I am not. Rather, I want to
suggest, in faithfulness to the Humean assumption of limited altruism
and to the Kantian assumption of limited readiness to comply with
duty for duty's sake, that the critics can live up to the requirements of

objectivity and impartiality if the public sphere is ordered in such a way that the costs of being objective and impartial are small enough, while the price to be paid for bias and partiality is sufficiently high.

This is a difficult task that cannot be carried out once and for all. There are powerful political and business interests that work against any arrangements that can successfully solve it. The emergence, consolidation and revision of the institutional norms of the critical public sphere are, themselves, an object of never ending political battles, which often seem to be uphill ones. But they are not doomed to be lost for ever. We can say this because the consumers of the products and services of the critics—the citizens—have a predominant interest in having a public sphere guided by the principles of objectivity and impartiality, and those struggling for an adequate regulation of public criticism can always try to derive support from this interest. Critics whose passion is politics but who are not running for political office or speaking on behalf of someone involved in political competition have some chance to carve out a solid place for themselves in democratic politics.

Suppose that the critical public sphere is tolerably well-regulated. In that case, its operation is likely to change the distribution of costs and benefits for the participants of power struggles. The critics may enlighten the electorate on both what the politicians are really doing, and on the availability of alternatives to a conspiracy between government and opposition designed to mislead the electorate. For the opposition party, the advantages from colluding with the party of government to mislead the public may shrink, while the disadvantages of such a collusion may grow as a consequence. The strategic interests of the players may come closer to supporting a public debate of good quality. Strategy itself may be transformed from an enemy of common deliberation into its friend.

7.4 Deliberation in indirect motivation

The previous section tried to show how well-regulated strategic action may help to raise the level of common deliberation. This section will explore the impact of deliberative communication on strategic interaction. In Section 7.1, I mentioned the possibility of the audience being divided into a group of intended listeners and a wider category of third parties. I added that this division may provide the speaker with an opportunity to influence the intended listeners indirectly, through the likely response of other segments of the audience to his speech. I will now address this possibility more closely.

The thesis is as follows: Utterances intended to contribute to common deliberation may also convey information of strategic value. Their deliberative content may target the public at large with the aim of affecting the distribution of beliefs and dispositions within it. The intended listeners may form a subgroup of the public whose success in carrying out its objectives depends on the general distribution of beliefs and dispositions. If that distribution is likely to change in response to the communicative act, the utterance with a primary deliberative content conveys secondary, strategic information to the intended listeners.

The reactions of the public at large matter for the contenders for power because the outcome of their struggle hinges ultimately on the electoral choices of the citizens. If the electorate changes its moral judgment about a contender and if that change in judgment is likely to affect the distribution of votes, then the contender whose electoral prospects are worsened has a strong non-moral incentive to amend his course of action. He may or may not be responsive to the moral reasons revealed by the deliberative process. If he is, the change in the distribution of beliefs in the electorate at large may provide him with an additional, concurrent reason. If he is not, the change may provide him with a surrogate reason, taking the place of his inoperative moral reasons.

There is a third possibility. An agent's responsiveness to moral reasons may depend in part on the magnitude of the non-moral costs of complying with them. The shift in electoral preferences may provide a contender for power with a non-moral incentive to change his conduct, either because it raises the costs of refusing to change or because it lowers the costs of changing. Thus, the conduct of the contender in question may respond to a mix of moral and non-moral incentives.

Let me tell a schematic story of the way the moral minima of political action are identified and enforced. As a rule, the process starts by a revelation. A politician is exposed as having violated some moral requirement. Typically, the facts now coming to light have been carefully suppressed by those involved in the affair—which proves that they considered those facts as not publicly defensible. Now the revelations are tested for their truth, and a discussion begins on whether the violation is really serious. Whatever the appropriate moral judgment on the story itself may be, it necessarily raises the further question of what is the adequate reaction to the story judged in that way. All these issues are controversial, and the controversies tend to be passionate and sharp. First, moral judgments are emotionally loaded: they express indignation, resentment, anger, scorn, contempt, and the like. Second, the public is usually deeply divided on such revelations, its large sections being committed either for or against the political colors of the person(s) under attack. The people who identify themselves with those colors are likely to perceive the revelations as a political maneuver aiming to undermine the positions of their side, and so they treat the revelations with suspicion, while members of the opposite camp are likely to see them as yet another proof of the moral corruption of the adversary. Therefore, more often than not, the scandal unfolds amidst heated public debates.

The politician under attack, of course, plays a central role in this process. He may try but cannot stay silent indefinitely: his silence would be interpreted as either conceding the truth of the allegations or attempting to cover up still unknown details of the story, or both. So what he will most probably do first is to issue a blunt denial. Once he has made a statement to that effect, he can wait and see whether the scandal will die away in the next couple of days. It may indeed disappear from the headlines because the evidence adduced is not sufficient, and no further information is provided, or merely because of a lack of interest on the part of the general public. But perhaps the original evidence is overwhelming, or the press succeeds in digging up additional incriminating facts, and the case reaches the sensitivity threshold of the electorate. In this case, the politician must change his tactics. He may dispute that what he has done should count as violation. Or he may try to belittle the significance of the act. Or else he may remind the public that politicians of other stripes have been implicated in similar scandals, and yet their careers continued unimpaired.

Suppose, however, that none of these maneuvers helps. Too many critics argue too persuasively that what was done was not right and not just a minor offense, and that it is not an acceptable defense that it was not unusual. Then a third tactic may be explored. The embattled politician may choose to concede some of the facts, for example, and to express his sorrow and regrets. In so doing, he presents himself as a person with the right sort of feelings. His acts may have been wrong, but he is a good man nevertheless. If successful, this tactics diverts the attention of the public from what he has done to how he feels, and he may be able to put the scandal behind him.

These tactics are not always successful, though. Rather than accepting the acknowledgment of a fault as a proper way to close the affair, the press may use it as a starting point for further attack. A political rival may ask awkward questions in parliament, and tell the disgraced politician that the proper way to assume responsibility for what he finally admitted to have done is to quit office.

At this point, the specter of the disgraceful end of his career makes its appearance. If he hangs on, he may suffer an inglorious defeat at the next elections. If he resigns, he may never have a come-back. What should he do? With the scandal going on inexorably, the dangers from the first option loom ever larger, bringing the agent fatally close to the turning point where departure from office becomes the most appropriate choice.

So far, I have told the story as if the politician acted in his own name alone. But, in modern democracies, this is an unlikely scenario. Almost all politicians run for office under the banner of a party. This has momentous consequences. It introduces a new and powerful player, whose interests may tip the balance in favor of the disgraced politician's departure from office even if he would want to hang on.

From the politician's own point of view, quitting his position is extremely undesirable because his come-back, if not totally excluded, is at least highly uncertain. By resigning he does not simply give up an office: he risks losing power and influence both within and outside his party. Thus, he needs to go a long way before he finds it rational to resign. His party, however, has its own interests with regard to the scandal, and these may part company with his own.

The disgraced politician will become a burden to his party. First, the scandal may make him a lame duck. If he acts, he will become visible, and if he becomes visible, the public will be reminded of his dubious dealings. In the crossfire of attacks, all he can do is to defend himself. Second, the moral taint is likely to spread by association from him to his party. While for that particular politician the loss of office may mean the end of his career, for the party it just means distancing itself from a representative who has become an electoral liability.[13]

The party will have to pay a price for this. By condemning a politician it allowed to occupy a public office of high visibility, it admits that it was not scrupulous enough in its dealings with a man of dubious moral character. But it has a good chance to keep the damage under control. The fall of the politician will remove the story from the headlines: what, for one individual, may be the end is a new start for the party. There are, thus, good reasons to assume that the party will reach the turning point much earlier than the compromised figure himself.

The first reaction of the party is probably an attempt to protect its man. If the culprit is a member of the government, the prime minister usually declares his full confidence in him. If he is the prime minister himself, the leader of the parliamentary group will announce that the premier has their unwavering support, and so on. However, as every day brings more heated public debates, and perhaps further revelations, the support that has kept him in office may begin to melt away.

In the previous paragraphs I have depicted the party as if it were a single agent with a unified informational and motivational setup. But it is not. Parties are invariably divided into coalitions of people with different values, preferences, and interests. As a further step, we can make these internal divisions visible.

The politician implicated in the scandal is likely to have his supporters within the party, whose organizational position may be weakened by his fall, while others—members of a rival group—may benefit from it. The outcome may, ultimately, depend on how effectively the rivals turn the scandal to their own strategic advantage, on how much the supporters are able to deflect their attacks, and on the two sides' ability to enlist the support of, or at least neutralizing, the non-committed party notabilities.

I began this description by claiming that political accountability works through processes that combine strategic interaction with common deliberation, non-moral interests with eminently moral ones. But my account of the conduct of the political actors was based on the electoral interests of individual politicians and their parties, and on the organizational interests of various intra-party groups. These are non-moral interests, through and through. What about the role of moral considerations?

First, the assumption that all influential members of all parties are always indifferent to the moral dimension of the scandals in which their party becomes involved is highly implausible. At least some members of some parties are likely to be outraged at least on some occasions by what has been revealed about a fellow party politician; they feel compromised and faced with a choice between being complicit in a cover-up on the one hand and publicly condemning the disgraced person and demanding that he be removed from office on the other.

Second, the politician under attack may himself be motivated by moral concerns. He may feel ashamed of losing face in the eyes of the public, or guilty about his past deeds that he should not have committed, as he now understands. On some rare occasions, the feelings of shame and guilt (perhaps in combination with prudential reasons) directly move the politician in question to resign. But, interestingly, even his obstinate refusal to quit may arise from moral considerations. The act of resignation stigmatizes: it confirms the charges and seals the moral verdict. It also raises the specter of irreversible moral defeat, for the fallen politician may never have the opportunity to make good the harm done to his public persona. Surviving the crisis, on the other hand, promises him a fair chance to rectify the wrongs or at least to reduce their significance for the overall balance of his career.

Most important of all, in the limiting case in which neither the target person nor any influential figure in his party or in the rival party is responsive to moral reasons, at least some significant group within the general public may still be responsive to them. This is no *ad hoc* assumption. After all, the democratic citizenry tend to see themselves as the principal, and the political office-holders as their agents. Any ordinary citizen takes it for granted that the office-holders ought faithfully to serve the good of the citizenry, avoid conflicts of interest, supply honest information on their activities, and so on. It is in the interest of the citizens that the office-holders comply with the moral norms that define their role as agents of the citizenry. One can, thus, safely assume that whenever an office-holder is exposed as having violated those norms, the citizens will feel betrayed. The natural attitude of a citizen towards the conduct of politicians is a moral one.

It seems to follow that the citizenry is the safest ally of the efforts to consolidate and enforce the moral standards of political conduct in a democratic regime, and I believe that normally this is indeed the case. But a caveat is necessary. Under certain conditions citizens may not regard the office-holders as their agents. When democratic procedures are grafted upon a social structure dominated by traditional oligarchies, citizens may see the elected offices as the natural due of the rulers, for example. In such cases, the citizenry may be nihilistic about the ethics of public conduct. Nihilism about public ethics is, however, a transition phenomenon. Once a society becomes more egalitarian in terms of the distribution of economic resources and of access to education, the holders of public office begin to be seen as representatives bearing heavy responsibilities for and to the represented. Citizens are very likely to develop high moral expectations towards their political leaders. In the long run, the real problem is that they may come to believe that the procedures of liberal democracy are incapable of making political leaders live up to those expectations.

A citizen may endorse the standards of political conduct as such while being utterly skeptical about the possibility of enforcing them through the democratic process. Skepticism is likely to dominate his reactions if he becomes convinced that all politicians at all times pursue their personal interests at the cost of the public interest and in contravention of their duties as agents of the citizenry.

The same citizen who condemns political deception or corruption in the most passionate terms may believe that all politicians are professional deceivers and thieves. Politics, he may conclude, is a trade that necessarily corrupts those engaged in it. Once a large enough part of the public settles on this judgment, it may happen that the electorate reacts with disgust and abhorrence to the revelations about the misdeeds of a particular politician but the electoral prospects of the offender remain unaffected by those reactions. The rise of skepticism about the politician as a social type tends to block the shift of the votes away from a disgraced politician and his party towards some rival person or group. Why bother to replace X by Y if Y is no more worthy of trust than X? The more the political establishment as a whole comes to be seen as lacking moral integrity, the better the chances of a politician caught in some serious wrongdoing to survive the scandal.

This is the concern that I raised in the previous section when I spelled out a model of the democratic process. I will discuss it in greater detail in the next section. For now, let me conclude the present argument by a brief remark. We started from very simple assumptions in order to advance towards greater complexities. At the beginning, we considered the disgraced politician as if he were a lonely agent; in the next step, we introduced his party as a collective agent in its own right; then, we paid some attention to the internal divisions of the party. But all along, we considered the dynamics of a political scandal as if it were a self-enclosed event, unrelated to the history of similar scandals. This is not true. Earlier cases tend to serve as precedents for later ones.

A case may become a precedent in two different senses. On the one hand, it may be a precedent in a *statistical* sense. Political scandals are perceived as belonging to a number of general types: sale of official influence for money or other economic advantage, advancement of the interests of friends and family, lies about official decisions, cover-ups, etc. Each type of scandal, observed over a sufficiently long period of time, displays a certain frequency with which it is concluded by the disgraced politician leaving his office. The participants of the struggles about a new scandal may be assumed to have a more or less correct assessment of this frequency. Given this assessment, they are able to estimate the probability of the offender going. The estimation of this probability helps the participants in determining their strategies; it enables them to weigh the relative costs and benefits of pressing for the offender's departure, supporting his stay, or remaining neutral in the affair.

On the other hand, individual cases are not simply particular events in a series of similar events. Earlier cases can affect the outcome of later cases not only through frequency distributions. Each case has its own history, and the public controversy about the facts of the matter, and about how those facts should be judged and reacted to, has its place in that history. The course of the debate and/or its main conclusions may be remembered together with its practical outcome and contribute to shaping the course of later cases. The conclusions of the debate and its practical outcome may diverge, as they do when a significant majority of the public agrees that the disgraced politician ought to go and he stays in office nevertheless. But they may also co-incide, and the cases in which they do are particularly relevant to later affairs. The message such cases convey is: This is how the issue was decided—and this is how such an issue should in fact be decided. Such cases serve as *normative precedents*. Their outcome is a particular solution for a particular issue, but the justification is given in general terms: A must go because he committed an offense of the type x, and the response to offenses of the type x should be the departure of the offender. The justification universalizes the particular issue. It sets a norm for the treatment of all those future cases that are relevantly similar to this one.

The normative aspect of the precedent may affect its statistical aspect. Once a normative precedent is cited in the debate about a relevantly similar case, it magnifies the costs of not doing what was done in the case that serves as precedent. The increase in costs of failing to comply with the standard increases the likelihood that it will be complied with.[14] If, before the first occurrence of a normative precedent, the probability that it will occur is of a certain value, then, other things being equal, that probability will take on a greater value when a relevantly similar case is interpreted in the light of this precedent.

This may suggest that once a normative precedent is set for the first time, the probability that the relevantly similar cases will be treated similarly is bound to increase progressively until it reaches full certainty. However, such a conclusion does not necessarily follow from the above reasoning. Once we have agreed that a community of equal citizens should not, and indeed cannot, strive to arrange its common affairs in conformity with the ideal proposed by the theory of deliberative democracy, our expectations regarding the role of normative precedents become more modest. Normative precedents provide those who want to see political action subjected to effective moral rules an opportunity to try to improve on the general practice by appealing to those rules. Common deliberation on their lessons plays an important role in translating abstract moral requirements into effective institutional rules without, however, settling a trajectory that would inevitably lead to strict compliance with a unique set of moral rules.

This said, let us return to the question of what may happen if the general public or a decisive sector of it is overcome by skepticism about the mores of the political establishment as a whole.

7.5 Populism

Skepticism about the mores of the political trade need not go on a par with nihilism about the ethics of politics itself. Actually, it does not as a rule. The more a citizen is convinced that politicians as a profession are corrupt, the more passionately he will condemn the immoral deal-ings attributed to them: lies, embezzlement, familism, and the like.

This is a dangerous tendency. Members of large-scale communities know all too well that their ability as individual citizens to affect po-litical decisions is negligible. The possibility that they become disaf-fected by politics is always there. No political regime is capable of containing the process of alienation unless it can infuse the citizens with a sense that as a community they matter collectively and that as members of the community they matter individually. Their individual vote is highly unlikely to be decisive, but together they decide the ul-timate political issues. This sense of collective sovereignty evaporates if the public adopts the view that the political trade as such is not only corrupt but unresponsive as well. The institutions of liberal democ-racy lose their social support, and the public becomes susceptible to the temptations of what is called *populism*.

Populists may harbor aspirations to replace democracy with an au-thoritarian or totalitarian regime, as was the case with Peronism or Nazism. Alternatively, they may be free of such aspirations and pre-sent themselves rather as advocates of vigorous democracy, the main target of their attacks being the political establishment, viewed as a self-contained and self-selecting oligarchy that is distant from the peo-ple in the physical and social space, and drives a deep cultural, eco-nomic and political wedge between itself and the rest of the commu-nity. Anti-elitism is the core of populism.

Populism, however, involves more than just a hostile attitude to-wards the "elites." It is a conception of how democracy should work; it expresses the very ideal of democracy distorted by anti-elitism.

The liberal conception of democracy also has a role for mistrust of both holders of, and contenders for, political office. This mistrust is based on the assumption that politicians are *no better* than ordinary citizens. In contrast, the mistrust characteristic of populism is based on the assumption that politicians are *worse* than ordinary citizens. The mistrust advocated by the liberal conception warns us that politi-cal institutions should not be built on the assumption that the political leaders are unusually virtuous people. It recommends to build institu-tions and practices that combine moral motivation with non-moral incentives in order to direct the office-holders towards faithfully serv-ing the citizenry. The mistrust characteristic of populism, on the other hand, is closely related to the belief that political institutions of the liberal type breed "elite" immorality and that, in order to restore the moral quality of politics, liberal institutions must be swept away. Three aspects of liberal democracy in particular are under attack from populism: party pluralism, the rule of law, and market-adapted social and economic policies.

The ongoing power struggle of competing parties promotes justice and the common good indirectly, while its costs are direct and immediate. The mechanisms of adjustment to the political market are highly imperfect, much more so than those of competition on the economic market (and even economic markets are far from being perfectly competitive). New entrants must overcome enormous obstacles in order to join the competitive game; the relationship between the voters and the contenders for power is burdened by serious informational asymmetries; the electoral system responds to the continuous shifts in the voters' preferences in discontinuous, periodic leaps; while the individual buyer has a decisive impact on the outcome of his market choice, of which he bears the full costs, the individual voter's chance to decide the outcome of the vote is negligible, but he is never supposed to bear the costs of bringing this or that party to government. As a consequence of such imperfections, it is not always the case—and never obviously so—that the aspirations of a contender for power or those of his party coincide with the public interest. Given the weak correlation between public interest and personal or party interest, the average voter finds it hard to accept the competitive and agonistic nature of democratic politics unless the participants of the struggle for power have a reputation of high moral integrity. Should they lose this reputation, the voter becomes easily convinced that democratic politics is exclusively about the selfish interests of those who seek power, and that their struggles, rather than promoting the case of justice and the common good, harm them. Skepticism about the mores of the political establishment breeds skepticism about democratic politics as an ongoing struggle between government and opposition. Populist anti-elitism is, thus, laden with animosity towards party politics perceived as putting factional interests first and neglecting the interests of the people.

Skepticism about the integrity of the political establishment breeds skepticism about the rule of law, too. The rule of law is a set of principled constraints on institutional procedures: it bans retroactive application of sanctions to offenses that have been committed before the promulgation of the relevant legal provisions; it demands that even the most vicious criminal should have access to the due process of law and to a fair trial, it insists that like cases be treated alike, and so on. Now these constraints involve unavoidable trade-offs. For example, the rights to a due process of law and to a fair trial shift the burdens of error from the person under suspicion or charge to the state and the community. They protect the innocent against unjustified penalty at the cost of improving the chances of the guilty to avoid just punishment. Sometimes it is argued that ordinary citizens, even if they understand the nature of such trade-offs, refuse to accept them because they believe them to be unfair. I find this argument unpersuasive. It is unclear why a reasonably well-informed citizen would resist the idea that, on balance, justice is better served by a legal system that protects the rights to the due process of law and to a fair trial than by a legal system that does not. The problem is that there is a kind of epistemic asymmetry between the benefits of the rule of law and its costs. The benefits are like the clean air: they are barely noticed as long as they are available; they become noticeable by their absence. It is no news that innocent, law-abiding citizens are not imprisoned under false charges. But it is headline news that a person everybody believes to be a criminal is acquitted. The costs of the rule of law are highly visible, and the more outrageous the offense, the more difficult it is to accept that the person under charge gets away without bearing the consequences of his wrongdoings just because he has a right to be treated in accordance with strict procedural restraints. So in order to accept those restraints, citizens must come to see that they are not unjust devices employed to protect the wrongdoer.

To see this is to recognize the nature of and the justification for the trade-off involved by the rule of law. What is to be understood is not just that the *type* of legal systems characterized by the features of the rule of law involves such a trade-off. Citizens live in a particular legal system that claims to be an *instance* of that general type. They must believe that their legal system provides a morally defensible trade-off between prosecuting the guilty and protecting the person under suspicion or charge against unfair treatment. No evidence, statistical or other, is sufficient to substantiate this claim. Unavoidably, there is a gap between the claim and the evidence that may support it. That gap is filled, if it is, by the people placing confidence in their legal institutions. The rule of law needs, for its acceptance, a certain degree of trust on the part of citizens.

Now the trust in the institutions depends, in part, on the trust in those who run them. It is a necessary condition for a legal system to be trusted that the men and women who run it are trusted, too. They must be viewed as persons of integrity, honest and dependable. So long as the public officials appear to be such the rule of law has a chance for enjoying public support. But if the trust in the officials withers, the trust in the institutions withers with it.

There is a corollary of this relationship. As long as the officials are trusted, the workings of the institutions are seen as an impersonal matter. But once the officials begin to be seen as unworthy of trust, the institutions are not merely believed to distribute burdens and benefits unjustly. The injustice attributed to them gets personalized. The institutional procedures come to be seen as means in the hands of those in control of advantaging the rich and the influential and of imposing disadvantage on the poor and the powerless.

This perception helps to translate the anti-elitist core of populism into an anti-institutional program. Once the trust in the political establishment's integrity gets lost, it becomes easy to convince large segments of the electorate that justice demands the abandonment of the procedural restraints of the rule of law for the sake of an effective clampdown on the corrupt and the dishonest.

Third, social and economic policies in a liberal democracy come into effect through rules and incentives that make the myriads of individual acts converge in the desired direction. The rules and incentives serve as correctives for the spontaneous workings of the economic market, but they take the basic features of the market economy and of the conduct of market agents for granted. Their benefits come to fruition through interactions motivated by different aims and, typically, with a significant delay. Their costs, however, have to be paid immediately. Suppose that the government proposes a package of health care reforms. Abandoning the rules under which medical services are provided in the present comes with a sacrifice, and the advantages the new system is said to provide are not likely to arrive soon. If the citizens are to support the reforms, they must believe that the true aim of the reformers is not to redistribute public resources away from the needy and towards the rich, but rather to make the national health system more efficient and fair. And this is highly unlikely to be the case unless they agree that their leaders are men and women of moral integrity who deserve their trust. If that trust is lost, the citizens will not find it rational to accept the present burdens of the reforms for the sake of distant and highly uncertain advantages. They will give priority to those policies that promise short-term benefits to be cashed in soon after the elections.

Such attitudes towards party pluralism, the rule of law and market-adapted social and economic policies favor populist demagogues, who break into the political arena by mounting an attack on liberal politics they accuse of being selfish and elitist; who campaign for replacing the parties that represent factional views and interests by a solidaristic all-national movement; who charge the rule of law with protecting the powerful, and declare that the corrupt elites should be put behind bars; who dismiss market-adapted social and economic policies and promise immediately to increase the immediate government allowances to the people.

Once the belief in the moral integrity of the political establishment is eroded, newcomer parties claiming to be outsiders to the ruling oligarchy may earn sweeping gains from one election to the next, dramatically redrawing the political landscape of the country. Such a shock is not necessary, however, for populism to make headway and to undermine liberal democracy. The atmosphere of general skepticism about the politician as a social type may push the mainstream parties themselves towards adopting the rhetoric of anti-elitism, of hostility to party pluralism, to the rule of law and to market-adapted social and economic policies, even in the absence of a challenge by a powerful outsider. Leaders with a reputation of moral integrity may be able to convince the electorate that by trying to gain and keep an elected office for themselves, they are promoting the interests of the community. Leaders with a reputation of lacking moral integrity have to pose as if they were above partisan politics and factional interests. Leaders with a reputation of moral integrity may be able to stand up against hostile sentiments towards the rule of law; they may win elections while honestly telling the citizenry that subverting liberal legal policies is wrong and dangerous. Leaders with a reputation of lacking moral integrity are forced to court the popular mood, and to come out with proposals that undermine the rule of law. Leaders with a reputation of moral integrity may be able to explain that it is rational to accept the short-term costs of socio-economic reforms. Leaders with

the reputation of lacking moral integrity must promise financial benefits and material services that can be enjoyed immediately.

The circumstances that favor the spread of the populist syndrome
are variable: they range from tensions due (or attributed) to immigration, through terrorist threats, to economic recession. Yet, the view
that democratic politics is in a state of moral decay favors populism
even in the absence of such factors. In this sense, populism is nothing but the general public's response to the moral problem of politics, distorted by the perception that the institutions of liberal democracy and those running them fail to react to the moral concerns
of citizens.

Our cursory look at this phenomenon has shown, I hope, how serious the problem of populism is. The moral deficit of democratic
politics is a disvalue in itself. And if it is left unattended it breeds further bad things. It gives rise to budgetary deficits, legal deficits and
political deficits. It may end in liberal democracy degenerating into
populist democracy—a parody of democracy.

One may hastily conclude that while the liberal conception of democracy is *morally superior* to its populist conception, it is *strategically
inferior* to it. After all, its success hinges on more demanding conditions. Party pluralism, the rule of law, and market-adapted social and
economic policies are not easily accepted unless the political leaders
enjoy a certain degree of trust on the part of the citizenry. The erosion
of the belief in the moral integrity of the political leaders badly damages the liberal institutions. Populism, on the other hand, does not
need trust in order to gain ground—on the contrary, it flourishes when
trust in the political establishment is decaying.

But populism has its own weaknesses. The guarantees of the rule
of law cannot be denied to a particular group without producing spill-
over effects on the way members of other groups are treated and, with
the passage of time, the threat those effects present to their cherished
rights is likely to become visible to the general public. The disintegra-
tion of parliamentary party politics makes the political leadership
seem markedly less, rather than more, trustworthy. Rather than eliminating social injustice, lavish spending policies sooner or later cause
fiscal crisis that makes severe austerity measures unavoidable. Thus,
liberalism has strategic weapons against populism. The struggle for
the soul of liberal democracy is not lost in advance. But neither is it
won in advance. It needs to be fought, again and again.

Note that the controversy with populism does not force liberals to take the side of elitism. Neither the moral principles acknowledged by liberalism nor the empirical assumptions it makes about the circumstances of politics commit its advocates to the mistaken view that upholding the moral standards of political action is the internal affair of the political establishment. Unlike populism, liberalism allows for the complexity of the processes of political accountability. It leaves room for the press, the civil groups, the competing parties themselves, and public bodies such as the legislature, to play their proper part in these processes. It can give an account of the interest of a party in preserving its good reputation or of a legislature in protecting its integrity. It has the tools to explain how these interests may govern the acts of holding politicians accountable between two elections. The explanation, however, is based on the expected electoral behavior of the general public as the ultimate regulator of this process. It shows that whether or not the disgraced politician himself or his party has a sufficiently strong moral reason to draw the practical consequences, the outcome hinges largely on the shifts in the voters' preferences, and those shifts respond, at least in part, to their moral judgements. In this account, the role of the final arbiter is allotted to the citizenry, not to "elite" groups that are supposed to "know better."

7.6 The Spiegel affair

I concluded Chapter Six by telling a real-life political story. In conclusion to this chapter, I will briefly tell another story with the aim of elucidating the interaction between deliberative and strategic communication in upholding a moral minimum.

On October 8, 1962 *Der Spiegel*, the Hamburg-based weekly, published an article about the state of the Bundeswehr. The report claimed that the German army had performed poorly at the NATO maneuvers in September of that year, and reported that the military leadership was deeply divided on strategic questions (some of the top officers, backed by the ministry of defence, held that in case of a Soviet invasion they should immediately use nuclear weapons; others sharply rejected that view). The attorney general promptly started an inquiry into the leakage. His move presented the personally implicated minister of defense, Franz-Joseph Strauss, with a golden opportunity to try to settle his scores with *Der Spiegel*: in 1961, the weekly had raised charges of corruption against him, followed by uncomfortable parliamentary hearings (the so-called Fibag affair). Strauss asked Chancellor Adenauer to give him a free hand, which he did. Eventually, the defense minister went as far as to by-pass his colleague, the minister of justice, and to subject the attorney general's action to his personal direction. The magazine was charged with threatening the existence of the Federal Republic of Germany and the security of the German people. On October 26, the police searched the editorial headquarters of *Der Spiegel* and the publisher's offices; the editor-in-chief, Rudolf Augstein, and the author of the article, Conrad Ahlers, were arrested (Ahlers being detained in a Spanish hotel by Franco's policemen, mobilized by the German military attaché). A vast solidarity campaign rallied behind *Der Spiegel*; the press, the radio and television spoke about a crisis of the rule of law, distinguished professors issued a protest, and there were solidarity meetings at the headquarters of *Der Spiegel*. The Free Democrats threatened to leave the cabinet unless the chancellor dismissed the secretaries of state of defense and of justice who had been instrumental in short-circuiting the liberal minister of justice. However, Adenauer resisted the pressure; he backed Strauss with his full authority as head of government, and accused *Der Spiegel* in the Bundestag of treason. Strauss himself at first denied playing any role in the affair. But on November 8, he was forced to admit in the Bundestag that he had had a telephone conversation with the military attaché in Madrid the night before Ahlers's arrest. From then on, the press identified him as the mastermind of the dirty action.[15]

Strauss displayed no sign of being touched by a sense of responsibility for the scandal, and it seems that Adenauer, too, was left unaffected by the moral implications of the story. For weeks, the chancellor failed to give any sign of being aware of how sweeping the political crisis was; towards the end of November, he asked his party's presidency "not to buy the tricks of the press, the radio and the television."[16] By the time he had finally come to realize that unless he dismissed his minister of defense, his government might collapse, his room for maneuver was severely restricted. He was the person who bore the ultimate responsibility for the Spiegel affair; he had made the charge of treason against the weekly's journalist and editor in the Bundestag; he had publicly defended the arrests. His position was further weakened by the blanket mandate that he had been rash enough to give to Strauss and that Strauss was audacious enough to use to blackmail him.

In the end, Adenauer had to resort to a trick in order to get rid of his minister who was desperately hanging on to his portfolio. The Free Democratic members of the cabinet had offered their resignation very early as a protest against the chancellor's refusal to back his minister of justice in his bid for redress after the invasion of his jurisdiction by Strauss. Many weeks later, the Christian Democrat ministers followed suit. Their move made the resignation of the ministers delegated by the CSU unavoidable—only Strauss himself was keeping tenaciously to his office. The resignation of all the ministers but one opened the way for Adenauer to form a new cabinet that did not include his main ally. Strauss lost his office without ever being dismissed from it.

This story was brought to its happy solution by strategic maneuvers conducted against the background of public outcry, while the key players—the minister and his boss—remained totally indifferent to the moral dimension of the conflict.

Clearly, the indignation of a significant part of public opinion was the ultimate regulator in the process leading to Strauss's departure. Public opinion, however, is not an agency that takes official measures: it neither appoints ministers nor relieves them of their office. Strauss's departure from his job could have been either his own decision or that of the chancellor. Neither of them was directly responding to the mobilization of the public opinion. In order to make at least one of them move, some intermediary agency with an influence on their conduct must have responded.

SPD, the opposition party, put some awkward questions to the chancellor and his minister in the Bundestag, and demanded Strauss's resignation quite early. That was what made the affair an issue for the Bundestag, confronting the chancellor with the question whether he would be able to preserve his majority throughout the crisis.

The government had the backing of a coalition of three parties, the CDU, its Bavaria-based sister party, the CSU, and the FPD.

The CSU stood firmly behind their leader, whose authority remained unchallenged within his party and its constituency (in the midst of the scandal, provincial elections were held in Bavaria and the CSU, led by Strauss, won by a clear majority).

As a party directly affected by Strauss's outrageous practices, the FPD confronted Adenauer with a choice between them and his minister of defense, and underlined their demand by the collective resignation of their ministers. The chancellor, however, believed that he could ignore the threat until his own party began to withdraw its support from his policy of firmly backing Strauss. Some Christian Democratic members of the Bundestag had serious misgivings about the political persona of the disgraced minister; the crisis revealed the loss of authority of the aging Adenauer, who was no longer able to keep his party and its parliamentary group under firm control; and the threat of the Free Democrats leaving the coalition evoked the specter of anticipated elections that most Christian Democrats were anxious to avoid.

Notes

1 See J. Habermas: Theorie des kommunikativen Handelns I. Frankfurt/Main: Suhrkamp, 1987, 141–151.

2 Ibid., 142.

3 See R. Goodin: *Reflective Democracy*. Oxford: The University Press, 2003, 75–90.

4 Benedict Anderson: *Imagined Communities*. London: Verso, 1991 (revised edition), 35.

5 See, for example, H. Arendt: "Truth and Politics," In Arendt: *Between Past and Future*. New York: Viking, 1968.

6 For a particularly clear statement of this view, see J. Cohen: "Deliberation and Democratic Legitimacy." In A. Hamlin–P. Pettit, eds.: *The Good Polity*. Oxford: Blackwell, 1989.

7 See R. Dworkin: "Why Must Speech Be Free?" in Dworkin: *Freedom's Law*. Cambridge, Mass.: Harvard University Press, 1996.

8 See D. Austen-Smith: "Strategic Models of Talk in Political Decision-Making," in *International Review of Political Science* 16 (1992) 45–58.; A. Lupia and M. D. McCubbins: *The Democratic Dilemma*. Cambridge: The University Press 1998.; and G. Mackie: "All Men Are Liars," in J. Elster, ed.: *Deliberative Democracy*. Cambridge: The University Press 1998.

9 See J. Schumpeter: *Capitalism, Socialism, and Democracy*. London: Allen & Unwin, 1943, and W. Riker: *Liberalism Against Populism*. San Francisco: Freeman, 1982.

10 This is not true of those who drop out completely from parliament. But their failure is evidence that they are too weak to challenge the rules of the game, at least when the elections are free and fair.

11 See J. Bentham: "Plan of Parliamentary Reform." *In Jeremy Bentham's Works*, ed. by J. Bowring. Vol. 3. Edinburgh: Tait, 1843.; cf. J. Mill: "Government," in Mill: *Political Writings*. Cambridge: The University Press, 1992. For a modern restatement, see A. Downs: *An Economic Theory of Democracy*. New York: Harper & Row, 1957.

12 Societies deeply divided on religious or ethnic lines may be better governed if the representatives of all the major groups share governmental power. Switzerland is a case where this model works successfully. Lebanon is a case where it fails. In other communities a national emergency or the inability of any one of the two sides to form a stable majority may lead to temporary grand coalitions. Grand coalitions may last long if there is a significant minority in the parliament that is not eligible as coalition partner.

13 "This is bigger than any single senator now. I am concerned that Trent has been weakened to the point that may jeopardise his ability to … speak to all Americans," declared Oklahoma Senator Don Nickles one day before Lott's forced resignation. See BBC News. December 15, 2002.

14 In the November 10, 1988 session of the Bundestag, commemorating the fiftieth anniversary of Crystal Night, Philip Jenninger, the Christian Socialist Vice-Speaker of the House of Representatives, expressed his regrets that the National Socialist regime that was so successful in its pursuit of laudable social policies had compromised itself by the atrocities of that notorious event. Although Jenninger did not make any anti-semitic remarks, his speech caused a public uproar. He had to leave public life abruptly. His resignation created a precedent of a normative kind. He had to quit office because equivocating about National Socialism was recognized to be impermissible for anyone holding or aspiring to elected office. The Jenninger affair extended the boundaries of prohibited conduct very far. If his ambiguous talk could not remain immune to sanction, neither could more explicit cases of anti-semitic discourse. In the fall of 2002, Jörg Möllemann, Vice-Chairman of the FDP, had to leave his party because of his attempts to woo voters with anti-semitic sentiments. Möllemann had admitted Jamal Karsli, a politician with Syrian origins, who was notorious for his anti-semitic criticism of Israeli politics, to the FDP caucus of the province of North Rhine-Westphalia. In an interview with ZDF, he blamed Israeli Prime Minister Sharon and Michael Friedman, at the time vice-president of the Central Jewish Council of Germany, for the anti-semitic atmosphere, and distributed anti-Israeli leaflets in his campaign. (In June 2003, after being charged with tax fraud and violating the law on parties by the prosecution, and having had his status of exemption suspended by the Bundestag, Möllemann committed suicide). See D. Cziesche–B. Schmid: Abschied vom Klischee? In *Der Spiegel*, 2002 June 10. At the end of 2003, Martin Hoffmann was expelled from the parliamentary group of the CDU for saying in his electoral district in Neuhof, Hesse, that the Jews were overrepresented in the Bolshevik revolution and especially in the Cheka, the terror

organization of the Bolsheviks, and therefore if the Germans were a "guilty people," then so were the Jews. See H. von Buttlar, etc.: Brodelnde Basis. In *Der
Spiegel*, November 17, 2003, 46. Both politicians' discourse was openly racist and
anti-semitic. If Jenninger had to go, then so had they.

15 See H. Köhler, *Adenauer, Eine Politische Biographie*. Frankfurt/Main: Pro-
pylaen, 1994, 1157–1183. I also used the November–December issues of *Der
Spiegel* for the reconstruction of the story.

16 *Adenauer*, 1175.

CHAPTER EIGHT

DIRTY HANDS IN POLITICS

8.1 A quasi-Weberian argument

In Chapter Six (6.2), I tried to show that the constraint on permissible dirty hands is no private business of the policial agent: rather, it expresses a principle of accountability. That argument seems to be open to the following objection: Yes, politicians are accountable to the public for acting wrongly in the course of their struggle to gain and retain office. But the problem of acting with dirty hands is not a problem of acting wrongly. The relevant instances of dirty-handed acts are acts that are morally objectionable in some sense, but not in the sense of being wrong. When an agent acts wrongly he makes himself responsible for something he ought to have refrained from doing. When he gets his hands dirty while doing what is right he makes himself responsible for the morally objectionable properties of an act that he ought not to have refrained from doing. Weber's ethics of responsibility applies to the second type of cases, not to the first. The argument deployed in the preceding chapters attacked the first type, not the second. It cannot be directly extended to the cases of justified dirty hands.

The present chapter will address this objection. I will begin by showing how it can be fleshed out so as to imply that the attempts to extend the reasoning of the previous chapters to the cases of justified dirty hands fails as of necessity. Since the argument I will be offering yields a conclusion close to Weber's, although its premises are different from his, I will call it quasi-Weberian.

Consider an act that is both wrong and dirty-handed. A is the father of B. As a student, B joins an illegal movement that aims to democratize the dictatorial regime ruling their country. The police offers rewards to those who will report on the members of the democratic movement. A betrays his son for gain. We believe that he has reason to feel guilty about his betrayal, and that third parties have reason to feel indignation and scorn at his act. The appropriate first-person and third-person reactions point in the same direction: both are condemnatory. The act that rightly arouses a sense of guilt in the agent is the same as the act that rightly arouses a sense of indignation in the observer, and vice versa. To state that the guilty agent is morally accountable to other people is to establish that the perspective of the agent and that of the others are correlated in this way.

Consider now an act that is dirty-handed but right. Suppose that B becomes involved in a terrorist plot against peaceful citizens of a democratic country. Believing that his father will endorse his project, he tells him about it. Frightened by the discovery that A condemns terror against innocent civilians, B makes A promise to remain silent about the information he shared with him. However, A breaks his promise. He alerts the police and his son is arrested together with his comrades before they can carry out their sinister plan. Since breaking a promise is morally objectionable, A has reason to feel very badly about his conduct. We would find him a worse character if he took the moral awkwardness of his act lightly. But since he did what was the right thing to do under the circumstances, we have no reason to react to the act with indignation or scorn. It is not appropriate for us to blame A for what he did, since we have no reason to believe that he should have acted differently. Compassion, not blame, is the proper third-person reaction. The correlativity of reactions is broken—the father has reason to feel badly about betraying his son, but we have no reason to condemn him for so doing. A person who does the right thing while getting his hands dirty does not make himself accountable to others. He makes himself accountable to his own conscience. Should he take the accountability to his own conscience lightly, we could properly condemn him *for that*—but we cannot properly condemn him *for what he did*.

So much about the relationship between the reactions of the agent and those of third parties. What about the relationship between the reactions of the agent and those of an innocent victim of his act? Suppose that B has a close friend, C, who is unaware of the terrorist plot. And suppose that the police ask A to tell them the names of all the friends of B whom he knows of. A mentions, among others, C, who is arrested together with the members of the terrorist cell, and remains in custody for months until he is finally cleared. Even if A

acted rightly, C suffers an unjust harm. He has a genuine grievance. This grievance is not offset by the fact that A's action has no satisfactory alternative. And so A owes an explanation to C. He owes C an expression of his awareness that he has done something morally objectionable to him. He owes C a communication that he feels pain as a result.

This may give the impression that the relationship between the agent who does the right thing with dirty hands and the victim of his action is one of accountability. But the first impression may not be accurate.

When the act is wrong, it creates an asymmetrical relationship between the offender and the offended. The perpetrator puts himself in a moral position of dependency on the victim. His moral standing becomes dependent on how the victim reacts to the offense. Whether he may be restored to his moral status before the offense depends to a large extent on the victim. Without a change in the victim's attitude from resentment to forgiveness (or some functional equivalent of forgiveness, such as condonation, oblivion, and the like) the perpetrator would have little hope of advancing beyond his present status in the interpersonal relationship as a blameworthy person (see again Chapter Six, 6.2). Typically, the victim has a margin of discretion regarding the question of whether to forgive or not, of whether to forgive unconditionally or on condition of a serious change of heart in the offender, of whether to inflict some punishment on the offender and forgive him only when he has suffered, and so on.

Such is the case when the agent is responsible for a wrongful act. Whenever this case obtains, it is correct to say that responsibility implies accountability.

In cases of justified dirty hands, however, the proper reaction on the part of the victim to the explanation of the agent cannot be described in terms of forgiving (or refusing to forgive) but in those of excusing, where "excusing" does not mean finding mitigating circumstances, but rather not finding the agent guilty at all.[1] The person who acted with dirty hands in a situation where no satisfactory alternative was available has not acted wrongly, and therefore even the victim has no good reason to blame him for having done what he did. Thus, the reconciliation between the offender and the victim, if it comes about, is not supposed to be based on things such as repentance and forgiveness.[2] It may be psychologically very difficult, perhaps impossible, for the victim to be reconciled with the offender who betrayed him, even if both agree that that was what the offender had to do under the circumstances. It would be a mistake on the part of a third party to blame the victim for being unable to excuse the offender. This does not entail, however, that a refusal to excuse is as appropriate a reaction as excusing. The adequate response to a justifiable dirty-handed act is acknowledging that the agent is not guilty at all. And where this is the only adequate reaction, the agent not make himself accountable to the victim in the sense in which I speak in this book about moral accountability: the victim doesn't gain standing to attach normative consequences (of blame and punishment) to his dirty-handed act.

To sum up, in the case of justifiable dirty-handed acts the relationship between responsibility for the act and accountability to other people seems to break down. Although the agent bears responsibility for such acts, this does not make him accountable to either third parties or even to the victim (if there is one). It makes the agent morally accountable to his own conscience and, in a way, only to it.

How is this finding related to the claim made in Chapter Six that the realist thesis is subject to a constraint and that the constraint makes the political agents accountable to the general public? The second step of the quasi-Weberian argument should deal with this question.

A justifiable dirty-handed act either respects or breaks the constraint. If it respects the constraint, it is permissible under the given political conditions, and the fact that it has morally objectionable features does not cancel its permissibility. The divergence principle is not overridden in such cases: although the agent has reason to feel remorse about his act, and although we would find him less good a character if he took these reasons lightly, neither third parties nor victims are justified to blame him for not doing something else instead.

Consider now the case when a dirty-handed act breaks the constraint. Such an act may still be justified if it is necessitated by some exceptional danger. If so, and if, consequently, the breach is morally permissible, then even in this case the existence of the constraint fails to overrule the divergence principle.

This is what I call the quasi-Weberian argument about dirty hands in politics. By now, it must have become clear to the reader why. Weber's own conception was based on a radically decisionist view of value. The adoption of ultimate values, according to this view, cannot be justified or criticized in terms of reasons, for it is a matter of blind choice. If this is so, nobody can be held accountable by others for his ultimate value commitments. To the extent that his secondary choices are consistent with his ultimate value choices, and to the extent that his acts conform to a consistent system of values, he is beyond ethical accountability. This is a sweeping claim. It applies to all dirty-handed acts that the agent believes to be right by the standards of his chosen set of values.

The present argument assumes that value judgments, including the judgments of ultimate value, are capable of being true or false. Its case against accountability is, thus, different and more restricted than Weber's. It holds that some acts are really right and really objectionable at the same time—something Weber would have ruled out as a meaningless claim—and it tries to show that those, but only those acts are beyond accountability for reasons Weber did not find it necessary to contemplate.

Can the quasi-Weberian argument be answered?

8.2 The "Catholic" model

In his much-cited article, "Political Action: The Problem of Dirty Hands,"[3] Michael Walzer proposes an answer to Weber that, if it works, shows that even if we grant that the moral issue of justified dirty hands is an essentially private matter, this does not make it improper to deal with it by public methods. This is because, as Walzer insists, the politician cannot master his problem of dirty hands without recourse to public procedures.

Walzer invites us to compare three broad traditions of thinking about dirty hands in politics. Let me call the Renaissance tradition the first that he associates with Machiavelli's political thinking.[4] The central idea of this tradition is, as we have seen, that the good prince must learn how not to be good. If he succeeds in this, power and glory are his rewards—even if his personal goodness is thrown away. However, Machiavelli "does not specify the state of mind appropriate to a man with dirty hands. A Machiavellian hero has no inwardness. What he thinks of himself we don't know. ... But then it is difficult to account for the strength of his original reluctance to learn how not to be good," Walzer concludes.[5]

For the Renaissance tradition it seems natural that the good prince acts unscrupulously. Since this is not at all natural, Walzer maintains, the Renaissance tradition must be abandoned. Therefore he turns to a tradition that he calls Protestant and associates with Max Weber.

According to Walzer, Weber's political leader is a tragic hero. He sacrifices his soul for a good cause. He allies himself with "diabolic forces," and the demon he follows through his career "is in internal tension with the god of love." He is a lonely figure. His charisma attracts and mobilizes large masses, but insofar as his moral problem is concerned, he is alone with it.

Weber's politician has a conscience; he sees that his acts are morally reprehensible, and he suffers for this, but his suffering is his private business and cannot be shared with the world. The Weberian politician does what he has to do, and is tormented inwardly.

> Here is a man who lies, intrigues, sends other men to their death— and suffers. He does what he must do with a heavy heart. None of us can know, he tells us, how much it costs him to do his duty. Indeed, we cannot, for he himself fixes the price he pays. And that is the trouble with this view of political crime. We suspect the suffering servant of either masochism or hypocrisy or both, and while we are often wrong, we are not always wrong. Weber attempts to resolve the problem of dirty hands entirely within the confines of the individual conscience, but I am inclined to think that this is neither possible nor desirable.[6]

Why is this "neither possible nor desirable"? Why should the problem of dirty hands not kept "entirely within the confines of the individual conscience"? Walzer does not say: because, against all appearances, the agent is accountable for his dirty-handed acts, even if these are justified. He says, rather, that from time to time, "the hero's suffering needs to be socially expressed." Its social expression serves two functions, according to Walzer. First, "it confirms and reinforces our sense that certain acts are wrong." Second, it socially limits the suffering. It is this second point that Walzer elaborates in some detail.

> We don't want to be ruled by men who have lost their souls, he says. A politician with dirty hands needs a soul, and it is best for us

all if he has some hope for personal salvation, however that is conceived. It is not the case that when he does bad in order to do good he surrenders himself forever to the demon of politics. He commits a determinate crime, and he must pay a determinate penalty. When he has done so, his hands will be clean again.[7]

This leads to the third tradition of dealing with the problem of (justifiably) dirty hands, which Walzer calls Catholic. The Catholic tradition offers us, sinners, a regular practice of confession, penance, and absolution. By periodically confessing his sins, and by undertaking penitence for them, the believer purifies himself. He remains vulnerable to the temptation to sin, but his relapses do not necessarily condemn him to eternal damnation.

The political community needs practices to keep the possibility of purification and salvation open to its leaders, Walzer insists. Those practices must be public. They require that there be some entity with the authority to establish the sin and to attach the appropriate penitence to it: some secular authority replacing the priest and the confessional.[8]

If this argument works, we do not need to face the quasi-Weberian argument head-on. Whether true or false, that account fails to lead to the conclusion that the political problem of justified dirty hands should be relegated to the internal forum of the conscience of the political leader.

Unfortunately, Walzer's argument is open to serious objections. First, Walzer characterizes justified dirty-handed acts as sinful, criminal, guilty, and wrong, and these adjectives, applied to a particular act, imply that the agent should have acted differently. However, the problem of justified dirty hands is a problem of doing something morally objectionable in the absence of any satisfactory alternative. This makes the idea that the agent deserves punishment for his deeds problematic. "We would honor him for the good he has done, and we would punish him for the bad he has done,"[9] Walzer says, but it is unclear how fairness would allow punishing an individual for doing something that had no better alternative.

Of course, Walzer could drop the claim that justified dirty-handed acts are appropriate grounds for punishment, and he could redefine the proper attitude of the agent to his own acts in terms of something other than guilt, without abandoning his central idea that politicians need some social practice to relieve them from time to time from the moral burden of dirty hands. For even if justified, dirty hands are still a moral burden for the agent.

However, and this is the second objection, it can be true that the character of someone who is not troubled by the moral burden of dirty hands is defective and that, at the same time, the common good is more effectively promoted by politicians who have such a defect than by those who are fully virtuous. We may agree, on the one hand, that a fully virtuous person would be hesitant to act with dirty hands even if this were necessary and that he would be tormented by his having so acted; on the other hand, we may also agree that, in politics, the common good is better served by someone who is less scrupulous than if a fully virtuous person would be in his place.

This statement is a summary of what I called, in Chapter Three (3.1), the second aspect of Machiavelli's paradox. As we saw, the claim that the good prince must learn how not to be good entails two different, albeit related demands. First, he has to commit morally reprehensible acts that a virtuous man would not be prepared to perform. Second, in order to be able to act in this manner, he has to unlearn the attitudes of a virtuous man. The stronger his moral commitment to the cause of the people, the more he must be ready to sacrifice his moral character for the sake of political success.

We found this claim to be fully supported by the unconstrained thesis of realism. In that version, the realist thesis does not expect the political leader to have any concerns about the moral awkwardness of his action. However, as we found in Chapter Five (5.4), the constrained thesis confronts the political leader with more complicated demands. It is true that, like the unconstrained thesis, it warns the leader that he must act without hesitation; if he were too tormented by moral doubts he would easily fall prey to his unscrupulous rivals. But the constrained thesis entails a second caveat. A leader without any moral scruples is not a good leader. Citizens have reason to want politicans who are capable of acting resolutely and at the same time responding to the constraints on permissible political action.

Even in this amended form, the thesis insists that a good politician does not have an ideal moral disposition. His or her character combines some degree of scrupulousness with the capacity for acting resolutely, i.e. for acting without too many scruples.

Thus, the good politician represents a sort of optimum compromise between perfect moral sensitivity and perfect moral indifference. But there is no guarantee that his character transformation stops at this optimum point. On the contrary, and this is the third objection, the pressures of the political career are likely to push it much, much farther.

Imagine Frank, a good man who, on entering the political arena, is told by his own Machiavelli that he must learn how not to be good. Let him be Walzer's "man of principles" with "a history of adherence to those principles." That is why we support him, Walzer says.

Frank and the ward boss. – Soon after starting his campaign, Frank learns that, in order to win the election, he must make a deal with a dishonest ward boss, "involving the granting of contracts for school construction over the next four years."[10] This is the first time in his political career he has to decide whether to get his hands dirty for the sake of political success or to keep them clean and risk dropping out of the game. We have to assume that he overcomes a very strong inner resistance when he accepts the deal and that, once he accepted it, he is seriously troubled by what he has done. Before he decided to run for elected office, he would never have listened to such dirty offers, let alone accept them. His self-image must be badly shaken.

This is how Walzer describes the conflict. But he does not continue the story. Suppose that Frank wins the election. Then, he will face new questions. Should he invite the ward boss to his victory party? What should he do if other investors who want an open tender for the projects of school construction protest against granting all the contracts to a single company? What should he do when the schools begin to complain about poor quality construction work? What should he do when the next election approaches? Should he renew the deal (or make a similar deal with someone else) or should he run his campaign with clean hands this time?

Throughout his career, a politician faces new and new choices between acting with dirty hands for the sake of the common cause and keeping his hands clean by not doing what the common cause would require him to do.

But the same thing repeated many times is not the same thing. The first dirty deal interrupts a personal history of clean hands. The distance between Frank's moral record before and after making it is immeasurable. The distance between his moral record before and after making the second dirty deal is smaller. After all, he has already lost his innocence before this second deal. The distance between his moral record before and after the third dirty deal is even smaller, and so on. As the weight of past dirty-handed acts increases, the relative contribution of each new one decreases. After each new dirty-handed act, Frank moves farther and farther from what he was before the first one. But it is not the *total* difference that matters for his *local* decisions. The relevant difference is incremental: it consists in the marginal change a particular decision involves for his moral record, and that change is represented by the distance between his moral record *now* and his moral record after his carrying out the decision. And as time goes by, the marginal loss caused by the successive decisions becomes smaller and smaller.

On the other hand, the costs of refusing to carry out the necessary dirty-handed act are likely to increase with time. When Frank starts his first electoral campaign, he has no office to lose. Next time he has. After his re-election, he may be appointed to chair a parliamentary committee. If he wins for a third time, he is likely to retain that position or to receive some other position equivalent to it; should he lose, he loses more than just his seat in the legislature. Notice that the marginal cost would rise even if Frank were to seek office and power for the sake of his ability to promote the common cause rather than anything else.

We should not imagine the successive dirty-handed acts as necessarily independent from each other. By getting his hands dirty the politician makes himself vulnerable to blackmailing or undertakes the risk of being exposed by third party investigators. In order to avert such risks he may be required to act with dirty hands again. Suppose that a journalist is investigating the illicit deal struck between Frank and the dishonest ward boss. Should Frank try to silence him? If he does not, his career may end in disgrace. If he does, he will get his hands even more dirty, and run the risk of provoking new occasions where the only way for him to save his career is to commit yet another dirty-handed act.

Thus, while the marginal moral loss from acting with dirty hands is likely to diminish over time, the marginal cost of keeping one's hands clean are likely to increase. It is highly implausible to think of

Frank as a tragic hero who suffers more and more as he sinks deeper and deeper into the morass of dirty-handed acts. It is much more plausible to see him as becoming more and more indifferent towards the problem of dirty hands. He is unlikely to remain the same man of principles whom his admirers persuaded to run for elected office because of his sincere dedication to the common good.

If, at the beginning of his career, he could have foreseen the character he was to become over time, he would have been appalled by the sight. But looking back with the eyes of his later self that he sees his earlier character as hopelessly naïve and idealistic.

In sum, the image of the political leader as a person overburdened by remorse for his dirty-handed acts is a romantic myth. Politicians, as we know them, are rarely if ever tragic characters. The danger they are facing is not one of being crushed by a sense of guilt but that of progressively losing the capacity to perceive the moral awkwardness of their dirty-handed acts. It is unclear how *this* problem could be taken care of by creating the opportunity for the politician to confess his deeds and to engage in expiatory acts. Walzer's account of the reasons why democracies ought to adopt a secular version of the Catholic model of dealing with the problem of dirty hands is utterly unconvincing.

Suppose, however, that the adoption of the Catholic model is well-motivated. The fact still remains, and this is the fourth objection to Walzer's proposition, that that model cannot be superimposed on the usual practices of democratic politics. One reason why this is so is mentioned by Walzer himself. Secular politics cannot rely on religious authorities, he intimates, and "[s]hort of the priest and the confessional, there are no authorities to whom we might entrust the task."[11]

This is true, but there is a deeper difficulty. Politicians are engaged in a continuous struggle for power. They know that their public statements are interpreted and used in that context. They know that a sincere public expression of their regrets about their past acts may be misused against them. Each confession may be taken as a cue for a new round of demands for apology. No serious politician who wants to stay in power can allow himself to speak about his moral doubts without giving due attention to the strategic aspect of his statements. If something like a practice of public confession and penance takes shape in the context of power politics, it is very likely to be instrumentalized and, as a consequence, turned into its own parody.[12]

One may retort that this objection is misdirected. Walzer speaks about what democratic politics would need in order to deal properly with the problem of (justified) dirty hands rather than about how democratic politics actually works. Even if the strategies of power politics are likely to distort the morally required practice of public confession and penance, this does not invalidate the claim that such a practice is morally required.

But I think the objection holds. It is a basic idea of this book that a satisfactory account of how moral deliberation and decision should proceed in a legitimate polity must be able to show that the processes it envisions can be successfully combined with strategic interaction. The struggle for power is constitutive of the general circumstances of politics; no theory that assumes it away can be a true theory of the political process, democratic or otherwise. It is a test of the validity of any conception of the moral problem of politics that the practices it recommends for dealing with that problem are not undermined and travestied by their combination with strategy.

If this is so, the therapy Walzer offers to the Weberian "suffering servant" must be abandoned. And if it must be abandoned, the quasi-Weberian argument of the problem of dirty hands in politics must be confronted head-on. We must be able to show that even justified dirty hands are within the scope of public accountability.

8.3 A fresh start

The way I read Walzer, he claims that the main reason why democratic politics needs something like a secularized version of the Catholic practices of confession, penance, and absolution is that it is bad for the community to be ruled by men who have lost their souls. Towards the end of his article, however, Walzer mentions another function that the proposed practice may fulfill. Political action is uncertain, he says, and

> politicians necessarily take moral as well as political risks, committing crimes that they only think ought to be committed. They override the rules without ever being certain that they have found the best way to the results they hope to achieve, and we don't want them to do that too quickly or too often. So it is very important that the moral stakes be very high...[13]

The idea seems to be this. To lie to the citizens for the sake of personal gain is not just morally awkward: it is impermissible. To lie to the citizens for the sake of avoiding some serious public disaster may be permitted, perhaps required, even if it is morally awkward. Unjustifiably dirty-handed acts are not simply morally awkward, they are plainly wrong. On the other hand, the same acts do not cease to be morally awkward if they are justified. This is a neat distinction, provided that we are able to tell without ambiguities whether, in a particular situation, there is, or there is not, a satisfactory clean-handed alternative for the political leader to adopt in preference to acting with dirty hands. The problem is that, typically, politicians cannot know for sure *ex ante* whether a dirty-handed act they are contemplating will prove to be justified *ex post*. It is important, therefore, that they do not lightly choose to act in ways that, even if justified, will make their hands dirty. People who are not troubled by the moral awkwardness of dirty-handed acts are likely to choose such options even if they are avoidable. It is, therefore, important that politicians should feel deep embarrassment at committing dirty-handed acts.

The same concern is expressed by Bernard Williams in an essay on the moral character of the politician: "[O]nly those who are reluctant or disinclined to do the morally disagreeable when it is really necessary have much chance of not doing it when it is not necessary."[14] This is so, Williams argues, because "there is no disposition which just consists in getting it right every time, whether in politics or anything else." All decision depends on judgment, and

> [w]hether judgment is well exercised, whether immediate moral objections are given the right weight, or any, against large long-term issues is ... something that involves patterns of sentiment and reaction. ... [Therefore,] a habit of reluctance is an essential obstacle against the happy acceptance of the intolerable.[15]

I will return to this claim later in this chapter. For the time being, I would like to call attention to another aspect of the problem of uncertainty as to whether a dirty-handed act is "really necessary." When we say that the outcome of a choice is uncertain, our assertion implies that the accessible evidence is not sufficient for predicting the consequences with confidence. Insufficient evidence, however, is not a problem for one decision-maker on his own. It also gives rise to an interpersonal problem. Where the evidence is inconclusive, disagreement is likely to arise between two or more persons facing the same issue. The greater the number of people interested in a case, the higher the probability of disagreement. This would be true even if all these people were similarly affected by all the decisions available in the given situation. However, participants in political processes in general are not similarly affected by alternative decisions, nor are they likely to perceive themselves as being similarly affected. The politician, for example, competes for the same elected office, and whatever decision he may take, it will typically affect the chances of his rivals to win in different ways: if it improves his chances, by the same token, it worsens theirs, and vice versa. Citizens support different contenders for elected office; their interests regarding the outcome of the competition conflict by definition, and so if a political decision has an impact on that outcome, then it will affect their own conflicting interests. Even those without a preferred candidate may be affected differently by a controversial decision, and may see themselves as being affected differently. Thus, whenever the evidence on the nature and circumstances of a political decision is inconclusive—and this is very often the case—citizens are likely to disagree among themselves on how to evaluate that decision, and the question whether acting with dirty hands is permissible in the particular case is as likely to be subject to disagreement as any other question raised by the politicians' acts.[16]

It may help, at this point, to recall the thesis of realism, for it is this thesis that spells out the conditions under which dirty-handed acts may be morally permitted. In Chapter Three I discussed an act-based version and two character-based versions of the thesis. The act-based version lists three conditions: insufficient general compliance, absence of any alternative that would bring about the same goal without involving the necessity of acting with dirty hands, and proportionality between the moral costs of acting with dirty hands on the one hand and the importance of the aim served by the act on the other. My point is that the question whether any of these conditions obtains is likely to provoke serious disagreements within the community.

Let us start with the issue of the level of compliance. It will be helpful to return to Frank's story.

Frank and the ward boss–2. Frank accepts the deal unwillingly and only because he thinks that if he refuses, the ward boss will turn to his rival, whom Frank believes to be totally unscrupulous. Given this assumption as to his rival's character, Frank must see himself facing a choice between buying a chance to win the election at the cost of getting his hands dirty and keeping his hands clean at the cost of condemning himself to certain defeat. But others may see the alternative differently on the basis of a different assessment of the rival's attitudes and dispositions. They may think that the rival is not very different from Frank himself. If he expects Frank to take the dirty-handed option in any case, he will not choose the clean-handed option, but if he has assurances that this is not the case, he will be happy to act without dirtying his hands. Thus, they may believe that Frank, rather than making a deal with the ward boss, should have publicly announced that he had received but refused a dishonest offer, and he should have publicly invited his rival to follow his example. In so doing, he would not have jeopardised his victory but, rather, made sure that the electoral competition became cleaner.

The disagreement about how likely Frank's rival is to comply with the principles of clean and fair elections has serious practical implications. Those who form optimistic expectations as to his conduct have reason to see Frank's choice in a different light than he and his supporters see it. They may believe that Frank has the option of refusing the dishonest offer and to announce publicly that he did so, inviting his rival to follow suit. The assumption that the rival is ready to play fair if he receives assurances that Frank will do the same makes this option seem the one that Frank has most reason to take. However, unless Frank indeed takes this option, one cannot know for sure whether there was a real chance of his rival cooperating. The disagreement is genuine and serious. If Frank opts for the dirty-handed alternative, he cannot expect the general public to agree unanimously that this was a necessary move.

Secondly, citizens may disagree about whether there is really no clean-handed alternative to the dirty-handed decision as a means to reach the desired aim.

Frank and the ward boss – 3. Some members of the community believe that even if Frank's rival were extremely unlikely to cooperate, Frank could still refuse the dirty deal without ruining his chances of electoral victory. Since his strongest political asset is his reputation of being an honest man, he could make it the central theme of the electoral contest by publicly announcing that he received an immoral offer and turned it down.

Again, unless Frank actually chooses this alternative, we shall never obtain any decisive evidence as to whether it could have worked.

Third, citizens may disagree on whether the political aim is such that it justifies the costs of dirty-handed action. Consider Two Politicians–5 again: DeLuca advocates generous spending policies, claiming with Keynes that economic growth is constrained by insufficient consumer demand. Dean is against deficit financing because he believes in the post-Keynesian macroeconomic orthodoxy, according to which economic growth is constrained by insufficient private investment.

One year before the elections, Dean is told by his economic advisors that unless he immediately introduces a package of radical austerity measures, the budgetary deficit will become unmanageable, the national currency will collapse, and the economy will be hit by runaway inflation. Dean knows that if he follows the advice to cut back government spending he will very probably lose the next elections. He is conscientious enough to make this sacrifice, provided that DeLuca can be expected to continue the stabilization policies now being contemplated. But he believes that this would not be the case. DeLuca advertises a very different therapy to the ills of the budget: cutting taxes to stimulate private investment and growth. Dean fears that if this man comes to power, he will implement those dangerous policies and, in so doing, ruin the economy. In full consciousness of his responsibility to his fellow-countrymen, he decides that this must not be allowed to happen. He instructs his minister of finance to manipulate the data concerning the budget and to issue misleading statements on the expected growth of the deficit. He paints a rosy picture of the state of the economy, presenting an electoral program full of attractive promises. He knows that he is gambling with the state of the national economy and that the risks are very high. But he succeeds, and in the wake of his victory in the elections, he announces that an austerity package must be urgently implemented. As to why he delayed telling the truth and introducing the austerity measures, he explains that he had to do this in order to prevent DeLuca—a dangerous populist—from becoming prime minister. Unavoidably, the stabilization policies announced after the elections are much more radical than those proposed by Dean's advisors one year before: they impose more serious direct losses on the average household, and involve more significant indirect losses for it by causing a deeper and longer economic recession.[17]

Does the danger justify the lies, the gambling, and the harm done to the citizenry? Dean and his supporters sincerely believe this to be the case. Not everybody agrees with them, however. Those who, utterly disappointed by the sudden turnabout in Dean's public assessment of the state of the economy, now see him as a professional deceiver, clearly do not. Nor do those economists who share DeLuca's unorthodox views. And even experts who disagree with A DeLuca's Keynesianism may see the political issue differently from Dean. They may point out, for example, that electoral programs do not necessarily lay bare the exact intentions of their makers. When the program is implemented the promised cut in taxes may be complemented with an equivalent rise in fixed contributions that were not mentioned during the campaign, so that the receipts of the budget are merely restructured without being reduced, while the cuts in spending initiated by the previous government may be left intact. Unless DeLuca wins the elections, there cannot be any conclusive evidence as to whether he would run amok or in the end pursue fairly prudent policies. Many people may genuinely believe that the justification Dean provides for his strategy is mendacious and manipulative, and only serves to cloud the real purpose he pursued in the year before the election: that of staying in power at all costs and by all means.

Let us now turn to the first character-based version of the realist thesis, formulated from the perspective of the necessary character imperfections of the good leader, that is, those imperfections that are indispensable for his success in the struggle for power. In this version, the thesis contains a further condition that may be sufficient to make dirty-handed acts morally permissible. It holds that dirty-handed acts may be acceptable even if they are not necessary to reach a valuable collective aim or if they involve disproportionate moral costs, provided that no leader who would not commit them has a chance to succeed in the struggle for power, and that the dirty-handed politician promotes the common good efficaciously. Citizens are likely to disagree, too, about whether this condition is satisfied.

Here is Dean's story retold to include the fact that the prime minister's own followers are skeptical about the justification he provides for his conduct after his post-election turnabout.

> *Two Politicians–6.* Dean's supporters do not lend much credit to the claim that his rival's accession to power would have involved a collapse of the national economy. But they believe that Dean is sincerely dedicated to a good cause and that the defects of character that explain his irresponsible strategy are indispensable to his success in the struggle for power. They tend to think, therefore, that although Dean's conduct is wrong, its wrongness is not a sufficient reason for holding him to account.

If Dean had been more scrupulous, he would not have made such grave mistakes. But, then, so his supporters tend to think, he would have had no chance of surviving among so many unscrupulous contenders. In this case, they accept Dean's dirty-handed acts not because they are necessary and because their benefits are proportional to their moral costs, but rather because good politicians from time to time unavoidably commit unnecessary or disproportionately awkward dirty-handed acts. The justification they give is shifted from the character of the act to the character of the agent. Their acceptance of the act is justified on the assumption that any leader with a "politically optimal" (neither too scrupulous nor too unscrupulous) character will commit acts of roughly the same type with roughly the same frequency.

Being neither too scrupulous nor too unscrupulous, however, is a vague criterion, and there is no way to make it more incisive. It demands judgment for its application, and no two people whose preferred politicians are competing for the same public office are likely to judge the character of each other's preferred politician in the same way. Rather than agreeing that any leader with a "politically optimal" character would commit dirty-handed acts of roughly the same type, they will disagree on whether the fact that a particular politician has committed such an act proves that his character is "politically less than optimal."

Finally, if citizens are unlikely to agree on whether the community should put up with an unjustifiable act that is explained by an allegedly necessary character imperfection, they will be even less likely to agree on whether the community should put up with the same act if it is explained by a character imperfection that is only contingently related to those dispositions of the politician that allegedly make him the best choice for leadership.

Two Politicians–7. Suppose Dean's supporters are ready to concede that he acted out of a single-minded passion for staying in power. They do not deny that, in the long run, he could be politically successful even if he were prepared to run the risk of losing this particular election by doing what the common good required him to do. But they believe that none of his potential intra-party challengers, who would be disposed to make a better choice in the given situation, have the ability necessary for success in the struggle for governmental power. And they are convinced that it is better for the country to be governed by their party than by DeLuca's. Therefore they tend to think that although Dean's conduct was plainly wrong, that was not a sufficient reason for holding him to account.

Again, the partisans of the rival political force have no reason to endorse this view unless they share the opinion that it is better for the country to be governed by Dean's party than by theirs. On some rare occasions, a deeply disappointed minority of a party's constituency may indeed form such an opinion. The outcome of some elections may be decided by the temporary defection of a smaller or larger number of committed voters. But even if badly shaken, the loser typically survives the electoral defeat because the majority of its supporters continue to feel and vote according to their old affiliations. It is therefore reasonable to assume that the citizens are divided on whether it is fitting, under the circumstances, to put up with such wrongs that are attributable to the contingent character imperfections of a politician who leads his party to victory, since they disagree on which party is better at governing their country.

In sum, disagreements on dirty hands are likely to be pervasive in a typical political community. This assertion has momentous consequences.

The quasi-Weberian argument relied on the finding that it is not appropriate to blame someone for not refraining from a dirty-handed act that it was right to perform. This is a general point that, if true, holds even in the relationship of the elected officials and the citizenry. Elected officials are in general accountable to the citizens, but their accountability is suspended, so the argument goes, with regard to their justifiable dirty-handed acts: the citizens should not fault or punish them for such acts.

Now suppose that the citizenry is divided by a genuine disagreement on whether a particular dirty-handed act was justified. How does the fact of disagreement affect the claim that justified dirty-handed acts should not be held against the agent?

8.4 "Democratic dirty hands"

A possible way to understand the effect of the disagreement is this: If the controversy involves large segments of the citizenry, it reveals the absence of consent on the acceptability of the disputed act. Elected officials, however, are supposed to govern with the consent of the governed. Whatever the circumstances of the dirty-handed act, the lack of consent undermines its legitimacy.

Dennis F. Thompson makes a similar argument in his *Political Ethics and Public Office*.[18] According to Thompson, the consent requirement confronts elected officials with a special dilemma.

> If they gain that consent, they are not uniquely guilty in the way that the problem in its traditional form presumes. If they act without that consent, they not only commit a further wrong (a violation of the democratic process), but they cast doubt on the justifiability of the decision itself.[19]

The idea is that no act of an elected official can be justified unless it carries the consent of the governed. If there is no such consent the legitimacy of the dirty-handed act is undermined. If, on the other hand, the consent condition is satisfied it does more than just removing a possible delegitimizing factor. It shifts the responsibility for the morally objectionable properties of the act from the politician to the community at large. As Thompson puts it, as long as officials are assumed to act with the democratic approval of citizens, officials cannot be burdened with any greater responsibility than citizens. Although the paradox would remain—politicians must sometimes do wrong to do right—the problem of dirty hands would no longer be a problem about how citizens should regard political leaders who commit wrongs.[20]

Either way, the problem of dirty hands in its traditional form is dissolved. If the requisite consent is given, the agent is not individually responsible for the dirty-handed act: he shares the responsibility with ordinary citizens, and he shares it equally with them. If the consent is denied, the dirty-handed act cannot be justified; it will be both morally reprehensible and wrong. Thompson calls this the dilemma of "democratic dirty hands."

If Thompson's view is correct it offers a knock-down argument against the quasi-Weberian view. It implies that the politician can never claim to be left alone with the moral problem of dirty hands: he cannot claim this when the public gives its consent, for in that case the problem does not burden him alone but rather the entire community; nor can he claim it when the consent is denied, for in that case he is acting without justification.[21] But I do not think that Thompson's view is correct.

There is a sense in which those who govern do need the consent of the governed in order to wield legitimate authority. To have the right to govern means to have the right to proceed in a capacity as office-holder, and none can act in such a capacity without first assuming his office according to the rules of succession of the system. In a democracy, the succession rule for the highest offices is based on popular election, and so those who occupy these offices can indeed be said to act (when they do so in their official capacity) with the consent of the governed.

Such consent, however, is given on the understanding that the elected official will exercise discretion within the rules of his office. So long as those rules are not violated, the official is authorized by the governed to act as he deems it best for the community. No further authorization is needed for taking specific decisions as long as these remain within the discretionary powers vested in the office.

This is an essential feature of representative government. Representative government, rather than direct self-government by the people, is needed because the collective affairs of large-scale and complex communities are hard to administer unless they are entrusted to officials who specialize in doing this job. This entails that the mandate given by the governed to those who govern must indeed allow the latter a wide margin of discretion. The idea that the elected officials would need popular consent for each particular decision plainly contradicts the rationale of representative government.

Nevertheless, suppose that consent is a necessary condition for a dirty-handed political act—for any political act—to be justified: is it also a sufficient condition? The positive answer would bring unacceptable consequences. There are certain conditions other than the consent of the governed that must be met for a dirty-handed act to be justified. For example, the aim of the act must be important enough for its significance and urgency to outweigh the moral costs of dirty hands, or the dirty-handed act must be necessary in the sense of there being no clean-handed alternative that would allow the agent to obtain political office at all. If consent were a sufficient condition for the justification of a dirty-handed act, then it would fully justify an act that violates one of these conditions—a truly embarrassing conclusion.

We are, thus, left with the assumption that consent is a necessary but not a sufficient condition for a dirty-handed political act to be justified. This assumption, however, has its own embarrassing consequences. Suppose that a dirty-handed political act is meant to serve a sufficiently important aim, so that its significance and urgency outweigh the moral costs of carrying it out, and that no clean-handed (or at least less dirty-handed) alternative is available. Suppose furthermore that the citizens do not consent to carrying out this act. Does the absence of consent imply that the politician in question ought to refrain from doing what he believes he should do as a servant of the community? Let us assume that his belief is true. If so, the absence of consent makes it morally binding to abandon a morally superior option for the sake of a morally inferior one. This would be intelligible if he needed some kind of formal authorization on the part of the citizenry for adopting the option in question, and if the lack of consent meant that the authorization was denied (as happens when the legislature rejects a bill designed to empower the president to declare war, for example). But, clearly, consent cannot be generally understood as formal authorization for the leader to act in a particular way (rather than exercising discretion within the bounds of the norms that constitute his official role). We must take it to consist in some kind of *informal* agreement. If this is the case, however, the moral requirement to abandon a morally superior act in favor of a morally inferior one becomes unintelligible. As we have seen, elected officials have the discretion and obligation to do what is best from the point of view of the citizenry. By hypothesis, the dirty-handed alternative in question is the best of all the alternatives open to a particular official in a particular situation. It follows that the official in question is morally required, or at least permitted, to choose it. If so, it is not understandable how the lack of an informal agreement on the part of the citizenry would make this choice morally dispreferable to the choice of another alternative that is less good, perhaps significantly so.

If the choice of the dirty-handed option is not made morally dispreferable by the absence of informal popular consent, then consent is not even a necessary condition for the justification of a dirty-handed act.

Let us now consider the second horn of Thompson's dilemma: when an elected official has the consent of the citizenry for taking a morally awkward decision, the problem of dirty hands shifts from him as an individual agent to the community. Although Thompson does not set out the argument that purports to underpin this claim in great detail, I believe that its steps can be reconstructed fairly easily. First, no individual can take official decisions without the consent of the many that he represents in his official capacity. As a consequence—and the second step of the argument—official decision-making is essentially a collective type of action involving all those whose consent is needed for it to take place. The proper unit of agency is the community, not the individual decision-maker. Third, if an individual acts in an official capacity on the basis of the consent of the governed, he acts in the name of the entire community, and his decisions commit the entire community, so that the entire community bears responsibility for them. Fourth, group members share the collective responsibility as a result of being parts of the group rather than as a direct consequence of what they do, one by one. And, fifth, what is true about an ordinary citizen as consenter is true about the official as decision-maker. The latter's responsibility derives from the responsibility of the group, and when it comes to considering the way in which the group's responsibility is distributed, "officials cannot be burdened with any greater responsibility than citizens."

Step one is acceptable, I think; its correctness does not hinge on the assumption that all official decisions need to be consented to by every citizen. Step two seems to follow. Step three spells out a true statement, although it does not distinguish clearly between two meanings of responsibility: backward-looking, meaning responsibility for having done something in the past, and forward-looking, meaning responsibility for doing something in the future (for example, redressing some harm). The two meanings are separable. A corporation, for example, may be responsible in the forward-looking, sense for compensating the victim of a harmful action of one of its employees, without necessarily bearing responsibility for the employee causing harm to the victim.[22] Therefore we must precisely identify the sense in which the community as a whole may be said to bear responsibility for an official decision taken in its name. I think we can say that it bears responsibility for it in the forward-looking sense, but we cannot say without further argument that it bears responsibility for it in the backward-looking sense. This distinction applies also to the way the collective responsibility for an official decision is distributed among individual members of the community. Assuming that the citizens were divided by the decision, some expressing their agreement and support and others vehemently opposing it, we can say that the first but not the second bear some responsibility for the decision in the retrospective sense, while both bearing responsibility for it in the prospective sense. The truly problematic step in the argument, however, is the last one.

The problem of the distribution of collective responsibility across individual group members is notoriously loaded with two difficulties: large numbers and overdetermination. Large numbers imply that the contribution of an ordinary member is negligibly small, so that if he alone fails to do his part the collective outcome remains almost the same. Overdetermination means that if the number of participants were diminished the group would still produce exactly the same collective outcome. Such a situation implies that the contribution of an ordinary group member is zero.[23] We have, thus, to assume that an individual citizen may have his part in the responsibility for the collective outcome even if he did not perceptibly contribute to it and had no opportunity to make any difference by failing to do his part. If, in such cases, an ordinary citizen has his part in the collective responsibility for some aggregate outcome, it must be sufficient for him to have it in virtue of belonging to the political community; his part must not be understood to be a function of his measurable contribution to the outcome.[24]

This is not how a political leader is responsible for the collective outcome to which he contributed by taking official decisions. If Dean had decided to implement the necessary austerity policies immediately, things would have turned out very differently from the way they did following his decision to postpone the move until after the elections. His part in the collective action, rather than being nil or negligible, is decisive. He is not just one of the many who agree that this or that is what ought to be decided. He owns the decision in a way mere supporters or citizens who voted against him do not.

In sum, if we have reason to assume, before asking whether the consent requirement obtains, that the problem of dirty hands is a private problem of the political decision-maker, then the considerations related to the consent requirement do not give us any reason to abandon this assumption. The problem of dirty hands remains a personal problem of the political decision-maker, whether or not he acts with specific authorization on the part of the community. Even if we were to accept that no official decision is justifiable unless it carries the special consent of the citizenry, this would not imply that the traditional problem of dirty hands is dissolved. It is not the case that, when the requisite consent is given, the problem shifts entirely to the community at large, nor is it the case that when the consent is denied the leader necessarily acts with no justification.

8.5 The moral risks from disagreement

The purpose of this section is to explain and defend the claim that far from dissolving the traditional problem of dirty hands, the fact of disagreement aggravates the risks inherent in it.

I have already spoken about these risks. At the beginning of Section 8.2 I cited Michael Walzer's assertion that politicians must act under the conditions of uncertainty: they can never be sure *ex ante* whether a dirty-handed act they believe to be required or at least permitted will not prove *ex post* to have been simply wrong and prohibited. I added that such uncertainty involves a further risk, related to disagreement. The dirty-handed act that the politician and his supporters believe to be justified may be believed by others to be unjustifiable and therefore morally impermissible, and the beliefs of the latter may have the effect of frustrating the aims of the dirty-handed action.

A responsible politician who believes that he is required by the common cause to carry out a certain dirty-handed act will be motivated to do so. Those who believe that he is prohibited to carry out this act will be motivated to react accordingly, and their reactions may undercut his plans. Herein lies the risk of disagreement.

The reason for committing a dirty-handed act is not that the agent *believes* that this is what he should do, but that this is what he should *in fact* do. And the reason for condemning and punishing a dirty-handed act is not that other people believe that this is what they should do, but that this is what they should in fact do. If the politician does what he should in fact do, and other people react to his action as they should in fact react to it, the politician runs no risk by acting with dirty hands. As I stated when I developed what I called the quasi-Weberian argument in Section 8.1, a person who did the right thing with dirty hands has reason to remember his own act with pangs of conscience, but other people have no reason to blame him or to express resentment, indignation, anger, or scorn.

These claims are based on what reasons there are, objectively speaking. But people do not act or form their attitudes for any reasons that exist independently of the information accessible to them and of their own motivational set-up against which they assess that information. They act and form their attitudes upon reasons they believe to exist, upon reasons in a subjective sense. And if two people disagree in good faith on a particular issue, the subjective reasons of one of them—the reasons he thinks he has—may be related to the subjective reasons of the other in a way that is different from the way their objective reasons are related.

Suppose that Frank believes that his rival will make corrupt electoral deals, no matter what he should do. If this is a warranted belief, given what he can know about his rival, Frank has good subjective reasons for accepting the corrupt ward boss's offer. Suppose, furthermore, that other people sincerely believe that his rival would cooperate if Frank were to give assurances that he preferred clean elections. Then, even if Frank has good (subjective) reasons to believe that by accepting the corrupt offer he does what he ought to do all things considered, he has no grounds to expect others not to blame him for so doing. His reasons justify his seeing himself required (or at least permitted) to act in a particular morally awkward way, but they do not justify his expecting the members of that group not to see themselves required or permitted by their own (subjective) reasons to object to his action. The fact that Frank acts believing in good faith that he is doing the right thing does not make him any less accountable to others, who in good faith disagree with him.

Thus, by choosing a dirty-handed option Frank runs a special moral risk. He runs the risk of becoming exposed as someone whose action is not simply morally awkward but morally awkward *in an inexcusable manner*. He knows that by getting his hands dirty he assumes a moral sacrifice in any case, but he does this in the conviction that he is throwing away his purity for the sake of his fellow-citizens' well-being. But he is threatened to be exposed as a mere wrongdoer, who has thrown away his purity with no decent justification. And if among those who believe this there are enough strategically well-placed individuals, his loss of face may involve his loss of office.

Deliberating about the choice between doing what he thinks the common cause requires him to do while acting with dirty hands, and refraining from the required action in order to keep his hands clean, he may of course put this risk in the balance, and prudence recommends him to do so. His decision would not be rational if he took the option of acting with dirty hands without getting convinced to have a fair chance to avoid being publicly exposed, or at least to avoid being publicly exposed too early, before he has carried his project to a successful conclusion. If he avoids being exposed altogether, the traditional problem of dirty hands still remains with him, but at least he is saved from publicly disgracing himself. If he is exposed, but not too early, he may hope that his political success will help him to convince enough critics that their first reaction was mistaken, or to create an atmosphere in which they will acquiesce in the outcome of the process. Such prospects greatly diminish the perceived risk and so they may make it reasonable for him to go ahead.

Yet a fair chance is no certainty, and the decision to do what seems to be right and what makes one's hands dirty at the same time always involves the danger of an untimely disclosure of the inconvenient facts.

Frank and the ward boss—4. The investigative journalist who I have said was after the deal between Frank and the ward boss publishes a well-documented report about the story two weeks before the elections. The revelations make Frank appear as a hypocrite who plays the part of a principled man but who is actually a scoundrel like "all of them." Frank's strongest asset, his reputation of a person of great integrity, is completely ruined. Disgraced, he loses the election and drops out of politics altogether, without any hope of ever gaining the opportunity to show the public that it misjudged his character and intentions.

One might say that this is utterly unfair. After all, Frank is no wrongdoer, but a victim of his selfless dedication to the common cause.

His social and moral demise is indeed a great personal tragedy. The fall of a good man is an undeserved outcome, and we would want Frank to avoid it both for his own sake and for the sake of the cause he entered the political arena to serve. But is that outcome due to unfair treatment? Would we blame it on the rules and practices of democracy? Do we have a reason to want those rules and practices to be changed so that Frank and his likes are saved from the danger of being exposed and ruined?

I think we have reason to feel compassion for Frank, but we have no reason to be angry with the investigative reporter whose article has ruined his career and reputation. Nor do we have any reason to want laws that would prohibit and punish what the reporter does. In other words, we have no reason to want laws that would prosecute the disclosure of the dirty deals of politicians.

Or perhaps we do. Why should we not want laws that protect those, and only those, politicians who get their hands dirty in the service of morally worthy aims, in the absence of any satisfactory clean-handed alternative, and who are concerned that the benefit from their acts should outweigh their moral costs? Why should we not want laws that refuse to extend the same protection to those, but only those, whose aims are self-serving or otherwise unworthy, who could have chosen a clean-handed option, or who allowed the moral costs of their conduct to exceed its benefits?

To begin with, this is not a distinction the law could draw with sufficient clarity. After all, we started from the finding that the question whether these criteria obtain in a particular case tends to be deeply controversial. How could one agree before Frank is elected that he is an honest and selfless person as his followers claim, and not a self-serving hypocrite, as is maintained by his adversaries? Secondly, and more importantly, whether or not there is a way to draw the distinction in a sharp manner, the community has an overriding interest that even those who do the right thing while getting their hands dirty are not protected against public exposure.

In a community that is not completely cynical, no deal such as the one offered by the ward boss and accepted by Frank can survive public scrutiny. If Frank gets away with concealing the truth, he is lucky. But he has no right to get away with it. On the contrary, the public has a right to know the truth about his dealings with the ward boss, and he has a duty to avoid violating this right. By concealing the deal, he violates the right of the public to know, and so he gets his hands doubly dirty.

Frank would not be the only lucky one if he got away with concealing the truth. Presumably, his electoral victory would benefit the community, and so the public would be sharing his luck. This may seem to mean that the public interest and the right of the public part company in this case and in cases similar to it. Should we not say, then, that the public has good reason to sacrifice an empty right for the sake of promoting a genuine interest? I don't think we should.

The risk from uncertainty—i.e. the danger that what seems *ex ante* to be the right thing to get one's hands dirty by doing will prove *ex post* to have been the wrong thing—is not a danger for the agent alone. It is a danger for the community as a whole because, if the act is wrong, at least some members of the community will suffer unjustifiable harm. The public has, thus, a weighty interest to make sure that this does not happen too often. Its right to know, and the procedural guarantees that protect those who provide it with the requisite knowledge, serve, among other things, this interest.

The threat of disclosure is an expected cost that those who intend to act with dirty hands must weigh against the expected benefits. It imposes caution and circumspection on them. It invites them to consider more carefully than they would otherwise whether the aim of the intended act is sufficiently important, whether acting with dirty hands is really necessary, and whether the benefits expected from the act are on a par with its moral costs. In the short run, it helps to reduce the number of the dirty-handed acts that are not really necessary or that are unjustifiable for some other reason. In the longer run, it protects the community from avoidable corruption of its leaders' characters.

In Section 8.2, I argued against Walzer that the circumstances of the political career push the leaders towards becoming less and less concerned about the moral awkwardness of their profession. The threat of being exposed is a powerful obstacle in the way of this change of character. The more effectively it works, the better are the chances that the process of corruption is halted before it goes too far. Suppose that this threat is really significant. In that case politicians must give serious thought to what would happen if the shaming truth about their dirty-handed acts were revealed to the public. They would have to contemplate carefully whether their action could be publicly defended against the charge of sheer immorality. This necessity holds even for self-serving opportunists, although their attitude towards the anticipated criticism is likely to be merely instrumental. But in the case of the leader with a passion for the common cause, the assumption of a merely instrumental attitude is not in place. We must suppose that he internalizes the point of view of the others who look at his deeds with a critical eye. And we have to suppose that the internalized regard of the others does not allow his scrupulousness to go away easily.

As Williams says about the emotion of shame:

"Even if shame and its motivation always involve in some way or other an idea of the gaze of another, it is important that for many of its operations the imagined gaze of an imagined other will do." The person who did something that, if discovered, makes him lose his face "might think that it was shameful to do it, not just to be seen doing it."[25]

For self-serving opportunists, to be seen engaging in dirty deals may not mean more than encountering an obstacle in the course of pursuing their immoral aims. For a leader who pursues the career of a politician not just for the sake of power, money, and the like, but driven by a passion for the common cause, the thought that he is seen making such deals is shameful. And such a person is likely to think "that it was shameful to do it, not just to be seen doing it." The demands of the struggle for power do not allow him to deal with the problem of dirty hands as scrupulously as an individual with a fully admirable moral character would do. But neither does the gaze of the others allow him to deal with this problem as unscrupulously as the circumstances of the struggle for power would in themselves recommend.

If our "good prince" were the only politician threatened by disclosure of his morally awkward deals, the impediments to his getting rid of his moral scruples would be a competitive disadvantage. But in a constitutional democracy the threat of being exposed is not directed against this or that particular politician or group of politicians. Freedom of speech and freedom of information are impersonal principles that protect inquiry and disclosure, no matter who should be involved. The more effective the general threat that politicians will be publicly exposed for their dirty-handed acts, the more confidently each politician can expect that the others will be deterred from getting their hands dirty easily and in ways that cannot be justified to the general public. In Chapter Five I asserted that a community needs leaders who are neither maximally scrupulous nor maximally unscrupulous, but whose dispositions are characterized by a certain optimum compromise between the two extremes. It is easy to see that the range of that optimum shifts with the changes in the general level of compliance. Other things being equal, publicity raises that level, and so it allows the character desirable in a good political leader to settle closer to the moral end of the spectrum.

Uncertainty and disagreement cannot be eliminated from politics. Honest politicians who are moved by impeccably selfless considerations to throw away their purity may find themselves ruined morally and politically. They may be disgraced not only when they mistakenly believe that the morally objectionable act is necessary, but also when they correctly believe that this is so. Politics cannot be made safe against such tragedies. But if the danger is meted out impartially by rules and procedures protecting the right of the public to know, then the politician who suffers an undeserved fall has no justified complaint against the workings of democracy. Politics is a voluntarily chosen profession. It promises great rewards in terms of power, influence, prestige, and privilege. It also involves risks including moral ones. Neither the rewards nor the risks of the political career are unknown to the general public, let alone to those who descend into the political arena. If a fallen politician laments that when he embarked on his career he did not suspect that such undeserved things might

happen to him, his lament is evidence of either objectionable ignorance or insincerity.

Let me take stock. Pace Weber, value judgments are not radically
subjective. We cannot believe that something is good (or bad) unless we
believe that it is really—independently of our or anyone else's believing
it—good (or bad), in other words, unless we are ready to allow that our
evaluative beliefs are capable of being true or false. This is not, in itself,
an argument for accountability. As I tried to show in Section 1 of this
chapter, agents are not accountable in the appropriate sense for the
morally objectionable features of their acts that are *really* right and dirty-
handed at the same time. However, the *claim* that something is really
valuable is not identical with that thing *being* really valuable. A belief
that is capable of being true or false may be false, after all. The reasons
that exist for us objectively and the reasons we are warranted to think
we have are different from each other. The second kind depends on our
informational and motivational set-up, personal history, etc., while the
first is independent of them. Rationality requires us to do our best in
order to bring the reasons we believe we have as close as we can to the
reasons that exist for us. But it is the reasons that we believe we have
that we have access to, not the reasons that exist independently of those
beliefs. And the reasons two individuals believe to exist may not be
identical. People may be divided by profound and lasting disagreements
on what are the correct evaluative and normative judgments that apply
to their interaction. They may disagree, among other things, on whether
an act is truly dirty-handed and, if it is, whether it is necessary to avert
some great harm, and whether the aim of averting harm is significant
enough to outweigh the moral costs of acting with dirty hands. Such
disagreements are ordinary facts of politics, democratic or not. And
they fail the quasi-Weberian argument. That they may act with dirty
hands does not free the political leaders from their accountability to the
public rather than to their private conscience.

8.6 Tony Blair's war

Following the pattern set in the previous chapters, I will conclude the
present argument by telling a real-life story.

As I am writing, four years after the overthrow of Saddam Hussein's regime by American and British forces, few would deny that the

war on Iraq has caused a disaster. Putting an end to a bloody dictator-ship is *pro tanto* a good thing, and the efforts to replace the cruel rule of a despot, relying on a religious and tribal minority, with something like a democratic regime uniting the three main ethnic groups in a confederation deserve applause. But the country has become a play-ground for international terrorism; there are no safe havens immune to suicide attacks; without external military support, the elected gov-ernment would not survive one day; arbitrary arrests and torture are practiced by paramilitary groups and by the new police force itself no less systematically and brutally than they were by the repressive old regime; violent deaths among the civilian population are no less and perhaps even more frequent than ever between Saddam's accession to power in 1979 and his fall in 2003; the specter of a full-blown sectar-ian war is still there; millions flee their homeland, and ethnic clean-sing is under way in various regions of the country, raising the most serious doubts about the possibility that Shia Arabs, Sunni Arabs, and Kurds can be brought together as one political community. The linger-ing crisis fuels anti-Western sentiments all over the Islamic world. Responsible political and military leaders in both the United States and Great Britain are beginning to speak openly about the impossibil-ity of winning this war. The occupation has replaced a ruthless dicta-torship with a Hobbesian war of all against all, reminding the world that the existence of states cannot be taken for granted and that by provoking the collapse of an unjust and oppressive state one may in-flict greater harm and suffering on its subjects than by allowing it to continue.

The Iraqi adventure undermined the reputation of the two politi-cians who bear the lion's share of the responsibility for it, George W. Bush and Tony Blair. It is not simply the case that they have been discredited as men of poor judgment and doubtful foresight. Their integrity, honesty, and truthfulness have been questioned. They not only led their nations into a war that many warned was going to be a disaster but they did that on the ground of evidence that they either knew to be false or that they bent to justify the military attack. And so large segments of the public opinion in their countries and in the community of the democratic states concluded that they are profes-sional deceivers and liars.

Although the major role in the run-up to the war was played by the American president, it is the British prime minister's part that attracts

222

the interest of a study of politics as a moral problem. Unlike George W. Bush, Tony Blair had a genuine sense and understanding of the moral dimensions of politics. In the years of his bid for power and, then, in his first years in office, he argued eloquently for higher standards of ethical conduct in public life. Before the 1997 elections that brought him to power he promised to lay down a code of ethics for ministers; on being elected, he made good his word. That code and the procedures for monitoring and enforcing compliance with its provisions are defective in many ways; they certainly need careful revision. In the last years of his rule, Blair himself was in clear violation of that code and of the principles of openness and accountability it was meant to serve. The "cash for honors" scandal exposed him in the eyes of many as a corrupt leader who approved the acceptance of secret loans to finance his last election campaign and then nominated four of the secret lenders for peerages. This story is banal. But the way it destroyed Blair's credibility was far from banal: what he did was trying to circumvent the rules that he himself had set up. Under the Conservatives no one knew where the campaign money came from. Under Labour, its origins could be traced. Blair was different. Unfortunately for him, he was not different enough.

He was not cynical about the war against Saddam either. Ever since he had come into power in 1997, he had taken a consistent stance in favor of liberal interventionism. It was his firm conviction that a systematic refusal to use military power against blood-thirsty dictators, dangerous warlords, or terrorist safe havens was an unwise and immoral policy. He was ready for air strikes against Iraq in 1998. In 1999, he convinced Clinton that NATO should intervene in Kosovo, and he pleaded for the deployment of military units on the ground in addition to the air campaign. He sent British troops to Sierra Leone to help the elected president against rebels in 2000. His stance on the invasion of Iraq in 2003 fits nicely into this pattern.

He had a number of reasons to lead Britain into the war against Saddam. As transpires from a confidential memo, he was aware as early as July 2002 that the American president had made his decision and could not be diverted from it.[26] He saw his choice as one between "standing shoulder to shoulder" with Bush and breaking with the practice his predecessors had pursued almost continously since World War II: maintaining Britain in a position of global power by making it the number one ally of the United States. Blair apparently thought that, given the interests of his country, refusing to participate in the war or even hesitating about it was not an option.

Refraining from arguing with Bush about the merits of the case did not strike him as a sacrifice of principle for power interests, because he firmly believed that going to war against Saddam was morally justified.

First, he apparently had an unusually permissive conception of liberal interventionism. Advocates of this stance tend to claim that military intervention may be justified to prevent genocide, ethnic cleansing or some other crime of a horrendous nature and dimension and on condition that all peaceful means of reaching that aim have been explored and have failed. Furthermore, liberal interventionists tend to hold that, apart from cases of extreme urgency, the intervention must be multilateral and should enjoy the sanction of the UN Security Council. Blair's own views were more relaxed. We have reason to credit him with a sincere belief that the invasion of a sovereign state may be acceptable from a moral point of view even if it violates international law, provided that it aims to bring down an oppressive regime and to promote democracy and human rights. He clearly thought that an Iraq without Saddam would be a better place for the Iraqis themselves and that this in itself was sufficient to make the war a good thing.

Second, he apparently nourished hopes that the success of the democratic experiment in Iraq would precipitate a chain reaction of democratization in the Middle East, opening the way towards economic modernization and sapping the social bases of religious fundamentalism and terrorism.

Third, he saw Saddam as a troublemaker whose presence was a factor of continuing instability in the region in general and in the context of the Israeli–Palestinian conflict in particular. He seems to have been hoping that Saddam's disappearance would change the power relations between moderates and radicals in Gaza and the West Bank, and thus unblock the negotiations towards a peace treaty between Israel and the Palestinians.

What about Saddam as a danger on a global scale? In the run-up to the war, Saddam was accused of conspiring with al-Qaeda, of restarting his nuclear arms program, and of rebuilding his arsenal of weapons of mass destruction (WMD) that had been largely dismantled under UN inspection between 1991 and 1998. These charges were based on secret intelligence. In hindsight, that intelligence seems to have been bafflingly unreliable: there were no connections between Saddam and al-Qaeda, and he had not made any serious attempts at restarting the nuclear arms program or stockpiling WMDs. But it would be unrealistic and unfair to charge Blair with being, at the time, cynical about the reports of the secret services. He must have believed that once the American and the British troops were in control, they would discover enough chemical and biological weapons to lend credit to the pre-war accusations.

Nevertheless, he did not argue for the invasion on the basis that Saddam *possibly* had some WMDs. He was claiming as *certain* that Saddam had the capacity to deploy within 45 minutes WMDs capable of hitting British targets. He inflated the image of the Iraqi dictator from a local tyrant and regional troublemaker into a global aggressor who presented a clear and imminent danger to the West, including the United Kingdom.

The claim about WMDs that could be launched within 45 minutes against distant objectives was part of a dossier the Joint Intelligence Committee submitted to the cabinet shortly before September 2002. That document warned, however, that the information had come from a single source and had not been checked for its reliability. It included similar caveats regarding other data. Thus, Blair was in a position to know that the claim of clear and imminent danger was based on insufficient and unreliable evidence.[27]

But he wanted the public to believe that the evidence was sufficient and rock-solid. Thus, when the Committee was working on a publishable version of the report, he sent it a request through Alistair Campbell, his communications director, that the document be freed as much as possible of any doubts and uncertainties.[28]

Tony Blair deliberately misled the public about the threat Saddam Hussein's rule presented to the British people. He was honestly convinced that the invasion of Iraq was justified, but he could not seriously think that it was justified by the need to preempt a deadly attack against Britain or its major allies. He believed that it was justified as a means to bring democracy and human rights to the Iraqi people, and peace, prosperity and stability to the Middle East. He knew, however, that neither public opinion nor Parliament or the international community was prepared to endorse the war on such grounds. He needed a different justification, one which would make the war legal or nearly legal even if the sanction of the Security Council was not obtained. In sum, he decided to act with dirty hands in the service of a cause he believed was morally clean.

He was clearly hoping that, finally, the terms of the public debate about the war would change in his favor, that the public would understand that he had done the right thing, and that he would be excused for misleading parliament, the British citizenry and world opinion in order to be able to do it.

But the terms of the debate changed against him rather than turning in his favor. No single stockpile of WMDs have been found in Iraq, and the military success was followed by a political disaster.

In his farewell speech delivered in his electoral district on 10th May 2007, Blair acknowledged—for the first time since the war started—that his Iraq policy might have been a failure, but he passionately defended the honesty of his intentions:

> "Removing Saddam and his sons from power, as with removing the Taliban, was over with relative ease. But the blowback since, from global terrorism and those elements that support it, has been fierce and unrelenting and costly. For many, it simply isn't and can't be worth it. For me, I think we must see it through. They, the terrorists, who threaten us here and round the world, will never give up if we give up. It is a test of will and of belief, and we can't fail it. Great expectations not fulfilled in every part, for sure. Occasionally, people say, as I said earlier, "They were too high, you should have lowered them." But, to be frank, I would not have wanted it any other way. I was, and remain, as a person and as a prime minister, an optimist. Politics may be the art of the possible but, at least in life, give the impossible a go. So, of course, the vision is painted in the colours of the rainbow, and the reality is sketched in the duller tones of black, white and grey. But I ask you to accept one thing—hand on heart, I did what I thought was right. I may have been wrong. That's your call. But believe one thing if nothing else—I did what I thought was right for our country."[29]

The same motive appeared in an editorial of *The Economist* endorsing Blair before the May 2005 elections. "[H]is willingness to bend facts to strengthen an argument" should not be taken as a reason for denying trust to him, the editorial insisted.

Mr Blair did genuinely believe in the threat posed by a WMD-armed Saddam Hussein. He was also convinced that it was not in Britain's long-term interest to withhold support from America. His judgment may have been faulty ... but it is wrong to doubt his sincerity. Mr Blair's supposed untrustworthiness ought not, therefore, to dominate the election.[30]

According to the available evidence, the intelligence Tony Blair had at hand did not provide him with any ground to believe that a "WMD-armed Saddam" could pose a threat that was great, direct, and certain enough to justify immediate military intervention. But even if he sincerely believed (on other grounds) that the intervention was justified, he deliberately misled his country and the world in order to have the war accepted for reasons other than his own. Was this a ground for the public to consider him untrustworthy? Clearly, it was for all those who refused to share his political instincts. Even if he had been as careful as possible in assessing the reasons for and against the war, he could not have a legitimate complaint against their judgment. But this is not a full answer to our question.

Suppose that his judgment was correct. Justified dirty hands are no ground for blaming the agent. Once the public had realized that the war was a necessity and that Blair could bring his country into it only by bending facts to suit his argument, it would have reason for forgiving him. But his judgment was faulty, and this brings us to the question whether the misjudgement was unavoidable, given the information available to Blair during the run-up to the war, or whether it was the result of serious moral failures. If he did what he could to avoid great mistakes in judging the odds of the war, there is no reason to blame him for his errors, and his public image as "Bliar" is unjustified. But if he recklessly disregarded the available information and the procedural restraints, he is rightly held morally responsible for taking Britain into war on faulty judgment and falsified reasons.

I don't believe Blair's errors were morally innocent. To say the least, the invasion of Iraq was of dubious legality, and a responsible leader does not treat the commands of international law lightly when he takes his nation into war. Blair knew that his conception of liberal interventionism was a long way from the mainstream, but he refused to give serious thought to the objections to his position. There were many warnings that the war would create more problems than it might resolve, and Blair decided to ignore them.

According to David Manning, British ambassador in Washington at the time, Blair was extremely exercised that the Americans did not have a clue what they would do after the removal of Saddam. In Manning's own words, Blair was deeply concerned that the American plans had not been "thoroughly rehearsed and thoroughly thought through."[31] Nevertheless, he went along with the White House without hesitation.

I do not want to defend the rigorist claim that no war can be just if it is started in contravention to international law. The law of war in force allows oppressive regimes pursuing traditional great power interests to veto humanitarian intervention of great urgency. The moral duty of liberal democracies to help endangered peoples against genocide, ethnic cleansing or other massive human rights abuses may demand them to act even in cases where the war is not initiated in self-defense nor has the mandate of the UN Security Council.

The war over Kosovo is an example. No state with an international standing was attacked by Yugoslavia, and the intervention was not sanctioned by the UN Security Council nor launched in self-defense. Therefore, under the *ius ad bello* in force it was unlawful, but it is hard to deny that for all its human and political costs it was a just war. It was envisaged as a response to ethnic cleansing, a crime against humanity. When the bombing of Yugoslavia started, the expulsion of the Kosovar people was already under way, brutal action of the Yugoslav army against civilian population was already under way. Documented atrocities were committed with the evident aim to expel the Kosovar Albanians from their homeland, so the intervention was of great urgency.[32]

This was not the entire justification, though. Even lawful military intervention requires great circumspection. The requirements of prudence are much more stringent in cases where the war is not permitted by the international regulations in force. The war over Kosovo satisfied those requirements to a very large extent.

First, if a resolution to sanction the military intervention had been submitted for a vote to the Security Council, it would have carried the majority. The only reason why the sanction of the SC could not be obtained was that Russia and China threatened to veto the motion. Second, in so far as the democratic governments were concerned, there was full agreement as to the necessity to intervene by force. Third, due to the consensus among the democratic governments, NATO—a long-standing and internationally recognized military alliance—could be gained to co-ordinate the operation. Fourth, since the population of Kosovo is 90 per cent ethnic Albanian, and the Serb minority is concentrated near the borders with Serbia, the NATO forces had a good chance to secure peace and stability in the province once it was under their control.[33]

Given the great urgency of averting a state-made humanitarian disaster, majority support among the Security Council's member states, full consensus among the democratic governments, availability of an internationally recognized military umbrella organization, and manageability of the post-war situation, the case for the war satisfied all the precautionary considerations. It was, thus, highly probable that after the surrender of Milošević's Yugoslavia the international community would smoothly return to playing the legal game.

None of the conditions that obtained in the case of Kosovo obtained in the case of Iraq. The war was not started to avert an imminent humanitarian disaster on a mass scale; the draft resolution that should have authorized it did not command a majority in the Security Council; major democratic governments like France and Germany vehemently opposed the action; NATO was unavailable to co-ordinate "the coalition of the willing"; and experts warned that once occupied, the country was likely to plunge into sectarian war and to become the theater of international terrorism.

Tony Blair played a major role in building up the coalition for the war over Kosovo, and he deserves our tribute for this. However, Kosovo became his hybris. He could have read its message as a warning that even if justice and humanity press for a departure from the norms of international law, one should not depart from them *too far*. Rather, he seems to have concluded that a just and humane cause easily trumps all cautionary considerations.[34]

This was a dangerous conclusion; it released Blair from much of the prudence characteristic of a responsible leader, and it removed those restraints that, had he formed uncautious judgments, could have prevented him from acting on them. Had he drawn the right lessons from Kosovo, he would have refrained from starting a war of doubtful legality that was not meant to avert genocide or ethnic cleansing and that could not gain the consent of major democratic allies such as

France and Germany. But he drew the wrong lesson, and became doubly responsible for acting on faulty judgment.

In sum, Blair made his hands dirty for the wrong reason. He did so because he substantially misjudged the situation; he misjudged the situation because he formed his views light-headedly; and he hastily acted on his erroneous judgment because he failed to take international law seriously. His wrong choices must be ascribed to morally questionable attitudes. That more than half of those polled in Britain in 2004 declared him a liar cannot be said to have been undeserved.[35]

Once the monumental failure of the Iraqi adventure began to take shape, Blair desperately needed a catharsis. But he could not have one.

In 1980, after the abortive raid to rescue the American hostages in Iran, secretary of state Cyrus Vance had resigned in recognition of his responsibility for deceiving the allies of the US over the intentions of the Carter administration: when he told them that if they cooperated in imposing sanctions on Iran, the US would refrain from military action, the maneuver was already under preparation. Although his departure was understood as an acknowledgment that he had misled his negotiating partners, Vance could quit his office in dignity. This was because his resignation meant that he was distancing himself from the plan he had had to serve as a subordinate official reporting to the president. Such an interpretation was not open to Blair. Unlike Vance, he was the supreme decision-maker. He had to bear the ultimate responsibility for all the decisions of his government, including the decision to mislead the public about Saddam's weapons.

Like Blair, Willy Brandt was the supreme decision-maker when he failed to treat the East German intelligence agent with the necessary caution.[36] But his fault consisted in reckless inaction rather than in a deliberate action of dubious morality. So he, too, could assume responsibility for his "role in the spy affair" and quit in dignity. Had Blair resigned at some time in 2004, he would have left the political arena in disgrace. This in itself made the option of resignation unavailable to him.

The option of acknowledging responsibility for taking Britain to war under false pretences while staying in office was not available to him either because such an avowal would have undermined his position. He could not confess to being guilty of deceiving the public; such a concession would have been taken as an acknowledgment that he was responsible for each violent death in Iraq. He would have been confronted by ever new demands for an apology until he had no choice but to resign. Thus, Blair's only hope was that if he consistently denied culpability and kept the parliamentary Labour Party firmly under his grip, he might succeed in muddling through until the elected government of Iraq found itself in control or until his own name was linked to some other political decision that could offset the shame of the Iraqi failure. His political tragedy was that the situation in Iraq could not be brought under control, and no other political event could permanently displace it from the headlines. Blair's career came to be identified with Iraq for good.

Under his governments, power was devolved to Scotland and Wales, the decisive step was taken towards peace and consociational government in Northern Ireland, the European Convention of Human Rights was incorporated into the law of the United Kingdom, Britain received a Supreme Court, the transformation of the House of Lords into a democratically elected senate was decided, and a number of important reforms were initiated. But all these feats are overshadowed by the Iraqi disaster.[37]

Notes

1 J. L. Austin: "A Plea for Excuses." In Austin: *Philosophical Papers.* Oxford: Clarendon, 1961.

2 Where there is no wrongdoing, there is no reason to forgive. J. Murphy, 20.

3 In *Philosophy and Public Affairs* 2 (1973) 160–180.

4 Walzer himself calls it Neo-Classical. In this book, I reserve that term for a different use.

5 Ibid., 176.

6 Ibid., 177.

7 Ibid., 177 f.

8 Ibid., 179.

9 Ibid.

10 Ibid., 165.

11 Ibid., 179.

12 In an article about the Abu Ghraib scandal, Tony Judt described this phenomenon very vividly: "For this generation of political leaders—and followers—it has always been important to have the right sort of feelings and to display them. Thus (according to his spokesman) President Bush feels sorry for the "pain caused" by the pictures and reports of US soldiers torturing Iraqis. In Bush's words he feels "bad," "sorry for the humiliation" of Iraqi prisoners. He might not

say that he "feels their pain"—a more Clintonian sentiment—but it is the same idea. In a generation raised on the cult of self-improvement, you are a better man if you feel better about yourself: and saying "sorry" unquestionably makes you feel better. It also makes the victim feel better—so you score a triple: you are good, you do good and you feel good." See T. Judt: The Cult of Contrition. *The Independent*, May 9, 2004.

13 Walzer: "Dirty Hands," 179 f.

14 B. Williams: "Politics and moral character," in Williams: *Moral Luck*. Cambridge: The University Press, 1991, 62.

15 Ibid., 62 f.

16 They may disagree even against conclusive evidence because some may object to the right option in bad faith. But we do not need to make an assumption of bad-faith disagreement here. There is enough scope for good-faith disagreement in any political community.

17 This story is not completely fictitious. It is a stylized version of the true scandal provoked by the leakage to the press of the "I lied" speech made by Ferenc Gyurcsány, Prime Minister of Hungary in May 2006, at a closed session of the parliamentary group of the socialist party, in the wake of their electoral victory. See my articles "Pengeélen" (On the Knife's Edge), in *Élet és Irodalom*, October 6, 2006, and "Pengeélen–2" (On the Knife's Edge–2), in *Élet és Irodalom*, November 3, 2006.

18 Cambridge, Mass.: Harvard University Press, 1987.

19 Ibid., 11.

20 Ibid., 22.

21 Thompson is aware that in any political regime there is a subset of official decisions that must be kept secret in order to succeed. This requirement creates a special paradox: if secrecy is given up for the sake of democratic legitimacy, the government is incapacitated in its pursuit of the common good; if secrecy is maintained for the sake of pursuing the common good, democratic legitimacy is lost. State secrets regarding nuclear and other military technology, and other matters of national security are obvious examples. This is a domain where Thompson believes that the traditional problem of dirty hands persists even in a well-ordered democratic community. He makes fruitful and illuminating suggestions as to how a democratic community could limit the dangers from secrecy: overseeing the secret decisions by a proxy to the citizenry at large (by a parliamentary committee, for example), reviewing the secret decisions at a later date (subject to a time constraint that allows citizens to effectively sanction the decision), and setting in advance the general policy of which the decision is part (so as to subject it to strict standards that must be pursued in the course of secret decision-making and covert operations). See *Political Ethics*, 24. Because all such methods are imperfect, the problem of dirty hands cannot be completely solved—at least as long as the world remains politically divided into separate states and as the threat of non-

governmental terrorism stays with us. But at least it can be kept under control, or that is what Thompson intimates. And insofar as the remaining (and largest) part of the official decisions is concerned, the problem of dirty hands in its traditional form is—in principle—absent from a well-ordered democratic community.

22 The employee may have violated the organization's code of conduct that he had had the opportunity to learn.

23 See D. Parfit: *Reasons and Persons*. Oxford–New York: Oxford University Press, 1984, Ch. 3. For an application to collective action in political communities, see C. Kutz: "The Collective Work of Citizenship." In *Legal Theory* 8 (2002) 471–494.

24 Belonging may be a necessary but not a sufficient condition: someone who de facto belongs to a group, but is treated by it in violation of the requirement of equal concern and respect, may be released from his part in the collective responsibilities of the group. See R. Dworkin: *Law's Empire*. Cambridge, Mass.: Harvard University Press, 1986, 195–202.

25 B. Williams: *Shame and Necessity*. Berkeley–Los Angeles–Oxford: University of California Press, 1993, 82.

26 For the "Downing Street 10 Memo" see the May 1, 2005 issue of the *Sunday Times*.

27 See "The 45-minute Case Collapses I" by Andy McSmith, in *The Independent*, February 8, 2004, and "The 45-minute Case Collapses II" by R. Whitaker and K. Sengupta, in *The Independent*, February 8, 2004.

28 Just one example: the September 17 version says that the Iraqi armed forces "may be able to deploy chemical or biological weapons within 45 minutes of an order to do so." The final version of September 24 says that they "...are able to deploy chemical or biological weapons within 45 minutes of an order to do so." Hutton Report, 153. The second version could hardly be said to be compatible with what the intelligence service claimed to know. "May be able..." means that "They may, but not certainly, be able...", while "...are able to" means that "They are certainly able to...." The so-called Butler report lists such stylistic changes through several pages, complete with tables. See Butler Report, 81, 82–86.

29 A. Grice: "The Legacy: Tony Blair Prime Minister 1997–2007." In *The Independent*, May 11, 2007.

30 "A Vote of Confidence." In *The Economist*, April 9, 2005.

31 For Manning's statement, see A. Rawnsley: "Iraq Is Not Just Blair's Dark Legacy: It Defines the Future." In *The Observer,* June 17, 2007.

32 See the *Kosovo Report* by the Independent International Commission on Kosovo. Oxford: The University Press, 2000.

33 One condition failed to obtain fully. It is not clear that the peaceful means to prevent ethnic cleansing were exhausted by the time the war started. Shortly before that date, negotiations were held in Paris between the representatives of the

Yugoslav government and of the international task force that was supposed to deal with the Kosovo crisis. At the Paris talks, the Yugoslav delegation was given an ultimatum including harsh conditions that they could be expected to reject (to allow NATO troops to occupy positions within Serbia in order to secure access to Kosovo, among others). Defenders of the Yugoslav position cite this as evidence that the Western powers sought the talks as a pretext to go to war, rather than as an opportunity to avoid war. On the other hand, as the Paris talks started, the military preparations for ethnic cleansing in Kosovo were completed, and the first steps towards expelling the Kosovar Albanians had been taken.

34 He has never publicly recognized that he had taken Britain into an unlawful war. On March 7, 2003, his Attorney General submitted a legal opinion in which he voiced some doubts as to the legality of the invasion. Blair did not let even members of his cabinet read the document. See C. Short: "How Ministers Were Misled on the Legality of Iraq Invasion," in *The Independent,* May 5, 2005. In Lord Goldsmith's speech before the House of Commons on March 17, there was no reference to his doubts. Something had happened to him in those ten days, and that, we may safely assume, was Tony Blair's insistence that he should stand by the legality of the war without equivocation. See A. Grice: "A Controversy that Still Damages Blair", in *The Independent,* May 5, 2005. This was a second case where the Prime Minister pushed his administration into misleading the public.

35 P. Waugh: "After Hutton the Verdict: 51 Per Cent Say Blair Should Go," in *The Independent,* February 7, 2004.

36 See Section 7.6.

37 In a poll carried out a week before Blair announced his departure, 69 per cent of the respondents said that he would be remembered most for the Iraq war; only 6 per cent mentioned the Northern Ireland peace process, 3 per cent the introduction of a national minimum wage, and 2 per cent the improvement of the public services. See Andrew Grice: "Blair's bloody legacy: Iraq." *The Independent,* May 1, 2007.

CHAPTER NINE

DIRTY HANDS AND MORAL DILEMMAS

9.1 Moral dilemmas: the tragic account

Machiavelli insists that in order to be able to promote the good, the good prince must learn how not to be good. A plain reading of this assertion, advocated by Johann Gottlieb Fichte, for example, seems to dissolve the paradox inherent in it. According to Fichte, an act that *seems* to be vicious (because it would be vicious if it were committed in the domain of private life) is not *in fact* vicious when it is performed (in the domain of politics) by a prince out of necessity and in the service of the common good (see Chapter Three, 3.3). We have seen, however, that the Fichtean reading cannot accommodate all the relevant passages from Machiavelli. There are strong statements in *The Prince* to the effect that a political act may be morally permissible without ceasing to be objectionable. If this is Machiavelli's last word on the matter, or if we have to acknowledge this view to be true, whether or not Machiavelli held it, then the paradox remains with us. This chapter will be dedicated to the question how, if we disown the Fichtean reading, we could nevertheless resolve the paradox.

I will discuss the paradox as one of general moral theory and not solely of the ethics of political leadership. Even though the phenomenon of acting with dirty hands was originally discovered in the context of political thought, any agent in any walk of life may be confronted with situations where the act he has most reason to perform makes his hands dirty.[1] Doing the right thing means doing something in a morally acceptable manner; getting one's hands dirty means doing something in a manner that is morally unacceptable. To maintain that an act is both right and dirty-handed seems to involve logical inconsistency. Thus sounds the paradox of dirty hands generalized.

Those who believe that an act may be right and dirty-handed at the same time, habitually discuss the problem of dirty hands as a side-product of moral dilemmas.[2] At first sight, this seems to be a promising approach. After all, an act that is both dirty-handed and right is chosen at the cross-roads of conflicting moral claims. It appears as morally acceptable in the light of one of those claims and as unacceptable in the light of the other. Since it violates at least one moral standard, it apparently ought not to be carried out. Why do we think it to be permissible nevertheless? Suppose the situation in which it is chosen is one of a moral dilemma. Then we have a clear answer. It is permissible because the alternatives are no less objectionable.

This answer suggests a workable strategy. We should seek the answer to the question how acting with dirty hands can be morally acceptable and morally unacceptable at the same time as an aspect of the answer to the other question how moral dilemmas are possible. Sections 1–3 will follow this strategy.

A choice situation is called a moral dilemma if it confronts the chooser with a conflict of moral reasons and if all available courses of action are morally unacceptable. Here is an example borrowed by moral philosophers from William Styron's novel, *Sophie's choice*:

> Sophie is deported to Auschwitz with her son and daughter. At the gate of the camp, a physician wearing the uniform of the SS (I will call him Dr. Mengele) divides the new arrivals into two groups. Those condemned to go immediately to the gas chambers are directed to the left, while those considered fit for labor are sent to the right. All the minors are put in the group on the left. When she reaches Dr. Mengele, Sophie hastens to say, "We are not Jews. I am a devout Catholic." "Alright, the physician answers, tell me which of your children should be taken away, and you can keep the other one."[3]

The offer is of utmost cruelty. If Sophie turns it down, she will abandon both children to certain death at the hands of the Nazis. If she accepts it, it will be she who pronounces the death sentence on one of the children. In other words, Sophie is confronted with a choice between *allowing* both children to be murdered and saving one of them at the cost of *betraying* the other.[4]

The choice leaves no room for a morally acceptable third option. Nor is there a way for Sophie to avoid it. Once the proposal is made by Dr. Mengele, Sophie has to choose.

Sophie bears no responsibility for having to choose between two morally unacceptable options, and her choice is constrained by the mortal threat to her two children. She takes her decision under extreme duress, and when the question of blame is raised, this fact counts as a fully exculpating circumstance. Nevertheless, it does not transform the choice into a non-intentional behavioral reaction, nor does it remove the burden from Sophie. It is still a choice, and it is *her* choice. It is *she* who makes the choice between abandoning both children and betraying one of them. If this were not the case, Dr. Mengele would not make the offer. He wants both Jewish children to die. But he wants even more to make the Jewish mother do what no decent mother would do on her own. He wants to enjoy the power not only to kill defenseless members of the hated race, but to force them to form and execute perverted intentions. Sophie is in the grip of a moral monster who is not satisfied with causing harm to her from the outside, but whose aim is to destroy her personal integrity from within. It is this wicked aim that invests the proposal with a meaning. It would not make sense to offer Sophie a choice if that choice were not genuine, or if Sophie could decline it.

But the choice is genuine, and a fairly complex one at that. It takes place in two steps. In the first step, Sophie has to decide whether to accept the offer at all. Her initial reaction is to refuse it.[5] She does not change her mind until Dr. Mengele tells her that, in that case, both children will die. Now the exchange proceeds with lightning speed, not leaving Sophie a second for reflection. She immediately exclaims: "Take her!" and pushes her daughter away at the same moment. The moment she decides to take the offer, Sophie also decides to betray her daughter in order to save her son. The two decisions seem almost simultaneous, but they are actually separate. We will return to the distinction between them later on.

Let us generalize Sophie's choice. I will call the person in Sophie's position—the subject of the dilemma—S. I will call the alternatives open to S (abandoning both children or betraying one of them, for example) a and b.[6] The choice between a and b is a moral dilemma if both choosing a and choosing b is in some sense morally objectionable. Traditionally, moral dilemmas are interpreted as conflicts of duties. In the conflicts-of-duties interpretation the morally objectionable nature of an alternative consists in entailing a breach of duty. But the vocabulary of moral requirements is much richer than that of duties, and moral dilemmas are not restricted to conflicts between duties.[7] For the sake of generality, I will rather talk about conflicts of moral "oughts": faced with a moral dilemma, S ought to do a, and S ought to do b.

Suppose that it is possible for S to adopt each of the two alternatives separately, but not to adopt them together. Thus, S can do a at the cost of not doing b, or b at the cost of not doing a, but not a and b at the same time. If S were either capable of doing a and b together, or incapable of doing a or b even separately, there would be no moral dilemma. For a dilemma to exist, it must be the case that

A1: S ought to do a, and S ought to do b;
A2: S can satisfy each of the two oughts separately, but
A3: S cannot satisfy both oughts together.[8]

Assumptions 1–3 define what we call a moral conflict. Not all moral conflicts are moral dilemmas in the sense that Sophie's choice situation is a moral dilemma. Dr. Mengele's offer to Sophie is such that no matter what she chooses, her action will be morally objectionable. Assumptions 1–3 in themselves do not entail that consequence.

This may suggest that moral dilemmas are such moral conflicts where the incompatible oughts are of the same stringency:

A4^{TR}: Neither "S ought to do a" overrides "S ought to do b" nor "S ought to do b" overrides "S ought to do a." Both oughts emerge from their encounter undefeated.[9]

Suppose that this is indeed the case. Then both oughts express a valid, in-force requirement. This brings us to the characterization of A1–A4 as being a moral dilemma in the following sense: A1–A4^{TR} jointly imply that whichever ought S chooses to disregard, she will violate a valid, in-force moral requirement.

Violating a valid moral requirement amounts to being guilty of a wrong. If the implication is correct, an agent involved in a moral conflict characterized by A1–A4 cannot do anything that would not be morally objectionable.

There is a further implication in A1–A4^{TR}. If these assumptions are sufficient to give rise to the implication that no matter what S

may do, it will be morally unacceptable, then the theory of moral dilemmas is complete: no further premise is needed. The irrelevance of any additional premises is an important consequence. At least some dilemmas are avoidable, that is, they emerge upon S having taken a prior choice between doing something that confronts her with a moral dilemma and refraining from doing it. Some other dilemmas seem to be inescapable: S becomes involved in them, whether or not she makes efforts to avoid this outcome. We may ask whether inescapable dilemmas are really possible. If A1–A4^{TR} are sufficient for a moral conflict to be a moral dilemma, then the answer is yes, because these premises do not include any condition that the subject of the dilemma must be responsible for being caught up in the dilemmatic situation.

The possibility of inescapable dilemmas makes the theory outlined here deeply troubling. Confronted by a moral dilemma, S cannot act but culpably, according to that theory. If no moral dilemma could emerge without a prior choice made by S between doing something that predictably would implicate her in a dilemmatic situation and not doing it, there would be nothing fateful in S's being confronted by equally culpable alternatives. Once facing the dilemma, S cannot but violate a valid, in-force ought, according to the theory outlined above. But she had the option of not violating any. If S violates one, the violation can be blamed on her earlier decision that was responsible for her involvement in the dilemmatic situation.

A1–A4^{TR}, however, allow for moral dilemmas that may impose themselves on the agent, no matter what she may do. If they are conflicts of valid oughts that can be satisfied separately but not together, and if they can be inescapable, then there is something tragic about them.

I will therefore call the theory of moral dilemmas based on A1–A4^{TR} the *tragic account*. It has robust implications:

I1^{TR}: Whichever ought S should choose to disregard, S violates a valid, in-force ought;

I2^{TR}: the situation described by A1–A4^{TR} is such that S may become involved in it innocently,

I3^{TR}: once in it, however, S has no chance of coming out of it innocently (a direct consequence of I1).[10]

If, however, we act culpably, then it is appropriate for us to feel guilty about what we are doing. Therefore

14[TR]: It will be appropriate for S to feel guilty about what she does.

The tragic view, to my knowledge, was first formulated by the young György Lukács, in early 1919. "There are situations—tragic situations—in which it is impossible not to commit a sin," he wrote in an essay dedicated to the problem of revolutionary violence.[11] Decades later Bernard Williams made a very similar claim: "In another, and more drastic, case..., which might be called the 'tragic' kind, an agent can justifiably think that whatever he does will be wrong."[12]

In what way are the tragic cases of moral conflict (the moral dilemmas) "more drastic" than the usual cases? One tends to think, with Joseph Raz, that their "drastic" nature consists "in the destruction they bring to the agent's own life."[13]

A moral dilemma may indeed involve disastrous consequences for its subject. Some dilemmas—like Sophie's choice—carry existential weight, threatening to undermine the very integrity of the person involved in them. Some others that meet the structural criteria of a "tragic choice" are less weighty or consequential, however. The tragic view identifies a moral dilemma as a conflict between two or more valid, in-force oughts; this definition says nothing about the weights of the conflicting requirements. A conflict between relatively weak oughts (between two trivial promises, for example)[14] would pass its test. Confronted by such a choice, S may feel in a quandary, and no matter what the choice should be in the end, she may feel remorse—but the quandary is not of existential dimensions, nor does the feeling of remorse threaten S's integrity.

But the idea of the tragic has a further aspect. Tragedies are, on the one hand, driven towards their fatal ending by some character trait of the tragic hero; it is Oedipus's determination to know the truth that brings about his fall, for example. On the other hand, greater forces than the hero himself are at work in a tragedy. Oedipus was predestined by Fate to commit the horrendous acts of killing Laios, his father, and marrying Iocasta, his mother. He was not a mere tool in the hands of Fate: both killing his father and marrying his mother were his own intentional acts. So even an observer who does not share the world view of ancient Greek mythology may agree that when the truth is finally revealed to him, Oedipus has good reason to feel that *he* ruined his own life. After all, it was he who had done these horrendous things. But we would not blame him for what he did in full ignorance of Fate's master plan. Although the act of killing his father was his intentional act, and so was the one of marrying his mother, he did not act with the intention of killing his father and marrying his mother. "Fear and pity" are the proper reactions to his tragedy, not contempt or indignation.[15]

It is not Sophie's fault that she and her children are forced into a freight car and taken to Auschwitz. It is not her fault that Dr. Mengele makes her a monstrous offer. But if the tragic account is correct, then no matter how Sophie should respond to that offer, her decision makes her culpable. She is damned if she accepts the offer, and she is damned if she does not.[16]

This second aspect of the tragic applies to all moral dilemmas, not only to those with a destructive potential. If it is true that no matter what S should do, her act violates a valid, in-force ought then S's act will be wrong, or culpable, or guilty, or sinful. And if S may become involved in a dilemma without having the option of avoiding it, then a moral dilemma is a choice situation that the agent may enter but cannot leave innocently.

This result threatens to undermine the ordinary view of the relationship between blame and responsibility. According to the ordinary view, one is not liable to blame for doing something morally reprehensible if one had no option to do something less morally reprehensible. No charge of fault, guilt or culpability can be legitimately made in such cases. We agree that the choice was Sophie's, we also agree that she has good reasons to feel ruined and that she would have felt ruined even if she had refused the offer. But we are disinclined to blame her for what she has chosen in the cruel grip of Dr. Mengele's master plan. The tragic account is troubling precisely because if it is correct, Sophie is liable to blame. If the tragic account is true, she is liable to blame, even if she had no option to act in a blameless manner.

This consequence is closely related to how, if the correct theory of moral dilemmas is the tragic one, that theory deals with the problem of dirty hands.

According to the tragic account, a person involved in a moral dilemma has to choose between disregarding at least one of two (or more) valid, in-force oughts. Acting in contravention of a valid, in-force ought however, means doing something wrong, or being at fault, or acting culpably, or committing a sin or a crime. Thus, according to this account, a person involved in a moral dilemma must choose between two (or more) wrongs, between two (or more) ways of being at fault, acting culpably, committing a sin or a crime. If she chooses well, the wrong resulting from her choice is at least no greater than the wrongs that would have resulted from any other choice open to her. Therefore, the act will be right or justified. But it will be wrong, guilty, culpable or sinful at the same time, since it will violate a valid, in-force ought. This is, then, what is meant by the metaphor of the agent acting with dirty hands, even if in a justifiable manner.

There are in fact quite a few philosophers who seem to describe the phenomenon of dirty hands in such terms.[17] Their description is simple and elegant. But its adequacy hinges on the adequacy of the theory of moral dilemmas it relies on and on the adequacy of the claim that dirty hands are a side-product of moral dilemmas. In the remaining paragraphs of this section, I will present an argument to the effect that the theory in question is defective.

A1–A4^{TR} are compatible premises. Combined, they do not imply mutually excluding statements. But if we add a sound principle of moral responsibility attribution, the theory becomes inconsistent. I have the 'ought implies can' principle in mind:

OC: If S cannot do a, then it is not the case that S ought to do a.

I1^{TR} and OC jointly imply that S must be capable of doing b. However, A3 entails that if S does a, she is not capable of doing b. Suppose that S ought to do b even if she does a. Then, in virtue of OC, S can do b. In virtue of A3, however, S cannot do b. Therefore, S both can and cannot do b.

In sum, A1–A4^{TR}, I1^{TR}, and OC together lead to the conclusion that S both can and cannot do a (or b). Either A1–A4^{TR}, or I1^{TR}, or OC must go.

Some philosophers deny the plausibility of A1–A4^{TR} or, more precisely, that of A1–A3; they deny the existence of moral conflicts. Richard Hare, for example, insists that, properly understood, no two moral requirements conflict with each other. In our ordinary lives we encounter moral principles in the form of moral rules. An act is right if it complies with the rules that apply to it. Hare proposes to call the relevant rules F and G. According to F, we ought never to commit an act if it is f (e.g. breaking a promise), while according to G we ought never to commit an act if it is g (e.g. lying). There comes a day when we cannot satisfy F and G together. We have to establish which of the two rules has priority over the other. Suppose that we do less harm by avoiding f than by avoiding g. If so, then we ought to do g under the circumstances. This conclusion, however, transforms rule G into rule G^*. It no longer holds that we ought never to do g, but that we ought never to do g except when doing g is the only way to avoid doing f. In sum, the solution of the conflict shows that the requirement G failed to apply in the first place: G^* is a better approximation to the correct rule, and there is no conflict between G^* and F.[18]

If this is the proper solution of the inconsistency, the tragic account collapses. Moreover, the very idea of a moral dilemma is revealed to be empty. Since the concept of moral dilemmas is predicated on the concept of moral conflicts, Hare's analysis concludes in the finding that there is no such a thing as a moral dilemma.

But this eliminative analysis of moral conflicts has serious weaknesses. In Sophie's case, suppose that f stands for allowing both children to be murdered and g for betraying one of them. And suppose that Sophie correctly judges that not doing f has priority over not doing g. Following Hare's argument, G (the rule according to which parents ought not to betray their children) is transformed for her into G^*, a rule according to which parents ought not to betray their children except when betraying one child is necessary to save at least the life of the other. But, then, how to account for our intuition that betraying one's child is morally reprehensible under all circumstances, including those of S's choice? Or should we revise that intuition? Hare's analysis seems to be defective as a general (eliminative) account of moral conflicts.[19]

This leaves us with a choice between I1[TR] and OC. Some insist that OC should be discarded.[20] But OC is inextricably interwoven with the practices and beliefs of our ordinary morality, at least as it has developed since the Enlightenment. It has pride of place in the shaping of our conceptions of moral responsibility and blame.

Moral dilemmas may appear to provide some support for the rejectionist stance. We tend to feel that persons involved in a moral dilemma are in a situation similar to that of Oedipus, in that they are unable to avoid making themselves *culpable*.

However, the *feeling* that, confronted with Dr. Mengele's offer, Sophie can only act culpably is no evidence that she does *in fact* act culpably. "Human beings are not so finely tuned emotionally," Terrance McConnell writes, "that when they have been *causally* responsible for harm, they can easily turn remorse on or off depending on their degree of *moral* responsibility."[21] In other words, the feeling that Sophie is acting culpably may be due to the low degree of emotional discrimination of which we are capable, and not to the allegedly culpable nature of her action. To appeal to the way we tend to experience moral dilemmas is to beg the question, because our experience is subject to interpretation, and the tragic interpretation entails already what it purports to justify.

There is, perhaps, a better argument. Our ordinary moral judgments sometimes condemn dispositions, attitudes, and conduct that are not under the control of the agent. As Robert M. Adams notes in a celebrated paper, "many involuntary states of mind are objects of ethical appraisal and censure in their own right."[22] We disapprove of the violent outbursts of a person, for example, even if we agree that they just happen and that no matter how hard she may try, she cannot bring her outbursts of rage under voluntary control. If so, we have no reason to stick to the 'ought implies can' principle. It may be replaced by a distinction between 'possible oughts' and 'impossible oughts'.[23]

I, for one, doubt that such observations undermine OC. In his article, Adams makes a distinction between the "ethics of acts" and the "ethics of states of mind." He claims that his argument refers to the second domain, not the first. Suppose, however, that it lends itself to an extension to the province of action. It does not immediately imply that there is such a thing as an impossible ought to act in a certain way. Let S do a, and let doing a be an object of ethical appraisal and censure. This is quite possible even when it is not the case that S acts culpably or that S ought not to do what she does. S may be blameless, for example, because of a lack of capacity for responsible action, or because of a lack of physical capacity to avoid doing the particular harm she does. Alternatively, S may be blameless because, although she could do something other than she does, none of the alternatives open to her are morally better than the one she chooses to carry out. S

may do something that, all things considered, is no worse than any of the alternatives open to her, and yet doing it may be morally reprehensible. The finding that an act may be both right and reprehensible at the same time is no argument, in itself, against OC.

If A1–A3 and OC remain, then I1^{TR} must go. A1–A3 and OC together imply that all things considered, S ought to carry out only one of the two acts: either a but not b, or b but not a.[24]

Once OC is incorporated in the theory, the claim that two conflicting oughts are simultaneously undefeated can no longer serve the tragic account. It does not follow that whatever S may choose she will violate a valid moral requirement. All things considered, S ought to do only one of the mutually excluding things. It is not the case that she ought to do, all things considered, the other thing. It is permissible for her to adopt either of the conflicting and undefeated options and to disregard the other, once she has made her choice. The conflict of two undefeated oughts does not involve any threat that S will become guilty, whichever ought she should decide to act upon.

If the condition for a moral conflict to be a moral dilemma is that regardless of which option the agent takes, she must violate a valid, in-force ought, then there cannot be any genuine moral dilemmas at all.[25]

9.2 The moral doubts account

Many philosophers claim that the idea of moral dilemmas must be abandoned, for it relies on an incoherent concept of a conflict between valid oughts. There are choice situations that *appear* to their subject as moral dilemmas, but are not *genuinely* so.

Those who insist that there are no genuine moral dilemmas must say something about their appearance. The belief that situations with a similar structure to that of Sophie's choice are moral dilemmas is deeply embedded in ordinary moral life. Nevertheless, one may adopt a radically revisionist stance and engage in the criticism of the idea of moral dilemmas as a means of therapy: once we realize that our typical attitudes and emotional reactions to a supposed moral dilemma rest on misperception, we shall see that these attitudes and emotional reactions should be discarded. I will call this the *therapeutic stance*.

The therapeutic stance is open to the same criticism as any theory of morality that proposes a radical revision of ordinary moral beliefs: it is unclear in what sense it may offer a theory *of morality* at all. Moral theory is supposed to take ordinary morality as its starting point so as to make sense of its principles, rules, and practices. In so doing it may depart from ordinary moral beliefs to some degree: it may propose determinate solutions to hard cases or a critique of some of the attitudes or rules or practices characteristic of ordinary morality. However, if it rejects too much of what it is supposed to account for, it cannot claim to be a successful account.

Most critics of the idea of moral dilemmas refrain from adopting the therapeutic stance. They take it for granted that a decent moral person would be reluctant to adopt any of the courses of action open in a situation that seems to be a moral dilemma and that, having adopted one, would feel a moral distress. They also tend to agree that it is not merely a psychological weakness on our part to resist the invitation to change our attitude towards apparent moral dilemmas. On the contrary, we expect each other not to change it. We would not blame Sophie for her choice and we would pity her for the despair and remorse to which she is liable, but if we discovered her to be free of any pangs of conscience we would think of her as a diminished person, and most critics of the idea of moral dilemmas agree with this judgment.

Richard Hare says, for example:

A man with good moral principles will very likely *feel* guilty whatever he does in [such] cases... If he did not, he would not be such a good man. For a person, on the other hand, who is mainly concerned with avoiding feelings of guilt, the best advice is to grow a thick skin. (...) Though (...) it is incoherent to suggest that one might 'sacrifice one's moral integrity justifiably, in the service of a sufficiently worthy end', it is not incoherent to suggest that one might so sacrifice one's peace of mind. And moral integrity and peace of mind are easily confused if one equates having sinned with having a sense of having sinned.[26]

So the appearance of moral dilemmas must not be explained away; rather, the explanation must show how clinging to the belief in their existence may make moral sense, and why someone who rejects that illusion and sheds the emotions corresponding to it "would not be such a good man."

Here is a typical account of this kind. Situations that appear to be moral dilemmas present the agent with an unusually hard choice between two or more oughts. All these oughts apply to the situation, and failing to act on all of them has weighty consequences, but the agent is uncertain about which ought should be attributed greater weight, either because he cannot precisely foresee the consequences of the alternative courses of action, or because the competing oughts do not lend themselves to non-ambiguous comparison as to their stringency. But the uncertainty about which alternative is the right one to adopt does not mean that none is. On the contrary, the deliberation on the conflicting alternatives rests on a conviction that there *are* better and worse choices and that it is the chooser's utmost responsibility to adopt the right one. The problem is that she can never be sure that the attempt has succeeded. If she adopts a wrong option, the chosen act will violate a valid, in-force ought.

There is, then, a right choice and a person who adopts it will not make herself guilty, culpable, or sinful. Thus, the situation is not a genuine dilemma. But the chooser can never be sure whether her choice is, indeed, blameless. The situation *appears* to be dilemmatic, and for good reason.

This explanation shows, too, why clinging to the illusion of the dilemma makes one a morally better person: for someone who is scared by the possibility that she may be acting against a valid, in-force ought is likely to do whatever is in her power to follow the right course of action.[27]

On this account, the moral emotions that respond to an apparent moral dilemma should be understood as expressing the agent's doubts about whether she has succeeded in avoiding acting culpably. Such doubts are painful enough in themselves, but human beings are not so finely tuned emotionally as to be able to distinguish them from emotions that respond to the certainty of having acted culpably.[28] In other words, a sense of doubt easily shades into a sense of guilt. This is a good thing, because "it may make agents more cautious about their actions and more sensitive about their responsibilities."[29]

I propose to call this the *moral doubts account*. Like the tragic account, it includes A1–A3. Unlike the tragic account, it affirms OC. Furthermore, it replaces A4^{TR} with the following assumption:

A4^{MD}: S is uncertain whether the requirement to do a overrides the requirement to do b, or whether the requirement to do b overrides the requirement to do a, or else whether both requirements are non-overridden.

A1–A3 and OC jointly ensure that the main implications of the tragic account are false. I1^{TR} is false because if S permissibly does a, then it is not the case that S ought to do b and, thus, by doing a while not doing b, S does not violate any valid, in-force ought. Therefore, although it remains true, as I2^{TR} affirms, that S may become innocently involved in situations described by A1–A3, I3^{TR} is false because it is not true that once in such a situation, S has no chance to act innocently (if S permissibly does a, then she does not act culpably by not doing b). Therefore, I4^{TR} is false because it is not true that no matter what S may do, it is appropriate for her to feel guilty about what she does.

On the other hand, A1–3 and A4^{MD} jointly involve

I1^{MD}: Even if S should permissibly do a (or b), it may be appropriate for her to be haunted by doubts as to whether doing a (or b) was not wrong after all.

The uncertainty described by A4^{MD} and the doubts reported by I1^{MD} are properties of the agent's beliefs. The situation appears to S as a moral dilemma. But the premises do not entail any support for the claim that it is a moral dilemma independent of S's state of mind. A1–A3 describe a mere moral conflict, while A4^{MD} reports about S's state of mind rather than about the state of the world. If the moral doubts account is correct, one can safely maintain that, indeed, moral dilemmas are nothing but appearances. Situations that appear to be dilemmatic confront the agent with serious moral troubles. But those troubles are due to epistemic limitations of the human mind: insufficiency of information and bounded rationality, not to the objective features of the moral situation.

The moral doubts account suggests that we interpret the phenomenon of dirty hands in terms of the unavoidable doubts that accompany the appearance of moral dilemmas. Suppose that S believes that she ought to do a and, that, she ought to do b at the same time. Suppose, furthermore, that S believes that the two oughts cannot be satisfied together. And she comes to the conclusion that, all things considered, *a* ought to be done and so it is not the case that *b* ought to be done. But *S* is at the same time assailed by doubts as to whether it is really *a* that should be done, or whether, if she had done *b*, it would not have been possible to satisfy the requirement to do *a* at the same time. If so, doing *a* appears to *S* as a morally doubtful and possibly wrong choice.

The moral doubts account rightly insists that uncertainty and doubt are important features of situations that appear to be moral dilemmas. But they accompany other situations as well. What is specific about the uncertainty and doubt characteristic of situations that appear to the agents as moral dilemmas is that they are parasitic on the judgment that the option which appears to be best is *awful* at the same time. The source of the doubts whether this was indeed the right thing to do is typically despair about having done it, and fear that it may have been done without justification.

Moreover, while the feeling of doubt is nourished by despair, the feeling of despair does not need any doubt to take hold of the agent. The feeling of doubt is dependent on the fear that there may have been *a better alternative* than this terrible one. The feeling of despair hinges on the chosen alternative being terrible *in itself*.[30]

Sophie may be certain that she had no better course of action than that which she actually took, and yet she may be horrified and desperate about having taken it. As Bernard Williams beautifully puts it with regard to Agamemnon's choice between sacrificing the Greek expedition against Troy and sacrificing his daughter Iphigenia: Having killed his daughter, Agamemnon has sleepless nights, yet "he lies awake, not because of a doubt, but because of a certainty."[31]

The moral doubt view fails to account for the rich phenomenology of moral dilemmas, and its failure is a source of theoretical instability. An adequate theory either dismisses all the significant phenomena characteristic of the experience that we tend to identify as moral dilemmas, or it explains them all. The moral doubt view is either pulled towards radicalizing its stance in the direction of therapy, or it is pushed towards acknowledging that moral dilemmas exist independently of the state of mind of the persons involved in them.

9.3 The tragic account revisited: moral residues

Since the therapeutic stance is not a tenable option, we are left with the option of trying to salvage the idea of the reality, as against the mere appearance, of moral dilemmas.

That attempt may take the direction of revising the tragic account so that it accommodates the 'ought implies can' principle. Bernard Williams explored this possibility in two pieces from the 1970s, "Ethical Consistency" and "Moral Conflict." In this section I will try to show why the revision of the tragic account fails. The following two sections will outline an alternative account.

"[N]o agent, conscious of the situation of conflict, in fact thinks that he ought to do *both* of the things," Williams acknowledges. "What he thinks is that he ought to do *each* of them."[32] "If I do *b*, it will then not be correct to say that I ought (then) to do *a*,"[33] he adds, noting that this is what logical consistency requires. But, so his argument continues, the dilemma remains, because even though it is true that if I do *b*, then I do not have to do *a* at the same time, "it does not follow from this that I cannot correctly say then that I ought to have done *a*; nor yet that I was wrong in thinking earlier that *a* was something I ought to do."[34] That I am now morally permitted not to do *a* does not entail that the requirement to do *a* was a mere illusion before I made my choice. And if it was not, then it does not become an illusion even if I can permissibly disregard it. In some sense it remains in force, we have only to establish in what sense.

A defeated ought is not a merely apparent ought, Williams argues. "[T]he *prima facie* obligations are not just *seeming* obligations, but more in the nature of a claim, which can generate residual obligations if not fulfilled."[35] A defeated ought still applies to the situation and exerts some moral force. This is the nerve of the argument of "Ethical Consistency."

"Conflict of Values" has more to say about the residual obligations in question:

> The evident fact that there is at most one of the two things which, all things considered, I should do, is taken to be equivalent to the idea that, all things considered, there is only one obligation. But this is a mistake. There are certainly two obligations in a real case of this kind, though one may outweigh the other. The one that

outweighs has greater stringency, but the one that is outweighed
also possesses stringency, and this is expressed in what, *by way of
compensation*, I may have to do for the parties who are disadvantaged by its being outweighed, whether I have merely to explain
and apologize, or whether I have to engage further in some more
substantial *reparatory action*.[36]

In sum, according to Williams, even if S is not supposed to satisfy
a defeated ought, the ought that S disregards in a permissible manner
leaves some moral residue behind, and that residue takes the form of a
requirement to do some reparatory action or at least to provide the
victim with an explanation and apology. The defeated ought has no
action-guiding force in the immediate context of the situation in
which the choice is being made, but it has action-guiding force in the
context of a later situation that emerges in virtue of S's action. It is in
this sense that an ought that was a valid one before its confrontation
with a conflicting ought remains, even if defeated, a valid, in-force
ought. We may call this the moral residue version of the tragic account or, briefly, the *moral residue account*.

If the idea of a moral residue works, the tragic view no longer depends on $A4^{TR}$ for its truth. To remind, $A4^{TR}$ holds that neither "S
ought to do a" overrides "S ought to do b" nor "S ought to do b" overrides "S ought to do a": both oughts survive their encounter undefeated. If this is understood to entail that by doing a and, therefore,
not doing b S violates a valid, in-force requirement (that of doing b),
then the tragic account is established. However, as we have seen, $A4^{TR}$
does not entail this consequence. The claim of moral residue seems to
entail it, but on the other hand, that claim does not presuppose $A4^{TR}$.
It is compatible with the original ought being defeated either because
the rival ought is more stringent or because the agent chooses to satisfy the rival ought that is no less stringent than the disregarded ought.
But the defeated ought leaves a derivative ought behind, and *that*
ought embodies a valid, in-force moral requirement.

Williams's suggestion allows the tragic view to be generalized. The
moral residue account is not in need of the assumption of equal stringency on the part of the conflicting oughts. Although the ought S fails
to satisfy may be non-ambiguously defeated, her failure to satisfy it
may harm some other person, and this, then, may call for compensation and/or apology.

The idea of a moral residue needs further elaboration, though. If, in a conflict of oughts, the right choice may involve some residual obligation, then the choice is more complex than it originally appeared to be. We assumed that S had to choose between doing a and doing b. But now we see that there is a follow-up to that choice, which S must consider in making up her mind. Suppose that if S does a at t_1, she will be confronted by a requirement to do c_b at t_2 (where c_b represents compensating the victim for the harm from S's failure to do b), and if S does b at t_1, she will be confronted by a requirement to do c_a at t_2 (where c_a represents compensating the victim for the harm from S's failure to do a). If so, the requirement of doing a and that of doing b will sound like this: "Do a at t_1 or, if you justifiably fail to do a at t_1, then do c_a in compensation at t_2," and "Do b at t_1 or, if you justifiably fail to do b at t_1, do c_b in compensation at t_2," respectively. The idea of a moral residue implies that when making the choice between doing a and doing b, S is expected not to look at this alternative in isolation from its follow-up. Clearly, it matters for her decision whether carrying out the requisite compensatory action is included in the set of feasible alternatives. Suppose, for example, that the requirements of doing a and doing b are of equal stringency, and S correctly thinks that she will be able to do c_a but not c_b. This consideration tips the balance in favor of doing b rather than a. If the moral residue is a reason for action that S has to weigh in the overall balance of her reasons, then her deliberation must not narrowly focus on the conflict between doing a and doing b at t_1. Rather, it must be extended to the alternative scenarios that include the immediate choice together with the tree of its follow-ups.

However, by hypothesis, c_a and c_b stand for what can fairly be claimed for the victim by way of compensation. If S does either a and c_b, or b and c_a, the victim will have no further claim against her. The moral residue evaporates together with the disregarded ought. The right choice does not leave any lasting moral residue behind, provided that S abides by all the implications of that choice. No valid, in-force ought is violated.

But suppose that S has most reason to do a, although doing a is not morally acceptable unless S also does c_b, and suppose that c_b is not feasible. If S does what she has most reason to do, then her act will inflict some *irreparable* harm on its victim. Sophie betrays her daughter, and her choice cannot be made morally acceptable unless the girl is emotionally compensated for the damage of parental rejection. But Sophie betrays her by sending her to her death. The daughter is murdered by the Nazis; she is not there to receive emotional compensation. The damage done by the betrayal is not reparable.

Suppose that Sophie's daughter miraculously survives Auschwitz and is reunited with her mother. Even then she may never recover from the trauma of being betrayed by the person on whom she depended emotionally. No matter how much maternal love and care is extended to her, the girl may remain a living corpse. There are, thus, many ways in which the harm from acting in a moral dilemma may be irreparable. And whenever it is, the moral residue cannot be eliminated. If it cannot be eliminated, however, then even if S should take the right choice, she seems to be doomed to violate a valid, in-force ought. The choices that lend themselves to such a characterization may be those with regard to which the moral residue account makes the tragic conception true.

We are now in a position to flesh out the moral residue account. A1–A3 and OC remain in force. $A4^{TR}$ drops out: the theory does not need the assumption that the dilemma is of a balanced shape. $A4^{MD}$ (stating S's uncertainty about the rightness or wrongness of her choice) is not negated but does not play a specific role in the argument. The key role is played by the following assumption:

$A4^{MR}$: At least a involves a non-eliminable moral residue, and b either also involves a non-eliminable moral residue or the requirement of doing it is not overriding.

Consider Sophie again. In the first stage of her choice there is an alternative without a moral residue (if she rejects the offer she will not wrong either of her children) but she is at least permitted not to adopt that alternative. In the second stage there is no alternative without a non-eliminable moral residue (whichever child were betrayed, great efforts at emotional compensation would be in order, but the child's death would preclude the possibility of any compensation taking place).

The assumption that the moral residue is non-eliminable has a serious consequence, though. As we have seen, if the requirement of compensation *can* be satisfied, the concept of a moral residue does not salvage the tragic account. That is why we added the assumption that the damage done by not acting on one of the conflicting oughts cannot be repaired. If it *cannot* be repaired, however, and if OC is true, then it is not the case that it ought to be repaired. And if it ought not to be repaired, then the defeated ought does not leave any valid, in-force ought behind. In sum, the concept of a moral residue does not salvage the tragic account when the compensation requirement embodied in it can be satisfied, nor does it salvage the tragic account when the compensation requirement cannot be satisfied.

This may suggest that it would be best to forget about A4^{MR}, but I don't think that advisable. In our discussion, in Section 9.2, of whether OC should be abandoned we found that an act may be an object of ethical appraisal and censure even if it is not the case that the agent acts culpably or that she ought not to do what she does. S may have most reason to adopt this course of action, and yet the act— her act—may be morally reprehensible. In such cases it is true that S ought to do what she does and also that it is appropriate for S to be horrified by her own act. S does not act culpably; and yet there is a sense in which she must take responsibility for the morally unacceptable features of what she does.

Thus, A1–A3 together with A4^{MR} involve

I1^{MR}: Even if what S does is no worse than any of the alternatives, it will be appropriate for S to feel badly about the debt of compensation that she incurs by her act but that she will be unable to discharge.

When I was writing the first, Hungarian, version of this book, I thought that this was the correct theory of moral dilemmas. It seemed to be consistent and fairly general. It certainly seemed to be capable of accounting for the phenomenon of dirty hands. If by doing the right thing S inflicted irreparable damage on someone else, her responsible choice would cause permanent loss of the well-being or of the moral status of that person. Thus, what we called acting with dirty hands seemed to admit an interpretation in terms of doing irreparable damage. Or so I thought.

Later on I came to realize that this view was mistaken. I now tend to believe that the fact of irreparable damage is neither necessary nor sufficient for a moral dilemma to exist. It is not a morally irrelevant fact, but it explains something other than the possibility and nature of moral dilemmas.

An irreparable damage is always a very great damage. And, as we saw in Section 9.1, the criteria of a moral dilemma do not include any appeal to the weight of the conflicting oughts. A conflict between two relatively trivial oughts may still be a moral dilemma in the requisite sense. The harm that S may cause to other people when she fails to satisfy a relatively trivial ought is likely to be a relatively trivial harm. Relatively trivial harms are likely to be relatively easy to repair. The less dramatic the ought, the more likely it is that the victims can be fully compensated. And conversely: the more dramatic the ought, the more likely it is that the victims cannot be fully or at least partially compensated. But if you inflict a very great harm on someone—so great a harm that there is no way for you to repair it—then by the same token you ruin your own life. After all, it is *you* who has done it, even if you did it in a moral dilemma which did not allow you to do anything better.

That is what the concept of irreparable harm may help to explain. It cannot contribute to the explanation of the possibility and nature of the moral dilemmas themselves, though. It cannot be necessary for their general explanation, because it is tied to a subclass: moral dilemmas with a destructive potential. Nor, interestingly, is it sufficient to explain even the cases belonging to this subclass. Sometimes the proper choice entails inflicting great damage on someone, but the situation is not a moral dilemma in the requisite sense. For a moral dilemma to exist, the proper choice must involve damage *done in a certain way*. Even if the damage is small, if it is done in a morally reprehensible way, the situation where there is no better choice becomes a moral dilemma. On the other hand, even if the damage is very great, if it is not done in a morally reprehensible manner, the mere fact that there is no better option does not transform the situation into a moral dilemma.

Consider a modified version of Sophie's drama.

Sophie's choice–2. Sophie enters the camp both children remaining with her. But the children contract a fatal disease. Sophie gets some medicine enough to cure one but only one child. She has to decide which child to save and which one to allow to die. The son has better chances to survive, and so Sophie gives the medicine to him.

By delivering the girl to the Nazis in Sophie–1, Sophie betrays her. By giving the medicine to the boy in Sophie–2, she does not betray the girl. Advocates of the doctrine of double effect would put this as follows: When Sophie chooses to give the medicine to the boy she *foresees* that, as a consequence of this choice, the girl will be allowed to die. But she does not *intend* that consequence, either as an end in itself or as a means of rescuing the boy. Betrayal is a deliberate act. It cannot be committed without the intention of committing it. Choosing to give the medicine to the boy does not entail that the mother *intends* to allow the girl to die. Foreseeing is not intending. In Sophie–2 Sophie does not act with the intention of allowing her daughter to die, and so she commits no betrayal.

Here we can set aside the question whether the distinction between foreseeing and intending is capable of providing a general explanation for the possibility of certain harmful acts being morally permissible. Whether or not that is the case, it is certainly true that Sophie does not betray her child if she does that what would count as betraying her if it were done with the intention of doing *that*. Therefore, the act of rescuing the boy does not count as betraying the girl at the same time.

Sophie–1 is a case of a moral dilemma. Sophie–2 is just a hard choice. But that choice involves irreparable damage. After all, Sophie allows her daughter to die.

A proper account of moral dilemmas must include a criterion for distinguishing between cases such as Sophie–1 and Sophie–2. Irreparable damage cannot be that criterion, for it is constitutive of both.

Finally, there are situations where the best choice gives reason for moral despair about what one has done, but where there is no need to compensate the victim because there is no true victim other than the subject of the dilemma himself.

Consider a much cited story constructed by Bernard Williams.

Jim and the Indians–1. Jim (a young scholar on a botanical field trip in South America) finds himself in the central square of a small country town. Tied up against the wall are a row of twenty Indians, facing them several armed men in uniform. The commander, whom Williams calls the Captain, explains to Jim that the Indians are a random group about to be killed to remind the inhabitants of the advantages of obeying the authorities. Since Jim is an honored visitor from a friendly land, the Captain is happy to offer him a guest's privilege of killing one of the Indians himself. He would point to one of the hostages, and if Jim shoots that man, the others will be let off. If Jim refuses, all of them will die.[37]

There is an important analogy between Jim's case and both Sophie–1 and Sophie–2. The hostage whose death is caused by Jim if he takes the gun and fires it would die anyway. Jim is not told to kill a bystander in order to save the lives of nineteen hostages. The proposal is that if he kills one of the hostages the others will be allowed to live. This is true about Sophie, too, in both versions of her story. The child who dies must die anyway. But Jim's case is also unlike Sophie's two cases.

In Sophie–1, if Sophie accepts the proposal, the girl dies, betrayed by her mother. If Jim fires the gun, he kills one of the hostages but the victim does not die betrayed by him. There is no personal relationship between Jim and the Indian who dies at his hands; to the Indian it makes no difference whether he is shot dead by Jim or by one of the armed men in uniform. He is no worse off for being killed by Jim than he would be if Jim refused the offer. Nor is he selected for death by Jim. One cannot say that he would have lived if only Jim had chosen someone else to shoot at. Although he dies at Jim's hand, he is not *Jim's* victim. The responsibility for his death lies at the doorstep of the Captain alone.[38]

Let us compare now Jim's case with Sophie–2. In Sophie–2, the mother does not do anything morally reprehensible. Jim does. In both cases, the outcome is better than it would be if the agent had done nothing. At least one of those facing death ends up better off, and none of the others end up worse off than they otherwise would.[39] But, in Sophie–2, Sophie simply lets her daughter die (since rescuing both children is not among the alternatives open to her), while Jim kills an innocent, defenseless, non-threatening human being. *He becomes a killer.*

The only person who is harmed by Jim's decision to fire the gun is Jim himself. He becomes morally tainted without causing additional harm to anyone. If he owes reparation to anyone, he owes it to himself. But this does not make sense. No one can be a claimant against his own person.

The upshot is that the concept of a moral residue cannot bear out the burden of a theory of moral dilemmas. This is a negative conclusion, but it has interesting positive corollaries.

First, an agent, while choosing the best alternative open to him, may cause irreparable damage to someone else. Second, he does not violate any valid, in-force ought by taking that alternative and by failing to compensate the victim. Third, the irreparable damage may be produced with the intention of producing it (as a means to a diserable end). Fourth, causing that damage intentionally may be morally reprehensible even if the agent pursues the best available course of action. Fifth, if such is the case, the agent has reason to be alienated from what he did. What matters is, however, not that irreparable damage is done but the way it is done: it is the morally reprehensible nature of the right action that justifies the bad feelings. It justifies the bad feelings even if there is no irreparable damage done to any person other than the agent himself.

The missing assumption, therefore, sounds like this: At least one of the available courses of action open to S is morally reprehensible, and the others are either no less reprehensible, or if they are less reprehensible, their disadvantages are significant enough to make the adoption of the morally reprehensible act permissible.

It would be wrong for S to adopt x, a morally reprehensible course of action, if the situation included an alternative that would be less reprehensible and would not involve a loss of such magnitude as to meet the critical threshold. But if x has no alternative that would be less reprehensible morally than x and that would not be accompanied by losses meeting the threshold, then adopting x may be the right thing for S to do.

Consider Sophie-1: in the first stage Sophie chooses between the option of betraying one of her children in order to give the other a chance to survive and the option of not betraying either of her children. To her great misfortune, the option of refusing Dr. Mengele's offer would involve too great a loss as compared to the option of accepting it. In the second stage, both alternatives amount to betraying a child.

In other words, our new assumption presupposes that S justifiably dirties her hands as the situation either includes no option to keep her hands clean (second stage of Sophie-1) or the option of keeping her hands clean involves a very great loss (first stage of Sophie-1).

We are, thus, gesturing towards a theory of moral dilemmas which, rather than explaining the phenomenon of dirty hands, presupposes it.

But then the theory of moral dilemmas cannot make the idea of justified dirty hands intelligible; rather, it must assume that that idea is indeed intelligible and consistent. In the next section I will try to show how this can be the case.

9.4 Dirty hands

I began this chapter by introducing the conceptual puzzle of dirty hands: doing the right thing means doing something in a morally acceptable manner; getting one's hands dirty means doing something in a manner that is morally unacceptable.

Three questions are raised by this paradox. First, what makes an act that it is right or morally acceptable to adopt under certain circumstances reprehensible or morally unacceptable under the same circumstances? Second, how can the two statements—that the act is right and that it is reprehensible—be reconciled with each other? The third question applies the second to the problem of moral responsibility. The standard understanding of moral responsibility insists that if S is responsible for doing a, and a is morally reprehensible, then S is liable to blame for doing a. Yet if S is justified in doing a then S does not make herself blameworthy by doing a. How can we resolve the apparent contradiction of S being blameless (because a is right) and blameworthy (because a is reprehensible) at the same time? The answers to these three questions jointly make up the theory of dirty hands.

I have already made various different claims regarding these questions at several points in this book. Now I want to bring those claims together and to show that they can be united into a coherent and conclusive conception.

1. What makes an act that is right to adopt under certain circumstances morally reprehensible under the same circumstances?

Ruth Barcan Marcus writes in an article on moral dilemmas:

These are actions in which the moral features, including intentions, circumstances, and immediate outcomes, are incorporated
in the description of the action. In that respect the attributive
content of that description is like an essential property—a property that the action has in all possible circumstances or, if you
like, in all possible worlds. ... There has been a tendency to con-
fuse two quite different senses of absolute—one in which it
means essential and the other in which it means having priority
under all circumstances.[40]

Some of our concepts unite description and evaluation in such a
manner that their descriptive content cannot be properly determined
without reference to the relevant evaluative criteria. Concepts such as
"betrayal" or "murder" belong to this class. The acts they describe
cannot be identified in morally neutral terms. Their "moral features"
are part of their essential properties: without them, the act is not the
same act. Thus, betrayal and murder remain loaded with negative
evaluative properties, whether or not they are committed under circumstances that may justify the act that counts as betrayal or murder
respectively.

It follows that an act that is right to adopt under certain circumstances may be morally reprehensible under the same circumstances.
It is in fact morally reprehensible if it has essential properties that
make it reprehensible.

Sometimes the fact that an act is carried under particular circumstances transforms the act into a different act, one lacking the essential properties that make it reprehensible. Suppose Jim pulls the trigger of the gun, but the gun is not loaded. And suppose the Captain
tells him: "Allright, you have done what I asked you to do. I let nineteen hostages go." What Jim does is the same act as it was in the
original story, at least under some descriptions: he pulls the trigger,
and he saves nineteen lives. But the same act does not involve killing
anymore: it doesn't meet *that* description.

This suggests that we should amend the criteria of an act being
morally reprehensible: An act is morally reprehensible if it meets
a description under which it has essential properties that make it
reprehensible, and if the particular circumstances under which it
is committed do not make it inappropriate to meet that description.

Sophie–1 satisfies this condition. Here, Sophie does not merely allow her daughter to die. She hands her over to the Nazis. And the girl being handed over to the Nazis is not a side-effect of the boy's getting saved but a means of saving the boy.

The choice is justified. Consequentialists would claim Sophie is morally required to accept the offer. Deontologists would claim she is at least morally permitted to do so. But what she is at least morally permitted to do counts as betraying her daughter. The circumstances that make her act permissible do not change it into a different act, one that is free of its essential and negative moral properties.

The same analysis holds for Jim's original case.

In sum, the class of acts that are right and that display some essentially reprehensible property is not empty. There are at least some cases when what the agent does is both morally acceptable and morally unacceptable or reprehensible.

2. How can the two statements—that the act is morally acceptable and that it is morally unacceptable—be reconciled with each other?

Human acts have two distinguishable aspects: one related to the states of affairs they bring about in the world, and another related to how they treat their object. In the following paragraphs, I will focus on the second aspect.

The object of an act may be of merely instrumental value, but some objects (persons, beings capable of experience, living creatures, works of art, and so on) have intrinsic value as well, and their intrinsic value sets standards for the ways we should deal with them. An object of intrinsic value is treated properly or improperly, depending on how well our treatment satisfies the relevant standards. An act may or may not express proper concern for the interests of the person affected by it; it may or may not express proper respect for her moral standing; it may or may not live up to the internal norms of the relationship (of friendship, for example) between the agent and the person affected by it, and so on. An act is morally reprehensible or dirty-handed if it fails to treat objects of moral concern as they should be treated or, to put it differently, if it expresses an improper attitude towards the way they should be treated.

Consequentialist theories tend to ignore this distinction. They hold that an act is right if it brings about a state of affairs that is, all things considered, at least as good as any of the alternatives open to the agent. They claim to give an account of the considerations regarding the way acts treat their object by adding this to the relevant states of affairs, but once the overall balance of reasons is set, it alone decides whether the act is morally acceptable or not. If the act results, all things considered, in a state of affairs that is no worse than any of the alternatives open to the agent, then it is acceptable, period. Once a particular reason has made its contribution to the overall balance, it has no further role to play. Thus, no act can be right and morally reprehensible at the same time—there are simply no conceptual resources to make a distinction between an act being morally reprehensible and wrong.

Deontological theories attach great importance to the distinction that consequentialism tends to ignore. They insist that the standards of dealing with persons and personal relationships do not compete with outcome-related reasons. Such standards, according to deontologists, are constraints that limit the scope of those outcome-related reasons on which we are permitted to act. If an outcome-related reason would conflict with a constraint, it is not balanced against the latter. The constraint does not win because the considerations that justify it have greater weight than the reasons conflicting with them. How weighty those considerations are may not matter at all. The constraint wins because it is a higher-order reason, which excludes certain considerations from the range of the eligible reasons for those actions to which the constraint applies.[41]

Deontologists tend to agree that the constraints admit of a threshold. Once a harm surpasses that threshold, it becomes permissible to act on the practical reason that counts in favor of averting it, even if the act continues to violate a standard of value. In other words, the agent is permitted, or perhaps even required, to act in contravention of the considerations that support a deontological constraint.

Thus, when we ask what, all things considered, we are permitted, or required, to do, the outcome-related considerations may defeat, even on a deontological account, the considerations regarding the treatment due to objects of value. When it comes to such a victory a new question emerges. The question asked by both consequentialist and deontological theories is: what are we permitted or required or prohibited *to do*? The new question is whether what we are permitted or required to do is compatible with the considerations regarding the treatment due to objects of value. Even if defeated as practical reasons, those considerations return undefeated as evaluative judgments. The aim of avoiding some great harm may justify treating a person in an improper way—betraying her, for example—but it does not change the treatment from inappropriate into appropriate. The apparent contradiction dissolves because, first, the claim that an act is right and the claim that it is morally reprehensible answer different questions—what I should do, all things considered, and whether what I should do pays proper respect to the value of the object of my action—and, second, the considerations of outcome may leave the considerations of treatment unaffected.

It certainly matters that what counts as improper treatment is the least bad means of preventing or reducing some very great evil, but it also matters that it is improper treatment nevertheless. It matters that when Sophie delivers one of her children to certain death she does so under the threat that both children will die. But it also matters that she delivers the child to certain death, and this is an aspect of her choice to which separate consideration must be given.[42]

3. If an act is right and morally reprehensible at the same time, how can the apparent contradiction between the agent being both blameless (since she does what is right) and blameworthy (since what she does is reprehensible) be avoided?

As we saw, Sophie's choice is not freely adopted. It is manipulated by Dr. Mengele under the coercive threat of having both her children taken away and murdered. Given the terms of the offer, Sophie is permitted to do what she does. She is blameless. Yet the choice is hers. She chooses to turn her daughter over to the Nazis. She acts deliberately. What she does is morally reprehensible (it counts as betraying her child) if it is done deliberately. Since it is indeed done deliberately, it is morally reprehensible.

The mitigating conditions exempt Sophie from blame. But they do not remove the morally reprehensible features from her act. Sophie has to take responsibility for acting in a reprehensible manner, even if she had no better choice. Does this mean that she is blameworthy? Does she act in a blameless and a blameworthy way at the same time?

According to the usual account of moral responsibility, if S could not do otherwise, there are no grounds to claim that she ought to have done otherwise, and the act is beyond the scope of her responsibility. Even if, by performing that act, S gets her hands dirty, nothing can be said about her conduct in terms of personal responsibility. One may regret that S had to act in circumstances in which no better course of action could be adopted, and S, too, has reason to regret this, but what is up for being regretted is the unfortunate circumstances and not the unfortunate way of acting in them.

In his celebrated essay "Moral Luck" Bernard Williams points out that the usual account may be too narrow. He cites the example of a truck driver who through no fault of his own has run over a child. The driver's part in the accident is neither intentional nor due to culpable negligence. Nevertheless, his agency is involved in the death of the child in a way that a third-person observer's agency could not be. Without necessarily believing that he did anything wrong, he regrets what he *has done* rather than what *happened* independently of him, and it is appropriate for him to feel this kind of regret. Williams suggests that we distinguish first-person regret from third-person regret, and he coins a specific term—agent-regret—for the former.[43]

The involvement of one's agency in an outcome does not mean that one is responsible for the outcome. But mere involvement of one's agency in bringing about an unfortunate outcome and personal responsibility for bringing about that outcome are arranged along the same continuum. And so their moral meanings, although certainly not identical, are not completely unrelated. When a person is morally responsible for something, that fact is a reason for other people as well as for himself to hold him morally responsible. And holding him morally responsible entails certain reactive attitudes towards him as the one who did *that*. The reactive attitudes in question are subject to standards. They may be appropriate or inappropriate, depending on whether they conform to the relevant standards. It is inappropriate to burst out in laughter at the sight of a terrible crime; it is inappropriate to react with anger and scorn to a mildly impolite gesture.[44] Williams' argument extends the same analysis to those persons whose agency is involved in bringing about some harm, but who do not bear moral responsibility for the result. The accident in which a truck runs over a child is a proper object of reactive attitudes, even if the appropriate reactions are different from those that would be in place if the driver were morally responsible for the death of the child. Third parties are not justified in reacting with indignation to what the driver did, nor is the driver justified in reacting with feelings of guilt. The third-person regret that properly applies to such cases definitely entails compassion towards the person whose agency became involved in bringing about great harm through no fault of his own. It is not only regret at the death of a child; it is also regret at an adult having had no choice to avoid causing the child's death. But even compassionate third-party observers would be unpleasantly surprised if the driver failed to display any distress about causing the death of the child.

The cases of (justified) dirty hands have their place along the same continuum, somewhere between the phenomena that properly involve guilt on the part of the agent and those where the appropriate first-person reaction is what Williams calls agent-regret. Guilt is not appropriate in these cases. It necessarily entails the wish that one had acted differently, and where the dirty-handed act is right, the agent has no reason to wish that he had done something other than what he actually did. But neither is mere agent-regret appropriate. It makes sense for the driver to regret that he acted in a certain way (so that the truck driven by him ran over the child) but it does not make sense for him to regret choosing to hit the child, because he had no such choice at all. Sophie, however, has good reason to regret that she chose to betray her daughter. The truck driver cannot meaningfully ask himself "What kind of a driver am I who did this?" This question does not make sense for him precisely because he had no choice. Sophie, on the other hand, may meaningfully ask herself "What kind of a mother am I who did this?" This question is unavoidable for her since she had a choice between refusing to betray either of the two children and betraying one in order to give a chance to the other, and she took the second option. Being the person who ran over the child is a great misfortune for the driver but it says nothing about him as a moral agent or as a bearer of some more specific role. Being the person who had to send her daughter to certain death in order to give her son a chance is both a great misfortune for Sophie and something that very understandably makes her feel a disastrous failure as a mother.

Unlike faultless involuntary contributors to accidents, agents who act with dirty hands have a choice, and they have to take responsibility for what they choose. If they choose a right course of action, they are not liable to blame and blame-related third-person reactions, nor do they have reasons to feel guilty about their choice and action. But the choice is theirs, and their position is much more dramatic than that of a person who becomes involved in the causation of harm without having any choice regarding it. Some philosophers recommend that we call the first-person emotional reaction appropriate to agents who act in moral dilemmas *remorse*, and distinguish it from guilt.[45] I accept this terminological distinction, and I also want to make a similar distinction between remorse and mere agent-regret.

There is a telling difference between the phenomenology of blameworthy wrongdoing and acting blamelessly but with dirty hands. Blameworthy acts invite condemnatory reactions on the part both of the agent and of third persons. Guilt feelings correlate with feelings of resentment, indignation, scorn, and so on. In the case of dirty-handed but blameless acts the correlation breaks down. The agent appropriately feels remorse and alienation both from the act and from himself. It is not simply the case that he is likely to nourish bad moral feelings. He ought to nourish such feelings. We would consider him a worse character if he did not. But we do not condemn him for his act. It is not appropriate for us to blame him, nor to nourish blame-related emotions towards him. The proper reaction to his quandary is not resentment or indignation, but "fear and pity."

In sum, the metaphor of dirty hands refers to acts that are essentially reprehensible, that is, reprehensible irrespective of the circumstances in which they are permitted or even required to be carried out. If acting with dirty hands means carrying out an essentially reprehensible act, then there is nothing paradoxical in an act being both justified and objectionable: it is justified under the circumstances, but the circumstances do not affect its objectionable character. By doing something that is justified under the circumstances and essentially reprehensible at the same time, the agent does not make himself guilty. He does not act wrongly or culpably. Therefore, he is not liable to blame. But the act is his, and it is his not in the weak sense that his agency is involved but in the stronger sense that he intended it together with its reprehensible properties. He has to take responsibility for it. Although feelings of guilt are not appropriate in his case, feelings of remorse are indeed.

9.5 The dirty hands account of moral dilemmas

We are now in a possession of the premises for a theory of moral dilemmas that I hope is robust and consistent at the same time. Before spelling it out, let us recapitulate the alternative accounts in order to place our findings in a comparative perspective.

The premises of the tragic account are as follows:

A1–A3 (moral conflict): affirmed
$A4^{TR}$: Neither "S ought to do a" overrides "S ought to do b" nor "S ought to do b" overrides "S ought to do a." Both oughts emerge from their encounter undefeated.
OC (ought implies can): denied

The moral doubts account is based on the following premises:

A1–A3: affirmed
$A4^{MD}$: S is uncertain whether the requirement to do a overrides the requirement to do b, or whether the requirement to do b overrides the requirement to do a, or else whether both requirements are non-overridden.
OC: affirmed

The moral residue account's premises are these:

A1–A3: affirmed
$A4^{MR}$: At least a involves a non-eliminable moral residue, and b either also involves a non-eliminable moral residue or the requirement of doing b is not overriding.
OC: affirmed

Finally, here are the premises of the conception that I propose to call the *dirty hands account*:

A1–A3: affirmed
$A4^{DH}$: At least a is morally reprehensible, and b is either also morally reprehensible or it is not overriding.
OC: affirmed.

Jointly, these premises imply that

I1^{DH}: Even if what S does is no worse than any of its alternatives, it is appropriate for S to feel remorse about her action.

Like the tragic account, the dirty hands account provides room for the possibility that an agent confronted by a moral dilemma may not be able to do the right thing and avoid taking responsibility for a morally reprehensible act at the same time. Since it, too, allows for inescapable dilemmas, it neither denies nor ignores the possibility of a person being confronted, through no fault of her own, by choices that destroy her life morally. But unlike the tragic account, the dirty hands account does not interpret this fatal outcome as the agent becoming guilty of a sinful action. Furthermore, the dirty hands account does not depend on the assumption that the conflicting oughts balance each other out. It is capable of explaining how cases where one of the options clearly defeats its alternatives may be moral dilemmas nevertheless.

Like the moral doubts account, the dirty hands account affirms the 'ought implies can' principle. Unlike that account, it does not restrict the phenomenology of moral dilemmas to the agent being in the grip of inescapable doubts. More importantly, unlike the moral doubts account, it does not end in the claim that moral dilemmas are only apparent. That the best available option has reprehensible essential properties is no mere appearance; it is a moral reality. It follows that the agent may actually *be* in a moral dilemma without realizing that she is. She may fail to see that the best option may actually be morally reprehensible. On the other hand, the dirty hands account is not incompatible with the recognition that uncertainty and doubt raise a special problem for the subjects of moral dilemmas. It allows for such problems as possible concomitants of dilemmatic situations.

Like the moral residue account, the dirty hands account both affirms the 'ought implies can' principle and interprets moral dilemmas as real. But it succeeds where the moral residue account fails, and in any case its explanation has a more general scope: it applies to cases where there is no residual duty to compensate. It explains cases with a moral residue as special cases where the essentially reprehensible nature of the act is related to causing (perhaps irreparable) harm to another person.

Finally, the dirty hands account draws attention to a type of dilemmas where one of the alternatives is essentially reprehensible, while the other is not. These are the dilemmas where the subject has to choose between getting his hands dirty and keeping them clean. The first stage of Sophie's choice is of such a nature, and so is Jim's choice. Situations such as these are not dilemmatic unless the option that permits one to keep one's hands clean involves so great a loss in comparison to the dirty-handed option that it becomes permissible to weigh that loss against the morally reprehensible character of the dirty-handed option. Thus, for Sophie's or Jim's choice to be moral dilemmas it must be the case that saving at least one life is important enough to make it permissible or required to take the dirty-handed option.

According to the most natural reading of consequentialism, Sophie and Jim are positively required to take that option. As I mentioned it earlier, deontologists deny this. They argue that the consequentialist claim involves what Bernard Williams once called the principle of negative responsibility.[46] If there existed an obligation always to choose that course of action which involves the best overall outcome, they object, individuals would be responsible for all the harms in the world that they could have averted but failed to avert. The principle of negative responsibility blurs the distinction between the responsibility of perpetrators such as Dr. Mengele or the Captain on the one hand and innocent people on the other who, like Sophie or Jim, are morally blackmailed into cooperating in an evil project, and so it is utterly unacceptable. But even deontologists acknowledge that, although they are not morally required to adopt the dirty-handed option, Sophie and Jim are at least morally permitted to do so.

If this is the case, however, then they are also permitted to take the option that allows them to keep their hands clean. But since the dirty-handed option is better in terms of averting or reducing harm, the adoption of the clean-handed alternative is subject to a special burden of justification. The mere fact that the chooser wants to keep his hands clean would not pass the test. Keeping one's hands clean comes at a moral cost in such cases: the agent avoids a moral sacrifice at the price of allowing some great harm to be inflicted on someone else. This makes him vulnerable to the charge that he is giving priority to having an impeccable moral record over preventing some great harm to strike other people. What he does, so the objection continues, is making others pay the price for his avoidance of a special—moral—kind of cost.

In other words, if someone becomes involved in a situation where he has to choose between averting some great harm and preserving his moral purity, and if, in that situation, he opts for moral purity, he will lay himself open to the charge of *moral self-indulgence*.[47]

One may think that the charge of moral self-indulgence is only another description of the principle of negative responsibility—but this is not the case. The principle of negative responsibility excludes the possibility of a justifiable refusal to act with dirty hands, provided that the dirty-handed act would produce the best overall outcome. The charge of moral self-indulgence, however, is compatible with such a possibility. What it does rule out is justifying the refusal by the desire to remain morally pure.

Consider Sophie–1. Suppose Sophie persists in her initial refusal to make a choice. She may do so for two very different reasons. She may refuse because she does not want to be a mother who does such a thing. In this case the charge of moral self-indulgence holds against her: she is acting on an intention that is liable to the charge of moral self-indulgence. But suppose that her refusal to choose is motivated by her feelings for her children. She loves both of them so much that she is incapable of doing to either of them what she would have to do to save at least the other. Her heart breaks for the child who would experience her betrayal. Sophie's failure to do what would dirty her hands results in a loss. However, that loss is not due to moral self-indulgence but to her inability to betray her child: a character trait that we admire in mothers.

I am not sure whether in Jim's case there is any conceivable motivation that would similarly pass the test. If there is none, then Jim, unlike Sophie, has no option of refusing the sinister offer and avoiding the justied the charge of moral self-indulgence at the same time.

9.6 Dirty hands in the absence of moral dilemmas

The dirty hands account differs from its alternatives in that it does not present the phenomenon of dirty hands as a side product of moral dilemmas. Rather, it presupposes an independent interpretation of that phenomenon. That a dirty-handed act is chosen in a moral dilemma where none of the alternatives is at least as good as the dirty-handed act itself, is *one* type of justification for taking it. Given the conceptual independence of dirty hands from moral dilemmas, other types are also possible. The present section will briefly explore their possibility.

I do not engage in this exploration with the aim of identifying the scope and limits of the theory of dirty hands. My aim is merely to show how acting with dirty hands may be justified when the choice is not morally dilemmatic.

I will proceed by way of examining some variations on Jim's case.

Jim and the Indians–2. Jim arrives in the square with his friend Tim. The Captain explains the situation to them and then turns to Tim with the offer. Jim knows Tim well enough to foresee that if Tim accepts the offer, he will be tortured for the rest of his life by the awareness that he murdered an innocent and defenseless person. To save him from personal disaster Jim interjects "Let me do it!" and before Tim can get his bearings, he takes the gun from the Captain.

Jim would not be liable to the charge of moral self-indulgence if he were to watch silently as Tim takes the revolver and fires it. But he is not to blame either if he steps in. Rather, we would praise him for intervening. His choice situation is not characterized by a conflict between two oughts. The choice between killing and not killing does not impose itself on him as an inescapable dilemma: he voluntarily chooses to redirect the offer from Tim to himself and thereby he makes himself responsible for whatever he should choose once he is authorized to make the choice. (By choosing to intervene he of course decides the alternative in favor of accepting the offer.)

Having received the Captain's offer, Tim would be permitted to accept it and to kill one of the hostages in order to save the lives of the rest. But, then, Jim must be permitted to take Tim's place, provided that his reasons for doing so arc good. And they are indeed.

It could be objected that although Jim is not himself facing an inescapable choice between two 'oughts' the permissibility for him to dirty his hands is parasitic on the fact that his friend Tim is confronted by such a choice. The reason why Jim is allowed to take on the bur-

den of Tim's dilemma is that the dilemma imposes itself on Tim inescapably. Although the Captain does not make the offer to Jim, Jim
does not add anything to the situation. He does not create a new
moral burden but rather shifts the burden that already exists so that it
does not fall on Tim but on himself.

We may test this objection by eliminating the offer altogether. Consider the following version of the story:

> *Jim and the Indians–3.* Jim arrives in the square alone. The Captain
> explains the situation to him without making any offer. But Jim
> knows the type and foresees that the Captain would prefer having
> him as an accomplice in killing at least one hostage rather than
> having twenty killed by his subordinates. So he makes the advance
> himself: "I will shoot one of them if you let off the rest."

Frances Kamm who devised Jim–3 points out that, in this version,
saving the lives of nineteen Indians comes at a heavier moral cost to
the young man than in the original version. In Jim–1, the responsibility for the death of the only hostage who is killed by Jim lies entirely
at the doorstep of the Captain, and so does the responsibility for the
immoral plot. In Jim–3, the responsibility for the immoral plot is
shared by the Captain and Jim. After all, the initiative comes from
Jim, not the Captain. It is Jim who creates a choice situation, not the
Captain.[48]

Does it follow that, in Jim–3, Jim is not permitted to make the offer
and, therefore, to take the revolver and fire, should the Captain accept
the deal? If it does, that may be an argument against the possibility of
justified dirty hands in the absence of moral dilemmas. For whenever
an agent decides to act with dirty hands without that decision being
taken in answer to a moral dilemma, he necessarily makes himself at
least in part responsible for the dirty-handed features of the action.

But I do not think making oneself (partly) responsible for those
features is a condition that would rule out *ab initio* the permissibility
of acting with dirty hands. Let us have a look at Sophie–1 again. The
responsibility for the death of the one child she turns over to the Nazis
lies entirely with Dr. Mengele. But the question as to which of the two
children should be sent to his or her death is decided by Sophie. By
defining the terms of the choice, Dr. Mengele makes himself co-
responsible for the content of Sophie's choice. But Sophie has her own

share in that part of the responsibility for what happens to her children. She is offered a choice and, after some hesitation, accepts it. The
choice is hers. "Take her!" she exclaims, and the girl is taken away. If
she were to say "Take him!," the boy would be taken away. By delivering the girl to the Nazis, she betrays her, and although Dr. Mengele,
who masterminded the choice, is the main culprit, she bears her own
share in the responsibility for the betrayal. In sum, Sophie cannot lay
all the responsibility for her action at Dr Mengele's door. And yet she
is morally permitted to accept the offer. She has good reasons to feel
remorse about accepting it, but she would have even better reasons to
feel remorse, had she rejected it.

A different type of objection may be leveled against reasoning with
Jim–3. It may be argued that this case, although it appears to lack the
properties of a moral dilemma, is in fact dilemmatic. There is a way
to save all hostages except one, as Jim discovers. He is the only person
in the square who may make an unsolicited proposal to the Captain in
the hope of a positive answer, and he knows this. The situation bears
the salient features of typical rescue cases: a number of human beings
are in mortal danger; on the scene of the impending disaster there is a
man capable of saving the lives of at least some of them; no other
individual capable of saving lives is near the scene; the rescue operation comes at a cost (in this case, a moral cost) for the rescuer, but the
cost is not prohibitively high as compared to saving lives. Given all
this, Jim ought to come to the rescue of the hostages. But since killing
one of the hostages is the only way to save the lives of the rest, Jim is
subjected to another ought as well, one that requires him not to carry
out the act that would save them. And because killing an innocent and
defenseless person is essentially reprehensible, yet at the same time
better than allowing all the hostages to be killed, the conflict of the
two oughts is a moral dilemma.

The objection does not show that the explanation of why Jim
may permissibly choose the dirty-handed option is not complete
without appealing to the dilemmatic nature of Jim–3. It merely es-
tablishes that, in Jim–3, justified dirty hands go together with a
moral dilemma. Thus, the objection can be met by changing Jim's
story again in such a way that the new version is exactly like Jim–3,
except for one feature which, when changed, leaves the justification
of the dirty-handed action intact while depriving the situation of its
dilemmatic character.

Jim and the Indians–4. Everything is as in Jim–3, except that there are many American citizens in the square and Jim is one of them. The Captain explains the situation to them, and makes no offer. However, his narrative suggests that if any of the Americans were to make the proposal Jim made in Jim–3, the Captain would accept the deal. Jim knows his fellow Americans well. He is confident that all of them understand the situation and are ready to take the initiative. But he prefers not to leave the moral burden of acting with dirty hands to others.

Unlike Jim–3, Jim–4 does not direct the task of coming to the rescue of the endangered Indians to Jim alone. He is not singled out by some salient property as the one who has to carry out the rescue operation. Nor is anybody else. In Jim–4, it is not the case that Jim ought to address the Captain with the morally objectionable proposal; and if it is not, Jim is not facing a moral dilemma. But the conditions that made it permissible for him to make the proposal in Jim–3 are not affected by this change. Thus, in Jim–4, Jim permissibly intervenes to save nineteen hostages by killing one of the twenty, even if his choice to do so does not answer a moral dilemma. Which is what we needed to show in order to defend the claim that there are permissible cases of dirty hands in the absence of moral dilemmas.

In Jim–4, it is true that each of the Americans could make the Captain spare the lives of nineteen hostages and that one of them ought to do what is necessary in order to achieve this. It is true that one of them ought to make the proposal. But it is not true that any one of them in particular ought to make it.

It is not true about Jim specifically. If he were to address the Captain, the justification of his move would not be that *he* had to do it. Rather, he could say, "*Someone* had to do it, and I decided to be that one." I did it because it had to be done. A subjectless ought was transformed into a personal ought by a permissible decision.[49]

If Jim, in Jim–4, turns to the Captain and puts a proposal to him, he does something that many others had to contemplate doing. Since he is not singled out as the one who ought to do it, Jim is permitted to leave it to someone else. But he has the moral courage to undertake a dirty-handed action that an unidentified member of the group must carry out in order to save the lives of nineteen hostages. Jim taints his moral record, but we would not, and ought not to, blame him.

But neither ought we to react to his action with "fear and pity." His moral sacrifice is not prompted by an inescapable dilemma; he has the choice of keeping his hands clean without making himself liable to the charge of moral self-indulgence. Undeniably, there is a certain greatness in his resolve. And then, as Hegel says in his *Lectures on the Philosophy of Art*, "our tribute to greatness is not pity but awe."

*

Politics is notorious about confronting agents with inescapable moral dilemmas. But even more characteristically, it confronts them, in the absence of any moral dilemmas, with choices between doing what someone ought to do at the cost of getting their hands dirty and leaving to others to do what someone ought to do so as to keep their hands clean. For remember: it is precisely this relationship between an impersonal ought and a personal decision that is the nerve of the morality of the struggle for power. The good of the people calls for someone willing to use political power as a means to promote the common interest, but—given the circumstances of insufficient compliance—nobody can gain power without dirtying his hands. If a good politician has the moral courage to act with dirty hands, he is permitted to do so, provided that his coming to power promises significant public benefit (see Chapter Three, 3.6).

Winston Churchill was not alone to recognize that the threat posed by Nazism should not be understood in terms of traditional national interests but rather in terms of deadly fight between Western civilization and barbarism. But he was alone among these people to have the will to power that enabled him to lead Britain in that fight. Convinced that the war with Nazi Germany was going to have only two outcomes—total defeat or total victory—he staked his fate as politician on "victory at all cost." And he knew that the costs were not going to consist in "blood, toil, tears, and sweat" alone; he was aware of the moral costs the fight for victory was going to involve. He was aware that the war could not be won without making an alliance with Stalin's Soviet Union. We admire him for his single-minded determination to bring about that alliance, even if it made the betrayal of the pledge Britain made to Poland inevitable, and even if it led to acquiescence in the Soviet dominion over Eastern Europe.

The judgment of greatness and the tribute of awe are particularly apposite in Churchill's case. Ordinary democratic politics is far from the world historic dimensions of the war against Nazi Germany, to be sure. Typically, it does not involve decisions of the war against millions of human individuals, and its morally doubtful aspects consist in things like routine lies to the public or diversions of public money for the aims of electoral campaigns. In this sense, the existential drama of Sophie's or Jim's choice is closer to the historical drama of Churchill's leadership than the everyday stories of democratic politics as we know it. But even ordinary politics shares dimensions with politics conducted on the stage of history that are lacking to Sophie's or Jim's choice.

The cases like that of Sophie or Jim are examined in the philosophical literature from a snapshot perspective. Focusing on the present moment is a permissible strategy when the inquiry is directed at momentary choices that involve morally reprehensible acts. All the essential features of acting with dirty hands must be discoverable in such choices. But the problem of dirty hands as it is raised in politics has a dimension that remains hidden in the snapshot perspective. It has implications that unfold over time. Although one may become political leader for one day amidst revolutionary upheavals, in ordinary politics, democratic or not, leadership is a career for relatively long periods. The snapshot approach is incapable of capturing the special problems related to time. The only question relevant for it is, whether the decision with the best direct effects has some essentially reprehensible feature, and if it has, whether it is permissible to act on it nevertheless. The repetition of situations where choosing to act with dirty hands is required or at least permitted, raises questions of a different nature.

Compare Jim's choice with that of Frank discussed in Chapter Eight (8.2). To remind, Frank is a freshman in politics confronted with the alternative of accepting or refusing a ward boss's corrupt offer. We found that accepting the offer has implications for the future: Frank is likely to face new and new choices between either keeping his hands clean at the cost of risking his career and getting his hands dirty in order to be able to continue. As the number of such choices increases, the marginal moral loss from acting with dirty hands is likely to diminish, while the marginal costs of keeping his hands clean are likely to increase. It is highly implausible to think of a career politician as a tragic hero, I said in Chapter Eight, who suffers more and more as he sinks deeper and deeper in the morass of dirty-handed acts. It is much more plausible to see him as someone who becomes more and more indifferent towards the problem of dirty hands. He is unlikely to remain the same man of principles whom his admirers persuaded to run for elected office because of his sincere dedication to the common good. Thus, the admiration for him is mingled with anxiety for the future of his character, and with a hope that the institutions and practices of democratic politics reduce as much as possible the risk of his moral corruption.

Notes

1 On some aspects of its history, not discussed in this book in any great detail, see note 12 in Chapter One.

2 See, e.g., B. C. van Fraassen: "Values and the Heart's Command," in *Journal of Philosophy* 70 (1973) 5–19; Donagan: *Theory*, 180–189; and S. I. Benn: "Private and Public Morality: Clean Living and Dirty Hands," in Benn and G. F. Gaus: *Public and Private in Social Life*. London–Canberra: Croom Helm, New York: St. Martin's Press, 1983, 169 ff.

3 In the original, Sophie is asked to name the child who *stays with her*, but she names the one who must go with the rest of the children. Like most other analysts of the case, I adjusted the offer to the answer. Furthermore, I disregarded the fact that Sophie sends her daughter to her death because she does not love her enough. That is a heavy burden on the choice. Sophie has very strong reasons to feel guilty if she marked her daughter for death because of her lack of love for her. I want to show that her pangs of conscience are justified even if she loves both children equally.

4 In the novel, the gesture of rejection is a vividly physical one. "Mommy! she heard Eva screaming as she pushed her away from herself and she got to her feet stumbling."

5 "Don't ask me to make the choice," she answers the SS-doctor.

6 The characters *a* and *b* may stand for two different courses of action, or one may stand for an act while the other may stand for refraining from that act.

7 See Peter Railton: "The Diversity of Moral Dilemma" in H. E. Mason (ed.): *Moral Dilemmas and Moral Theory*. New York—Oxford: Oxford University Press, 1996.

8 The number of conflicting alternatives may be greater than two. So whenever I speak about a conflict between two courses of action, a conflict of two *or more* options is to be understood.

9 The index [TR] is added because, as we will see later, A4[TR] is an assumption specific to the tragic account; alternative conceptions replace it with some other assumption. There could be another interpretation of such a case. Rather than claiming that neither of the conflicting 'oughts' is overridden, one may claim that both are overriding. For example: "The strongest cases of conflict are the genuine dilemmas where there is decisive support for two or more incompatible courses of action or inaction." See T. Nagel: "The Fragmentation of Value" in Nagel, *Mortal Questions*. Cambridge: The University Press, 1979, 128. This reading, however, is self-contradictory, as Walter Sinnott-Armstrong has shown: "[M]oral requirements cannot be stronger overall than each other. The reason is that, if one requirement overrides another, and the other also overrides the former, then the former must override itself; but this is impossible." See W. Sinnott-Armstrong: *Moral Dilemmas*. Oxford: Blackwell, 1988, 17. So we are left with the interpretation that both requirements come out of the encounter undefeated. This seems to be Bernard Williams's view, for example: as he puts it, the subject of a moral dilemma is confronted by "conflicting moral requirements, and ... neither of them succeeds in overriding or outweighing the other." See B. Williams: "Conflict of Values," in Williams: *Moral Luck*. Cambridge: The University Press, 1981, 74.

10 For the aspect of the tragic account summarized by I2–I3, see C. Gowans: *Innocence Lost*. Oxford: The University Press, 1994.

11 Lukács: "Taktika és Etika" (Tactics and Ethics), in Lukács: *Forradalomban*. Budapest: Magvető, 1987, 132.

12 Conflict of Values, 74.

13 J. Raz: *The Morality of Freedom*. Oxford: Clarendon, 1986, 363.

14 A staple example is this: *S* promises *A* to go with him to the cinema on Tuesday at 7 pm, and promises *B* to take her to a restaurant on any evening of her choice; *B* proposes Tuesday 7 pm.

15 For the complexities of the involvement of Oedipus's agency in his destruction, see B. Williams: *Shame and Necessity*. Berkeley–Los Angeles: University of California Press, 1993, 69 ff.

16 Ruth Barcan Marcus makes use of the saying "You are damned if you do, and you are damned if you don't" to describe the impact of moral dilemmas on their subject. See Marcus: "Moral Dilemmas and Consistency," in *Journal of Philosophy* 77 (March 1980), 127.

17 See, for example, the discussion of Michael Walzer's views in Chapter Eight, 8.3.

18 R. M. Hare: *Moral Thinking*. Oxford: Clarendon, 1981, 33. Cf. Hare: *Essays on Political Morality*. Oxford: Clarendon, 1989. Hare's argument is made with regard to two rules of which one is overriding and the other is overridden (and, therefore, changed). But it can be extended to the case where both rules are undefeated. In this case, G* says: "Never do *g*, except when you have to choose between doing *g* and doing *f*, and the requirements to do *g* and to do *f* are both unde-

feated, and you have chosen to do *f.*" Hare was a consequentialist, but the above argument is neutral between consequentialism and non-consequentialism. A very similar argument is made, for example, by Alan Donagan. See his *Theory of Morality*, 93.

19 See Bernard Williams as cited in Section 9.3, notes 33–35.

20 In the literature on moral dilemmas and dirty hands, Michael Stocker takes this position, for example. See M. Stocker: *Plural and Conflicting Values*. Oxford: Clarendon, 1990.

21 "Moral Residue," 38.

22 R. M. Adams: "Involuntary sins," in *The Philosophical Review* 94 (1985) 3–31 (12).

23 For the concept of an "impossible ought," see M. Stocker: *Plural and Conflicting Values*. Oxford: Clarendon, 1990.

24 See D. O. Brink, "Moral Conflict and Its Structure," in H. E. Mason (ed.): *Moral Dilemmas and Moral Theory*, 107.

25 Interestingly, this result does not apply to choice situations that *S* had the opportunity to avoid, and that she entered knowingly or negligently. If *S* has wrongfully confronted a choice between two conflicting oughts, then the wrongness of not avoiding that choice is inherited by the choice itself: whichever 'ought' *S* chooses to satisfy, by failing to satisfy the other she does something wrong. This is not related to any assumption that all the conflicting oughts are valid requirements. The reason why *S* cannot avoid doing wrong is that she could have avoided facing the choice.

26 R. Hare: "The Rules of War and Moral Reasoning" in Hare: *Essays on Political Morality*. Oxford: Clarendon, 1989, 58.

27 See T. C. McConnell: "Moral Dilemmas and Moral Consistency in Ethics," in C. W. Gowans, ed.: *Moral Dilemmas*. New York–Oxford: Oxford University Press, 1987, and A. MacIntyre: "Moral Dilemmas," in *Philosophy and Phenomenological Research* 50, Supplement (1990) 367–383.

28 T. C. McConnell: "Moral Residue and Dilemmas," in H. E. Mason, ed.: *Moral Dilemmas and Moral Theory*. New York–Oxford: Oxford University Press, 1996, 38.

29 Ibid.

30 As Joseph Raz has pointed out, the moral characteristics of an act may be unrelated to whether the agent could choose anything better. See Raz: op. cit., 363 f.

31 Williams: "Ethical Consistency," 173.

32 He shows this by way of arguing that the so-called agglomeration principle is to be abandoned. The agglomeration principle holds that if *S* ought to do *a*, and *S* ought to do *b*, then *S* ought to do (*a* and *b*). Consistency requires that we give up either this principle or the "ought implies can" principle. We have good reason to stick to the "ought implies can" principle. Therefore, we have to give up the ag-

glomeration principle. See B. Williams: "Ethical Consistency," in Williams: *Problems of the Self.* Cambridge: The University Press, 1973, 181.

33 Ibid., 183.

34 Ibid.

35 "Ethical Consistency," 176. The term "prima facie obligations" makes reference to W. D. Ross, and the idea that an overridden prima facie obligation may leave some residual obligation behind also comes from Ross.

36 "Conflicts of Value," 73. (Italics added.)

37 See B. Williams: "A Critique of Utilitarianism," in J. J. Smart and B. Williams: *Utilitarianism—For and Against.* Cambridge: The University Press 1973, 98 f. The original version is silent about who selects the Indian to be shot: it may be Jim or the captain. But if Jim both chooses and kills, his acceptance of the captain's offer is morally reprehensible on two accounts. In Sophie's case the choice carries the whole moral burden of the story; she does not participate in the killing. It is better, for the sake of analysis, to have one single act carry the moral burden. Since Jim receives the offer to kill, I decided to make it explicit that the choice of the potential victim does not belong to him.

38 The fact that Jim bears no responsibility for the death of the Indian he shoots is pointed out by Frances Kamm in her article "Responsibility and Collaboration," in *Philosophy and Public Affairs* 28 (1999) 169–204.

39 In Sophie–2, the daughter is not betrayed. Nothing worse happens to her than what she would have been subjected to anyway.

40 See R. Barcan Marcus: "More About Moral Dilemmas," in H. E. Mason: *Moral Dilemmas and Moral Theory.* New York–Oxford: Oxford University Press, 1996, 25 f.

41 See T. Nagel: *The View from Nowhere.* New York–Oxford: Oxford University Press, 1986, Ch. 9.; E. Anderson: *Value in Ethics and Economics.* Cambridge, Mass.: Harvard University Press, 1993, Ch. 2.; R. Dworkin: *Life's Dominion.* New York: Knopf, 1993, Ch. 3.; T. S. Scanlon: *What We Owe to Each Other.* Cambridge, Mass.: Belknap, 1998, 103 ff.

42 M. Stocker: *Plural and Conflicting Values.* Oxford: Clarendon, 1990, 12 ff.

43 See B. Williams: "Moral Luck." In Williams: *Moral Luck.* Cambridge: The University Press, 1991.

44 See Chapter Six at 6.2.

45 See e.g. Sinnott-Armstrong: *Moral Dilemmas.*

46 See Williams: "Critique," 93 ff.; Kamm: "Responsibility."

47 See J. Glover: "It Makes No Difference Whether or Not I Do It," *Proceedings of the Aristotelian Society* 49 (1975), Suppl. Vol. 171–190.

48 See Kamm, "Responsibility."

49 In the year of Terror, many thought—and not just the royalists but Girondin republicans as well—that the slaughter could not be stopped unless the Jacobin leaders were killed. "Let's Marat's head fall and the Republic is saved.

(...) Marat sees the Public Safety only in a river of blood; well then his own must flow, for his head must fall to save two-hundred thousand others," a leaflet by Pézénas, a deputy from the Hérault county declared, and Charlotte Corday of Caen decided that she would be the one to carry out this must. ("I have killed one man to save a hundred thousand," she said at her trial). See S. Schama, *Citizens: A Chronicle of the French Revolution*. New York: Knopf 1989, 730, 738.

CHAPTER TEN

SUMMARY

Politics is a profession involving high moral risks. Political leaders regularly face situations where they either refrain from doing what is best for the public or get their hands dirty.

The problem of dirty hands is not unique to politics—it is a problem of general morality (see Chapter Nine). But as a political problem, it has special dimensions. For example, since politicians do not merely act *in* office but also compete *for* office, they often face choices where their responsibilities as office-holders conflict with what the struggle for (staying in) office demands from them (see Chapter Two, 2.1). Or, because politics is a long-term career, the momentary dirty-handed choices may involve cumulative effects on the politician's moral record and on his character (see Chapter Eight at 8.2).

The problem of dirty hands is first of all a problem for the agent himself: his dirty-handed act makes him liable to justified remorse; it gives him reasons for trying to explain his act to others, particularly to those adversely affected by it, or for offering compensation to the latter. But it is also a problem for other people. It gives reason to the affected persons for reacting with resentment, for asking for an explanation and for demanding rectification, and so on. And it gives reason to unaffected third parties for passing judgment about the act and the agent, for pointing out that those affected by the act have a right to be given an explanation and that, perhaps, apology and compensation are owed to them. In other words, acting with dirty hands makes the agent morally accountable to other individuals.

Moral accountability has, again, a special dimension in the context of political action because elected officials are accountable to the citizenry in a special, political way (see Chapter Six, 6.2). Nevertheless, the problem of dirty hands is often discussed as if it belonged to the internal forum of the politician's conscience (for Max Weber's classical discussion of the issue, see 6.1). The viewpoint occupied by this book is different. Rather than focusing on the question how the political leaders should respond to their dirty-handed choices, I asked how (democratic) political communities should deal with politicians who dirty their hands by doing the right thing.

Citizens of modern democracies are deeply perplexed by this problem. As the Introduction of this book observed it, a deep malaise is getting hold of the public in both the new and the old democracies. Various different factors cooperate to give rise to that malaise but I identified increasing skepticism as to the moral integrity of the holders of elected office as one of its distinct causes. I also noted, however, that the democratic public seems to be extremely uncertain about the way it should react to the apparent immorality of its political leaders. On the one hand, it seems to agree that the moral standards applying to the holders of elected office are more stringent than those applying to ordinary citizens in their private lives. On the other hand, it seems to agree that in their public capacity politicians are subject to more relaxed standards than as private individuals.

My book has been written with the ambition of providing a unified account for the conflicting views of the public. It began with an outline of what I dubbed the classical doctrine. The question of the classical doctrine was, why political leaders should not be expected to act in compliance with moral requirements that apply to private life, and why institutions should not rely on their being morally motivated. Here are its answers, in a nutshell.

It is a fact that too many politicians engage in objectionable transactions on too many occasions. Under such circumstances, an honest politician suffers serious competitive disadvantages unless he does the same. Doing such things for private gain is not morally permissible. But doing them for the sake of a public cause is prohibited only if enough others refrain from it on enough occasions. Under the conditions of pervasive non-compliance anything goes (at least in so far as it is necessary for promoting the common good and its beneficial consequences are proportional to its moral costs). Even if dirty-handed, the act is justified. Or so does the unconstrained thesis of realism insist (see Chapter Three).

But why would a politician pursue the aim of promoting a public cause at all? The classical doctrine does not rule out the possibility that people seek political office out of a concern for the good of their community. What it does rule out is that it would be rational for political institutions to rely on a sufficiently large number of politicians being effectively motivated by that concern. Such motivation is not strong or stable enough to make a typical individual regularly comply with institutions worthy of support. Thus, in order to make non-compliance less pervasive political institutions must replace the agents' moral reasons by non-moral reasons. Morality's requirements are typically conformed with if and only if the acts recommended by self-interest coincide with those demanded by moral considerations. Or so does the narrow thesis of indirect motivation insist (see Chapter Four).

It is not necessary to repeat at this point the objections leveled towards the end of Chapter Four (4.4) to the classical doctrine. Let me state only that the classical doctrine is incapable of uniting in a consistent account the two apparently conflicting beliefs held simultaneously by citizens of modern democracies. Immanuel Kant, for example, claimed that "true politics" always pays homage to morals. That claim sits well with the ordinary view that political action is subject to high moral standards and, that, the community needs honest and trustworthy leaders who are directly motivated by moral concerns (rather than just responding to non-moral incentives that indirectly motivate them to conform to the requirements of morality, see 4.2). Kant understood this as an outright rejection of the realist thesis in any form of it: no pragmatic reasons can ever justify political acts that depart from the general requirements of morality, he maintained. At the same time, he endorsed the narrow conception of indirect motivation. But he was unable to show how that conception may cohere with the claim that "true politics" always pays homage to morals.

This book may be read as an exploration of how to revise the classical doctrine. Since it takes the circumstances of politics on which the classics relied for granted, it proposes to amend the classical doctrine, not to reject it altogether. Hence the adjective "neoclassical" in the name of the revised theory. The neoclassical theory shares with the classical doctrine the empirical assumption that the moral norms of the struggle for power are not sufficiently complied with, and it agrees that this assumption has bearing on what honest politicians who aim

to promote the cause of justice and the common good may be permitted to do in order to gain and keep power. But it modifies the theses
that are built on the assumption of insufficient compliance.

The neoclassical version of the realist thesis holds that 1. there is a
moral minimum that no political action may permissibly disregard
and, that, 2. the bottom line of the moral minimum is raising as the
general level of compliance with the demands of political morality
rises. According to the neoclassical version of the thesis of indirect
motivation, institutions must not fully close the gap between the demands of morality and the self-regarding concerns of the political
agents; rather, they should aim at merely narrowing that gap: they
should economize on virtue rather than making it completely inert
(Chapter Five).

These amendments change the political questions raised by the two
classical theses. The unconstrained thesis of realism asks, what is
permitted to the political agent engaged in the promotion of the
common cause. The constrained thesis asks, what is *not* permitted
even to such an agent; it focuses on the limits to which the permission
is subjected. The narrow thesis of indirect motivation asks what kind
of non-moral incentives may replace moral motivation; its question
directs the attention to the agent's self-interest. The wide thesis asks,
how the conflict between non-moral and moral motivation may be
reduced in order to make moral motivation effective; rather than restricting the attention to the self-regarding concerns of the individual,
it asks how to enable his moral concerns to guide his action.

For the aims of the classical doctrine, politics is a domain of (adversarial) strategic interaction. The neoclassical theory does not deny
strategy plays a legitimate role in politics but it gives room for common deliberation as well (see Chapter Seven, 7.1). It builds into the
two theses a reference to processes of critical reflection on the moral
constraints of political action and on how political agents should be
motivated. Constitutive of that reflection are appeals to the high
moral standards that apply to elected officials and to the reasons why
such standards apply to them. One argues, for example, that as representatives of the community, elected officials are agents who bear
special responsibilities towards the citizens. Or one argues that the
action of the elected officials is backed by a monopoly of coercive
force, and in order for its coercive nature to be justified, unusually
stringent requirements must obtain. Or else one argues that the offi-

cials in question act in the name of a community of equals and are, therefore, supposed to treat its members with equal concern and respect in a special and very demanding sense. Such arguments are part of the process in which the constraints of political action are identified and the expectations about the moral character of politicians are settled.

The unified account does not eliminate the tension between the conflicting beliefs on the ethical standards of political action. Rather, it explains that tension. It shows, for example, that many political choice situations justify dirty-handed action, and the frequency of such situations makes the disposition to act without too much scruple and to avoid being too much haunted by feelings of remorse after having acted a virtue that the public has reason to value in a politician. But it also shows that the democratic public is not condemned to oscillate back and forth between its conflicting beliefs. It identifies that tension as a driving force encouraging progression from more lenient towards more stringent expectations and from lower-level towards higher-level compliance. It does not predict any unilinear tendency towards improved compliance and more demanding standards. It has room for developments of the same tension enabling a populist leader to gain control over large segments of the public by promising them to wipe out the very motivational assumptions on which the theses of realism and of indirect motivation rely.

One of the objectives of the neoclassical theory is to explain why and under what circumstances populism may emerge victorious (see Chapter Seven, 7.5). But its main ambition is to show that there is a practical alternative to populist abuse of the moral concerns of citizens: it is possible to improve the moral quality of democratic politics in ways that, rather than undermining the principles and procedures of liberal democracy, affirm them and stabilize their hold over the community.

The liberal view is often identified with the classical doctrine, especially with the narrow thesis of indirect motivation. This book tried to show that this identification is not justified. Nor is it justified to claim that, on the contrary, liberalism is a conception according to which political action is directly subjected to the general constraints of morality. The liberal account takes it for granted that in order for the moral constraints on political action to become harder and more demanding, the general principles of political morality must be translated into specific institutional rules and procedures. What it denies is that those rules and procedures are to rely on mere self-interest.

This book had something to say about the institutional properties of those rules and procedures, too. Often, they are adopted as laws (on freedom of information, on conflicts of interest, on campaign financing, for example), and they are enforced by the coercive apparatus of the state. But, as I tried to show in Chapter Six (6.4), there are limits to the capacity of the law to provide the requisite rules and procedures. The task of making political action comply with moral principles presupposes non-legal rules as its indispensable means.[1]

Sometimes, the non-legal rules in question resist any formal definition, and have no other existence but that of a convention implicit in the practice guided by them. At other times, the community is free to choose between leaving non-legal rules and procedures fully informal and laying them out in something like a code of ethics (a code for members of Parliament, a ministerial code, etc.). Whenever the choice is open, more formalization seems to be preferable to less.

A written code of ethics is easier to appeal to than an unwritten convention. Its provisions may be made fairly specific, it may admit of elaborate procedures of investigation, and it may attach specific sanctions to specific violations. Finally, an independent agency may be set up to monitor the conduct of those under the code's application.

If such a monitoring agency is established, how wide its competences should be? In particular, should it be entrusted with the authority to investigate particular cases and to mete out specific sanctions?

I do not know of any democratic polity where an independent agency supervising the ethics of public conduct would be empowered to decide about the dismissal of a politician from his office. And I know only of one case where such an adjudication panel had the mandate temporarily to suspend an elected official for flagrant misconduct. The question is, whether it is desirable to make further progress in this direction and to give such panels the power to decide questions of suspension or even of dismissal.

Good arguments can be forwarded in support a positive answer. Sometimes the democratic process yields paradoxical outcomes if the decision is entrusted to elected officials. As an analogy to our problem, consider legislation on speech. Democratic parties of all stripes

tend to agree that freedom of speech is a political value to be protected against government interference. They all tend to agree that it is
valuable because, among other things, it serves as a check on the government's mistakes and abuses. Now whenever a party is in opposition, its principled agreement with the value of the freedom of speech
is supported by the interest related to its role of an opposition. To be
sure, when the same party comes to government, its short-run interests regarding freedom of speech undergo a reversal. Freedom of
speech is a friend of a party's power-related interests so long as it is in
opposition and an enemy of those interests as soon as it becomes the
party of government. In the long run, the alternating interests cancel
out each other. Suppose, there are two parties struggling for parliamentary majority, and both have an equal chance to be on government. Then, their long-term interests will be indifferent towards freedom of expression. What remains is their agreement that, from the
point of view of the community freedom of speech is a great value. So
both parties are reasonable to support freedom of speech, and to oppose any attempts at abridging it.

This is not what the simple model outlined above predicts, though.
Parties are indifferent towards freedom of expression, from their own
point of view, only in the long run. In the short run, their interests are
either friendly or hostile towards it. And it matters a lot that they see it
as their enemy when they command the majority in the legislature
and, that, they see it as their friend when they are the minority. We
must not suppose that all parties try to abridge freedom of speech all
the time when they are on government. It is sufficient to suppose that
they do so more often than they engage in undoing the restrictions
adopted by the previous majority. If this prediction is correct, then the
support that the attempts to curtail freedom of speech are likely to
enjoy over time will be stronger than the resistance they are likely to
meet. Even if there is general long-term agreement that freedom of
speech must be protected against legal interference, freedom of speech
will be massively interfered with. The upshot is that the will of a democratic community is better served by an institutional system where
the rule of legislative majorities is constrained by constitutional constraints than by one where it is left unconstrained, and it is better
served by constitutional review being entrusted to a body that is fairly
well insulated from the electoral process than by leaving it with a body
of elected representatives. In other words, rather than compromising

on the democratic principle, constitutionalism seems to be demanded by it.[2]

This book argued that similar paradoxes are at work in the domain of identifying and upholding the moral principles of public conduct, and it tried to show that the democratic mechanisms of the struggle for power do not completely eliminate the causes of those paradoxes (see Chapters Three and Seven, 3.2 and 7.3). The analogy with constitutional review suggests that independent monitoring agencies are invaluable means of improving the moral quality of the democratic process. We have also seen that there is no political accountability without sanctions and, that, the relatively weak sanctions of reprimand or apology get emptied if no stronger sanctions such as that of dismissal or forced resignation are available (see Chapter Six, 6.2). But the parties that alternate in government and in opposition may collude to allow their compromised politicians to stay in office. Thus, there is a reason to think that authorizing some independent agency to decide on the sanctions of political misconduct, including removal from office, would improve on the moral quality of the democratic process.

But I think decisive reasons argue against adopting such a solution. Morality, whether private or public, is a matter of the beliefs, attitudes and dispositions of the group of individuals whose relationships and interactions it is supposed to guide. It is not a set of rules and incentives that would regulate the group from the outside. Its standards must be identified and upheld by practices internal to the community.

These practices may receive help from externalized instances. A committee on the standards of public life may conduct general inquiries and it may investigate particular charges of misconduct as well. It is more likely to collect the relevant facts with sufficient care and to weigh them with the requisite impartiality than any panel consisting of politicians. So it helps to have the inquiry into political scandals entrusted to such an independent body. This body may even make proposals to the relevant political instance on what kind of sanction is appropriate to impose, if any. But the decision itself must remain with the latter.

What democratic communities need are not politicians whose moral aspirations are effectively regulated by such external stimuli but rather ones who take guidance from morality as a specific source of inspiration. It needs individual political agents and a political profession of moral integrity.

Entrusting the enforcement of the code of public ethics to bodies whose members are insulated from the electoral process would replace the public deliberation on moral reasons by indirect motivation in the narrow sense. And we have good reasons to be suspicious about narrow strategies of indirect motivation.

There is a further important consideration. If, for example, an independent agency is allowed to decide whether a cabinet minister should suffer some sanction for improper conduct, the prime minister is relieved of responsibility for what his subordinate does. It ceases to be his business. If that agency makes a proposal concerning the sanction and leaves the decision with the prime minister, then the latter remains accountable for the conduct of his subordinate. Should this be the case, then the outcome of the scandal will hinge ultimately on the expectations regarding the electoral choices of the citizenry. The relationship between the fate of the minister and the expected reactions of the voters is indirect, to be sure; it is mediated by political struggles within the ruling party and between government and opposition, by the alertness of the critical press, and by many other factors (see Chapter Seven, 7.4). Even so, the relationship exists, and it is important that the citizenry could *see* that it does exist.

Notes

1 Let me remind the reader that this book drew heavily on a public political debate for inspiration. That debate was provoked by the question whether there was good reason for Péter Medgyessy, Hungarian Prime Minister between 2002 and 2004, to resign over his being exposed to have hidden his past of a covert officer of the Communist counter-intelligence. Those holding that he had no such reason argued that 1. the law in force failed to mandate that candidates for elected office disclose the fact of their past cooperation with the counter-intelligence of the Communist regime; thus 2. Medgyessy did not violate the law. They hastened to add that 3. politicians should not be held accountable for ethical misconduct unless it counts as violating the law. It is this third premise that I subjected to criticism in the Introduction showing that the arguments proposed in favor of it were defective. That was a negative argument. Now we have a positive argument at hand. If, as we have found, an elected official's responsibility to the voters cannot be fully specified by the law; if, therefore, public morality cannot dispense

with rules and procedures that resist being legally codified, then the claim that politicians should not be held accountable for ethical misconduct unless it counts as violating the law is untenable.

2 One might ask how general the scope of such a democratic justification for judicial review is. To remain with the issue of freedom of speech: many forms of expression (revolting works of art, or hate speech, or pornography, for example) fail to contribute to the public control of the government or to give rise to phenomena of preference inconsistency over time. Stable legislative majorities may agree that such expressions should not be protected. How could we say that the overruling of the majority agreement by judicial decision enforces the will of the democratic community? I think such a claim is defensible. Freedom of speech, as Ronald Dworkin reminds us, is an abstract principle that needs interpretation to provide a ruling in a specific case. The questions of interpretation admit of right and wrong answers. If a community endorses the abstract principle, it commits itself to seeking and enforcing the right answer to each such question, rather than the answer that the majority believes to be the right one. Suppose the question is whether an expression of unpopular content or form counts as protected speech. It is easy to see that in all such cases entrusting the decision to a body insulated from the electoral process is more likely to track the democratic community's will to live under the rule of freedom of expression correctly interpreted than under provisions that distort the meaning of that abstract principle. In other words, disagreement over the correct interpretation of constitutional principles is likely to generate similar kinds of paradoxes to the one we uncovered with regard to the public accountability of government, and they call for the same institutional solution.

APPENDIX

"LIVING IN TRUTH"

The title of this appendix quotes the key term of Václav Havel's seminal essay, "The Power of the Powerless." "Living in truth" was meant by Havel to encapsulate the experience of political engagement on the part of the democratic oppositions in Soviet-dominated East Central Europe during the decade and a half before the collapse of the Soviet empire. It depicts the choice of political action as a choice of a way of life. It suggests that political strategy is based on, or even identical with, personal moral reform.

This is an unusual attempt to facilitate the self-understanding of a political movement, but it fits the unique circumstances and profiles of dissident politics at the time very well.

Dissidents distinguished themselves from reformers, progressive party people, regime critics, or internal emigrés by their mode of action. Unlike all the others, they demonstratively disregarded the rules of conduct prescribed and enforced by the communist regime. Rather than circumventing those rules, they rejected them—and they did so publicly and defiantly. They opposed higher principles, those of human rights, to the laws, habits, and procedures of the regime. They declared that the state had no legitimate power to restrain and prosecute any speech or assembly or association, since the right to express one's ideas publicly, to hold meetings and to associate with others is not granted by official fiat but is owned by each individual by virtue of being a human person. A dissident was someone who practiced *principled disobedience.*

Principled disobedience is in fact a way of life. A rights-bearer does not ask for favors but demands his due. Rather than lamenting his grievances, he loudly protests against any offenses to his moral status. He rejects the petty deals with the power-holders. He opts for personal independence and integrity. This is a liberating experience, which allows the person to be in harmony with his conscience.

Some dissidents did not seek any other aims beyond this internal satisfaction. They engaged in the dissident way of life to testify for their religious faith, for example. Or they did so in defense of their autonomy as artists. For others, principled disobedience was not only constitutive of their personal life but also a means for approaching more distant aims. By demonstratively practising human rights, they wanted to confront the communist party state with a choice between unleashing enough repressive violence to crush the dissident move-ment on the one hand, and using its power with a certain moderation that would allow for islands of civil society to emerge, to grow and to consolidate, on the other.

The party-state had all the necessary means to suppress the opposi-tion movement. It had legions of policemen, informers, judges and gaolers at its disposition. It exercised firm control over the people's sources of income, their movements and their contacts. Thus, the dissidents ran a genuine and serious risk. But, rather than hoping for the glory of martyrdom, they took that risk in the expectation that the repressive apparatuses would not be mobilized at full capacity.

This expectation presupposed that the communist power-holders would not react to the challenge with blind vindictiveness, but with rational calculation, leading them to assess the costs of a clampdown to be greater than the advantages they could hope to derive from it. In Poland, where the democratic opposition was best organized and where it enjoyed the widest and most active social support, an explicit bargain was offered to the political leadership: you resign yourselves to the rise of an independent civil society, and we accept in exchange your continuing monopoly control over the state.[1] But the offer was supported by pressure from a political movement launched in a de-monstrative exercise of human rights. Even in the Polish case, the moral ends and the strategic means were indistinguishable from each other.[2]

This unique coincidence is analyzed in Havel's celebrated essay.

"The Power of the Powerless" starts with an assessment of the situation. The totalitarian era of the communist regimes is over, it states. The passion to change the world is gone; the regime is about mere self-preservation. Things have become more regular and predict-able; power is no longer wielded in the form of brutal, arbitrary, and mass-scale terror. The communist rule has retained its total character insofar as it forces the multiplicity of human relations into "predetermined roles," demanding strict conformity, and making any deviation appear as a rejection of the entire institutional system as such. Its rigid structure violates "the ends of life," the plurality, variety, and spontaneity that is constitutive of a human being.[3]

But then, how is the regime that Havel calls post-totalitarian sustained? By a combination of promises and threats, he maintains. Expressions of loyalty are the bargaining chips in the hands of the subjects. Those who are prepared to express publicly their agreement with the official ideology are offered various small advantages: promotion, fringe benefits, summer holidays in a socialist country, and the like. At the same time they are threatened with the loss of all that and more if they stop sending out signals of agreement: their children may not be admitted to the university; they may lose the chance of obtaining an exit visa to the neighboring socialist countries; the oppressive apparatuses may be let loose on them.

Havel's paradigmatic figure is the Grocer who manages a small shop under state-run franchise. His position is negligible, but he has to pay for it. The price does not seem to be very high: "he puts the slogan, 'Workers of the world unite!' in the shop window, between the onions and carrots."[4]

The primary addressee of the message is the Grocer's boss. Its content, needless to say, is unrelated to the manifest meaning of the text. The Grocer does not inform his superior of his ardent desire for the workers of the world to unite. He means to say something entirely different: "I act the way they expect me to act. I can be trusted; I am impeccable. I obey you, so you can leave me where I am."[5]

The slogan couches the naked act of submission in the trappings of the Cause. The regime kindly allows the Grocer to pretend that he is not performing an act of submission, but rather making a stand for the international alliance of the proletariat.

No one expects the Grocer to actually believe in the slogan. He only needs to put it in his shop window. If he does so without believing in it, he is viewed as even more reliable. He is someone who consistently obeys the order to put slogans in the window without thinking for a moment that they convey anything true or important. The more he is assumed to believe that the notices are sheer lies, the better. Repeating lies is demoralizing, and the regime is better sustained if its subjects are demoralized cynics than if they are true believers. That is why the Grocer and his fellows are forced to "live in lie."[6] Living in lie is to degrade oneself, and diminished people are easy to control and manipulate.

There is another aspect to the problem of "living in lie." The slogans are not repeated in face-to-face conversation between the Grocer and his boss. They are put into the window, for all to see. The act of submission is expected to be *public*. Everyone must see that the Grocer is cooperating with the regime. To "live in lie" means to take part in the maintenance of the false appearance of general ideological consensus that keeps the regime going.

If the Grocer were the only one to express his loyalty publicly, he would be humiliated in front of everyone, and most likely it would not cross his mind to collaborate. However, everyone else in a comparable situation is expected by his boss to do the same, and according to general experience, most people conform to the expectation. There is nothing conspicuous in the Grocer's conduct, which fits well into the overall picture. Passers-by are not interested in the slogan in the window; what they notice is no more than a general panorama of slogans in all the shop windows, and that only as an inescapable background to their lives. It does not occur to them that the Grocer personally has done anything that should be the object of moral judgment.

> People do not take note of the slogan, but only because such slogans are to be found in other shop-windows as well, on lamp posts, on clipboards, in the windows of apartments, on buildings. In fact, they are everywhere. And while people do not notice the slogan, they are well aware of the panorama itself. And then, what else would be the Grocer's slogan than a tiny part of the enormous background view of everyday life?[7]

Consider the Office Girl. She passed by the shop an hour earlier without paying any attention to the slogan, and now she may be placing a similar one on the wall of her office, which, in its turn, will not receive any attention from the Grocer, should he pass by. Everyone acts on the understanding that everyone else does the same. "Metaphorically speaking, the Office Girl's banner could not exist without the Grocer's, and vice versa."[8] They sustain the panorama together, each taking the contribution of the other for granted. But what they jointly sustain overpowers them and grows into a seemingly impersonal mechanism. It creates a sense that it is "natural and inevitable," that it would not change at all if they stopped playing the game, and that those who stay out of it are simply abnormal.[9]

The practice of "living in lie" forms a system, and its systematic and impersonal workings help to calm the participants' conscience. They may tell themselves that nothing depends on them, since their contribution to the overall picture is negligible. They can say: if I had not accepted the deal, there would have been others to accept it. Without my participation, the world would be exactly the same; by staying out of it I would not change anything. I have no responsibility for the way it is, for my action makes no difference.

Havel rejects such excuses with contempt. Participation in the collective reproduction of the big lie is degrading, he explains. Sustaining the ideological panorama is morally problematic even if there is someone else waiting to do one's job if one were to withdraw. Although the outcome would be the same, it matters that it is produced with the collaboration of one particular person rather than another. It matters for the person who is involved in the process:

> One's position in the hierarchy of power determines the extent of responsibility and culpability, but it does not allot full responsibility and culpability to anyone, nor does it fully exculpate anyone. Thus, the conflicts between the ends of life and the ends of the system are not generated between two socially distinct and clearly demarcated communities. (…) In the post-totalitarian system, the demarcation line runs, *de facto*, within each individual, because every one is in his own way a victim and an enabler of the system.[10]

This is not Havel's last word, though. He describes a third character, the Beer Technician. The Beer Technician does not live in lie for the sake of his own career. He is a committed and conscientious expert; he has a profession, and his profession has internal norms, which he takes seriously. He joins the Party and repeats the obligatory lies in order to be left alone to do his job, and to do it well. His good deeds, tiny as they are, do not change anything essential. But was it not President Masaryk who emphasized the importance of "small deeds"? The Beer Technician can tell himself in good faith that even though it is morally objectionable to participate in lies, he does the objectionable thing for the good of others.

Havel acknowledges that the masters of "small deeds," who try to achieve the best compromise between the norms of their profession and the expectations of the regime, are able to produce genuine good.[11] He is inclined to admit that the goodness of the outcomes may affect the moral judgment about the personal compromise. The Grocer considers his own interests when he chooses to get his hands dirty, while the Beer Technician dirties his hands for others. But Havel insists, the game that the Beer Technician plays is a dangerous one, for the balance between the moral concessions and the tiny goods from the "small deeds" is delicate and uncertain. The reference to the interests of others can easily become self-serving; once he has made the deal, his fear of losing his job may force the Beer Technician into ever softer compromises; the lies may multiply, and the professional quality may drift ever farther from what is still worthy of the moral sacrifice. The initial difference between the conduct of the Beer Technician and that of the Grocer may erode. On the other hand, the Beer Technician's attempts to avoid the trap of moral decay and to live up to the internal norms of his profession may easily involve him in a collision with his bosses. The boundary between what counts as a local conflict and what is perceived as global contestation is vague; one may never know whether a particular step remains on this side of the invisible line or crosses it.

We would think that the dynamics of the Beer Technician's dilemma have a potential to spill over from "living in lie" into "living in truth." This is because the Beer Technician is no self-serving opportunist but an individual with his own norms and ideals. Yet Havel chooses to depict a different route towards personal moral reform. One day the Grocer changes his mind for no specific reason. He decides not to put the banner in his window in order to secure the boss's good will. "He renounces the rite and breaks the rule. He rediscovers his pent-up identity and dignity. He gives concrete meaning to his freedom. With his revolt, he makes an attempt to live in truth."[12]

This sudden change may strike the reader as implausible. We would find it easier to understand why a character like the Beer Technician might turn from collaborator into dissident. Havel has his own reasons to make the Grocer the hero who breaks with the everyday panorama of lies. His claim is that literally everybody has the chance of moral reform. Whoever is capable of choosing to live in lie also has the capacity for choosing to live in truth. Humans are equipped for both types of choice. On the one hand, the reason why people may be made to live in lie is that "they can in fact live so."[13] On the other hand, "attraction to truth" is inherent in their nature;[14] they harbor "the elementary human need to live in harmony with oneself."[15]

We are finite beings, but we are moral beings at the same time, and we can never know when the moral self, inherent in every person, will make its voice heard, or how that voice might change our lives. Concealed under the surface of lies is a "hidden sphere" of life, i.e. "life's hidden openness to truth."[16] What matters is not that particular motives may emerge to move an individual towards rejecting collaboration. The important thing is that rejecting collaboration is a moral decision, and whatever else may support it, it certainly needs the inspiration of the moral self. Every human being harbors the possibility of one day hearing that inner voice. At least it can be said that among the many people who live in lie there are a few who at some point in their life will suddenly and unexpectedly choose truth.

These people reject the petty compromises. They sacrifice a great deal but they also gain a great deal in exchange. They come to live in harmony with their conscience, and they need not look for false rationalizations and excuses. They are granted the experience of taking responsibility for themselves and for the world.

The consequences of such a moral redemption do not stop at the boundaries of the self. "Something very dangerous has happened." Even though the Grocer's revolt is of a purely moral nature, it has "a clearly political dimension." As long as our hero took his share in the collective practices of sustaining false appearances, his personal acts went unnoticed. But breaking with collective practice is something visible, something conspicuous. It shows that "it is *possible* to live in truth." It becomes dangerous for the system, not "out of its physical or real power, but because his act went beyond itself, because it casts a sharp light on its environment, and because the consequences of this illumination are unpredictable."[17]

Retribution may not be far away. The Grocer is removed from his position of shop manager and transferred to a supermarket. His salary is reduced, and he can say farewell to holidays in Bulgaria. The admission of his children to university is at risk. His bosses start to harass him. Of course, the oppressors are not acting out of conviction but for the same reasons that had earlier made him put the banners in his window. They are demonstrating their loyalty to the regime. In their position this is what corresponds to the "general panorama."[18]

But liberation from the web of lies is worth the sacrifice. The practice of "living in lie" does not merely force individuals to accept petty compromises. It completely erodes their sense of personal responsibility. It makes them incapable of understanding that we are all responsible for ourselves and for the world. "And if this sense of responsibility ceases (...), then with it disappears [the individuals'] sense of self-identity," the sense that "they have a determinate, irreplaceable place in the world."[19]

Breaking with the practice of "living in lie" may deprive one of many external advantages, but it restores one's personal identity, it gives back the individual the experience of being unrepeatable and irreplaceable, a sense of having a unique life and a unique position within society and nature. And this sense matters more than anything else.

It may be objected that this view is dangerously aristocratic. No matter how important the sense of uniqueness and the sense of responsibility for one's own life and for what one may do in the world, ordinary people have other, more pedestrian concerns: raising their children or taking care of their elderly parents, for example. These concerns may be overwhelming, and the demand that they all should opt for truth would be not only hopelessly irrealistic, but with its extreme demandingness also inhumane.

Havel is aware of this objection. He writes in the "Power of the Powerless" that

> thousands of unknown people try to live in truth and millions would like to but cannot, may be just because under their circumstances doing so would take ten times the courage than for those who already made the first steps.[20]

Under the circumstances of the post-totalitarian regime, Havel intimates, most people would have to pay a disproportionately high price for choosing truth, and he recognizes that the "millions" cannot be required to pay this price.

But how can these two thoughts be made compatible with each other? Havel might have replied that there is a difference between the balance of the "existential" choice as it appears to the chooser before and after the turn. Before the turn, it appears too costly, because individuals tend to overestimate the external advantages of life, and to underestimate what is to be gained by restoring one's moral integrity. After the turn, however, the weights look very different. Once the Grocer has rebuilt his autonomous personality in the wake of choosing "living in truth," he will attribute much less value to external goods, and much more to his moral integrity. Thus, whatever may explain the turn, once it has taken place it is likely to sustain itself. Something of this sort may be the congenial answer to the spirit of "The Power of the Powerless."

It is precisely the self-sustaining potential of the moral turn that makes its scattered cases so dangerous. No matter how rarely a person "living in lie" may choose to "live in truth" instead, it is even rarer that once he has rebuilt his integrity and autonomy he should relapse into the practices of "living in lie." The change is irreversible.

Once the number of those choosing truth reaches a critical mass, they may begin to associate with each other for coordinated action. Samizdat publishing ventures, private seminars, home theaters, independent academic forums may be established. Should their rise reach a critical level, their total suppression would require a mobilization of the oppressive machinery that the post-totalitarian regime can no longer afford. The "independent life of the society" begins.[21]

As a next step, the dissident movement proper may emerge on the basis of the infrastructure of civil initiatives such as the samizdat to issue an open challenge to the system of official lies.[22] Human rights groups, incipient trade unions, and other associations may be created. While the life of the independent educational, cultural, and professional communities is inward-looking, human rights groups, trade unions and the like have goals beyond themselves. They extend public protection to the persecuted, and serve society as self-conscious examples of how personal and collective independence may be regained.

But the dissident movement cannot live up to its promises unless it is animated by the spirit of "living in truth" all the way down. It must, Havel warns, be nurtured by the "living humus" of this spirit and adjust its own strategy to its high demands. Dissident politics is first and foremost a moral project, and must stay that way. The participants must not be moved by the aim of personal advantage. Dissidence "is not a profession but first and foremost an existential attitude."[23]

This attitude is not unique to the dissidents, but they are the ones who bring it to politics. It cannot be preserved in politics, however, unless those who share it engage in practices that are wholly different from those of politics as we know it. They must keep out of the struggle for power;[24] they must avoid becoming the opposition of the government, and they must refrain from presenting positive political programs.[25] Clearly, at the time when "The Power of the Powerless" was written, gaining power or having one's political programs put into practice seemed to mean nothing less than allowing oneself to be co-opted by the regime. But this was not what Havel had in mind. Even if the dissidents had hopes of replacing the communists in government, he warned, what they would gain by the takeover would not be worth the loss caused by returning to the routines of customary politics:

> To oppose the [post-totalitarian system] merely by presenting another political platform and then trying to effect a change of government is not just not realistic but also inadequate, because in this way we never get to the heart of the problem.[26]

One could read this as suggesting that a change of government would not mean anything without the whole system being changed. But Havel leaves little doubt that what dissident politics should strive for is goes far beyond even regime change: "dissident movements see something superficial, something secondary in changing the regime," he writes.[27] Their mission points beyond trying to replace one regime with another. They anticipate and thereby prepare the ground for the "existential revolution" that humankind needs both East and West, and which would bring with it "the moral restoration of society, (...) the radical renewal of interpersonal relationships, (...) our renewed presence in the universe."[28]

Even under democracy and capitalism mankind is severed from the moral content of its existence, the "higher responsibility" that, if made self-conscious, can lend a precious meaning to human existence. Citizens of capitalist democracies are not forced to give up their moral identity as a matter of daily routine. However, this is a dangerous advantage, Havel insists. It frees ordinary life from the challenges that make a human being aware of the existential dimensions of his choices and his acts. As a consequence, people may drift among the

shallow goals of consumer civilization, without so much as sensing
the fundamental falsehood of their mode of existence.

In Havel's reading, the communist regimes represent only one aspect—admittedly, "a specifically drastic aspect which, for that very
reason, puts the real nature of the phenomenon in sharp relief"—of
the "general incapacity of modern humankind to exert control over its
own situation."[29] Consumer societies, "The Power of the Powerless"
intimates, make individuals the slaves of "mass civilization" and force
them to pursue worthless goods, allow their identity to dissolve and
their personality to lose its moral stature.[30] This is the basic problem
of humankind, and this is what denizens of Soviet-type regimes experience in an especially intensified form.

In the contrast between "living in lie" and "living in truth," capitalist democracies are on the same side as communist post-totalitarian
regimes. Both are incapable of addressing the general crisis of human
civilization. That crisis is internal to them: in modern democracies,
everything is decided by large-scale impersonal processes. It is not
only life in general that loses the dimension of personal responsibility,
but also politics in particular:

> In our time, (...) rulers and heads of state are replaced by manag-
> ers, bureaucrats, apparatchiks, the professional agents of govern-
> ance, manipulation, and grandstanding, by a certain impersonal
> amalgam of power and functional relations, a device of the state
> machinery designed for some specific purpose, an "innocent" tool
> of an "innocent power" that is shrouded in anonymity (...)[31]

What the post-totalitarian regimes do is to make the gap between
the meaning of life and the falsehood of ordinary existence painfully
obvious. Thereby, they inspire a passionate longing in many after "a
life in truth" and, in this manner, they give an impulse to the "existential revolution" that is so badly needed by the whole of mankind. It is
this aspiration to an existential revolution that the dissident movement
has the calling to make apparent in politics, Havel maintains—and
this is why dissidents must be careful not to allow their movement to
degenerate into the practices of politics as we know it.

He calls the politics he expects the community of dissidents to pursue "counterpolitical politics." "Counterpolitical politics" does not
depend on the expectation that the state of the world will improve as a

consequence of their actions. It is, Havel writes, "an all or nothing bet, and it is hard to imagine that someone would choose this route because he thinks that today's sacrifices will reap their rewards tomorrow."[32] It is not the likelihood of external success that makes the choice of "counterpolitical politics" reasonable but its inner moral worth.

Suppose that one must choose without having any information on the probabilities attached to the possible outcomes. Even so, there remains something one may know for certain: "living in truth" is morally right while "living in lie" is morally wrong, whatever the consequences. One chooses to step out of the collective practice of lying, and fate will take care of the rest. If, and only if, the dissidents are capable of persisting in this attitude, Havel intimates, they may carry out their historic mission.

This idea deserves our admiration but it also raises some serious difficulties. It is doubtful that moral assessment could so completely disregard the consequences of human choices in any walk of life, but it is certain that the ethics of *political* action may not be indifferent to the consequences. As so many have pointed out since Max Weber, political responsibility is first and foremost responsibility for the consequences. Dissidents may not be neutral towards the question whether their action improves or worsens the state of the world. If they have reason to believe that the situation will at least not become worse as a result of their intervention, they can safely regard their choice as an all or nothing bet: *they* may not gain anything and may well lose everything personally, but at least *others* will not pay the price of *their* adventure. If, however, the risks include that of the situation of many other people becoming worse as a consequence of dissident action, then the bet may well be morally problematic.

This charge was directed, one way or another, against all the dissident movements in East Central Europe. Its gist was that the dissidents put other people's well-being at risk for the sake of their own moral comfort. Censorship would be reinvigorated. Police persecution of religious groups would become harsher. The reform-minded technocrats would be ousted from the party leadership. Dissidents have the moral advantage, but they are not the only ones to bear the costs. The ethical literature calls this objection the charge of *moral self-indulgence*.[33]

The democratic oppositions of the region were right to reject this charge, but only because the alleged connection did not obtain. At most, they caused transient and local deterioration in the state of affairs, if that.[34] The likelihood that other people would suffer lasting losses as a consequence of dissident action was indeed negligible. But that is very different from the claim that the consequences did not matter.

Once we agree that consequences do matter, we have to face the task of assessing them. And whatever our moral ideals may be, the assessment of the consequences of our actions must be based on realistic assumptions. We have to assume that most people do not experience moral rebirth without a sudden and dramatic change in their circumstances.

Responsibility—a moral value ranking very high on Havel's list—required dissidents to take this consideration seriously and to assume that the turn to "living in truth" was and would remain a relatively rare event. Dissident politics had to count with the typical motives and reactions of the people. It had to calculate how to increase the costs of a violent clampdown for the power-holders, and how to decrease the costs of independent conduct for the groups subjected to state power. It had to be careful not to isolate the democratic opposition from the many who found the dissident way of life—or the mere contact with dissidents—prohibitively costly. To the extent that it came to satisfy these requirements, it was very close to what Havel wanted to dismiss as conventional politics.

There is simply no way for politics to become a moral venture indifferent towards non-moral costs. Those setting and realizing political objectives must always keep in mind that people have respectable non-moral interests, and they must adopt strategies that do not involve larger costs in terms of those interests than what people in general are ready to accept and able to bear. They must adopt strategies that tend to reduce the expected non-moral costs and/or increase the expected non-moral benefits of the people whose co-operation is needed for political success.

It seems to follow that no politics may ever overcome the internal moral tensions characteristic of politics as we know it. Reducing certain specifically targeted tensions is a meaningful aim, and the aspiration to make political action more moral should never be abandoned—but this aim is very different from that of completely eliminating the tension between morality and politics.

I do not simply mean that full harmony between morality and politics is a vanishing ideal that we may infinitely approximate but never reach. I do mean that, of course, but I also mean that a world that functions well if, and only if, nobody cares about the costs of acting morally would not be a good place to live. During the early period of their Sturm und Drang, the communist regimes demanded from their subjects an unconditional readiness to sacrifice everything to the ideals of morality, and they in fact sacrificed people in the name of this demand. Opposition to communism was based on the hope that a world where the pursuit of justice and of the common good does not require unlimited sacrifices is possible.

Or at least that was the hope of the author of this book. I was not expecting the Grocer to undergo moral rebirth. My attention was drawn, rather, to characters like the Beer Technician, who was cautiously but relentlessly groping for the increasingly shifting boundaries of the regime's tolerance. I understood dissident politics to be aiming to make the limits of enforceable conformity recede for all, so that everybody could experiment with enlarging the scope of his autonomy without undergoing radical moral reform.[35]

But I can see why Havel's imagination was captured by the Grocer and his sudden change of heart.

At its birth, the democratic opposition had no chance, in any country of the region, to be transformed into a movement of national dimensions. It had to rest contented by reaching firm ground so as to survive the attempts at oppression and manipulation. What dissidents needed first and foremost in the initial years of the movement was integrity and resolve, and a strong conviction that what they were doing was right. In other words, they needed something like what is described by "living in truth." Havel was talking about what was most important initially for dissident politics.

The initial years were concluded in Poland by the birth of Solidarity. In Hungary, they came to an end during the political erosion of the 1980s. In both countries, dissident politics had begun to resemble conventional politics already before the collapse of the communist regime. In Czechoslovakia, by contrast, the regime held fast till the Fall of 1989. It did not become apparent until the mass demonstrations of August 21 and the subsequent events that even here, under the surface of steadfast intransigence, the party state had been undergoing an irresistible process of erosion over the years. The "velvet revolution" brought with it the moment Havel had to abandon the attitude of the heroes of "The Power of the Powerless." The change of fortune was breathtaking: overnight, yesterday's "castaway"[36] found himself in the highest office of the land.

His "counterpolitical politics" had come to an end. Rather than persisting in his rejection of conventional democratic politics, Havel started a new and different adventure: that of joining the political game of liberal democracy. But while accepting the rules of the game he never accepted that playing by the rules would mean abandoning the ideal of politics as a matter of moral commitment and personal responsibility. It is his relentless efforts to act in conformity both to the circumstances and to the moral ideals of politics at the same time that makes his second adventure fascinating and worthy of our admiration.

Notes

1 See Adam Michnik: "Le nouvel evolutionnisme" (The New Evolutionism), in P. Kende–A. Smolar, eds.: *Pologne/Hongrie 1956–1976.* Paris: Le Seuil, 1976.

2 For a more detailed account of the structure of dissident politics, see my "Das Erbe der demokratischen Opposition" (The Heritage of the Democratic Opposition), in *Transit* 1/2000.

3 V. Havel: "The Power of the Powerless," in J. Keane, ed.: *The Power of the Powerless.* London: Hutchinson, 1985, 29.

4 "Power," 127.

5 Ibid., 28.

6 Ibid., 31.

7 Ibid., 35.

8 Ibid., 36

9 Ibid., 37.

10 Ibid. The claim that *everyone* was at the same time a victim and an enabler of the system is exaggerated, and in no way follows from Havel's analysis. Not everyone became a shop manager, not everyone contributed to the ideological mystification that surrounded the regime in exchange for the smaller or larger benefits granted to collaborators.

11 Ibid., 61.

12 Ibid., 39.

13 Ibid., 38.

14 Ibid., 41.

15 Ibid., 51.

16 Ibid., 41.
17 Ibid., 40.
18 Ibid., 39.
19 V. Havel: "A személyiségtudat válsága" in Havel: *A kiszolgáltatottak hatalma*, Budapest: Európa, 1991, 220.
20 Ibid., 59.
21 Ibid., 65.
22 Ibid.
23 Ibid., 59; cf. 44.
24 Ibid., 42.
25 Ibid., 68.
26 Ibid.
27 Ibid., 71.
28 Ibid., 92.
29 V. Havel: "The Power of the Powerless," in J. Keane (ed.): *The Power of the Powerless* (London: Hutchinson, 1985), 90.
30 Ibid., 45.
31 V. Havel: "Politika és lelkiismeret" in Havel: *A kiszolgáltatottak hatalma,* 250.
32 Ibid., 45; cf. 81.
33 See Chapter Nine, note 49.
34 Early in 1977, a series of anti-Charter rallies were organized, and millions were made to sign petitions that condemned the Charter. Those who were forced to the rallies or to sign the petitions were undoubtedly in a difficult moral situation. It is worse to make a stand against an identifiable and evidently honest project than to put meaningless banners in a shop window. But first, this was a transient phenomenon, as the regime quickly learnt that such mobilization only increased the political weight of its opponents. Secondly, and more importantly, the charge was untenable in precisely this case, because if those who let themselves be steered into the rallies and signed the petitions had not lent their signature or their attendance, these shameful events could never have taken place to begin with. To put it briefly, the claim that the appearance of the Charter worsened their situation was made true by their own conduct.
35 See my articles "Gondolatok a közeljövőről" (Thoughts on the Near Future) and "Másfél év után ugyanarról" (On the Same Thing Again After One and a Half Years), in *Beszélő* 3 (1992), and *Beszélő* 9 (1994), respectively.
36 See his piece "Ma még hajótörött, holnap politikus" (Today's castaway, tomorrow's politician) October 7, 1989. in Havel: *A kiszolgáltatottak hatalma.*

INDEX